Praise for *The Coming Food Crisis*

"*The Coming Food Crisis* shines a light on the vulnerabilities of our current food system and the farmers caught in the middle. Klar traces the forces reshaping our food supply in a way that's both gripping and deeply human. His analysis invites readers to question assumptions and look beyond the supermarket aisles to the soil itself. It's a timely, compelling read for anyone seeking a deeper understanding of where food, health, and freedom intersect."

—Dr. Sina McCullough, author of *Hands Off My Food!* and *Beyond Labels*

"This book is a vital, courageous defense of small farmers and local food systems at a moment when corporate consolidation and toxic inputs are pushing our food supply toward a breaking point. It exposes how policy, industry, and captured institutions have systematically undermined soil health, rural communities, and true food security, while pretending to 'feed the world.' Most importantly, it offers readers a path back to sanity: rebuilding living soil, supporting independent farmers, and reclaiming food sovereignty before crisis forces the issue."

—Kelly Ryerson, cofounder of American Regeneration

"The war on farmers is a war on us all. This is the message of John Klar's passionate book. The author not only exposes the threats to agriculture posed by globalism, ecomania, powerful bureaucracies, interest groups, and ideological fads, but also, like his great predecessor, Cato the Elder—a Roman senator, soldier, and farmer—presents farming as a dignified pursuit that builds bonds between people, connects us with nature, and allows for a better understanding of our existence in the world. A fascinating narrative about brave, hard-working people in confrontation with the soulless machinery of the powers-that-be."

—Ryszard Legutko, author of *The Demon in Democracy* and *The Cunning of Freedom*

"Are we facing famine in the age of plenty? Could supermarket shelves loaded with thousands of products mask an inherent fragility in the world's food supplies? *The Coming Food Crisis* paints exactly this scenario, chronicling elitist efforts to consolidate food production and eliminate farmers, especially livestock producers. 'Climate change' is just the latest propaganda salvo to criminalize the independent peasant farmer. John Klar paints a sobering picture while pointing to a solution: know your farmer, buy direct, and eat real food."

—Sally Fallon, founder and president of the Weston A. Price Foundation, and author of *Nourishing Traditions*

"The human arrogance to think that we can outsmart nature through technology has been eroding our health and destroying the ecosystem. To think that killing the cows and producing lab-grown meat is a solution to our problems is insanity. Toxic chemicals on our food are destroying our health and increasing the wealth of the pharmaceutical empire. This book will help you understand why the path we are now on is unsustainable and may ultimately lead to human extinction. Returning to the model of the small family farm is the only way forward."

—Dr. Stephanie Seneff, author of *Toxic Legacy*

"John Klar, a lawyer turned farmer, has seen the food supply fiasco we face up close and personal, and this lucid, concise book beautifully maps out the struggles ahead. You'd better listen up and learn!"

—James Howard Kunstler, author of *The Long Emergency*

"I talk to hundreds of farmers every year who tell me that they feel that the cards are stacked against them. Well, as John Klar explains so vividly in his exceptional book, the war on farmers profoundly affects every one of us because everyone eats! I highly recommend this book."

—Gabe Brown, regenerative farmer and author of *Dirt to Soil*

"John Klar chronicles the challenges our country faces to have true food independence and access to clean, untainted meat and produce raised by farmers who embrace regenerative practices, without cumbersome government red tape and interference from big food and big ag companies that are focused on profit over health. More Americans are learning about the corporate corruption of government agencies and how big food and big ag companies contribute to the chemicals in our food supply that are partly responsible for the nation's chronic disease epidemic. In *The Coming Food Crisis*, Klar uses firsthand experience cultivated as a lawyer and a small independent farmer that brings attention to how America's food supply is at risk, and what can be done to improve the figurative and literal health of our nation."

—Jeff Louderback, reporter for *Epoch Times*

THE COMING FOOD CRISIS

How Corporations, Activists, and Climate Alarmists Are Waging War on Farmers

JOHN KLAR

FOREWORD BY JOEL SALATIN

MAHA
BOOKS

A portion of the proceeds goes to MAHA Action 501(c)4.

MAHA Books may be purchased in bulk at special discounts for sales promotion, corporate gifts, fund-raising, or educational purposes. Special editions can also be created to specifications. For details, contact the Special Sales Department, Skyhorse Publishing, 307 Fifth Avenue, 4th Floor, New York, NY 10016 or info@skyhorsepublishing.com.

MAHA Books is an imprint of Skyhorse Publishing, Inc.®, a Delaware corporation.

Visit our website at www.skyhorsepublishing.com.

Please follow our publisher Tony Lyons on Instagram @tonylyonsisuncertain.

10 9 8 7 6 5 4 3 2 1

Library of Congress Cataloging-in-Publication Data is available on file.

Cover Design by David Ter-Avanesyan
Cover image credit: Getty images

Print ISBN: 978-1-63144-102-8
Ebook ISBN: 978-1-63144-103-5

Printed in the United States of America

This effort is dedicated to my beloved bride, Jacqui, whose patient support and encouragement have made my writing possible, to our delightful grandsons, Jonah and Julian, and to all the children and grandchildren of the world. May the food system they inherit be healthier and more secure than the present travesty, and may small rural family farms reclaim the American countryside.

Contents

Foreword by Joel Salatin *ix*
Preface *xiii*
Introduction *xxi*

Chapter 1: It's Living Soil, Not Dead Dirt! 1
Chapter 2: From Soil to Computer Chip 11
Chapter 3: The Uniquely Modern Threat of Famine 27
Chapter 4: Food Inflation: Thousand-Dollar Gallons of Milk? 43
Chapter 5: Cows, Climate, and Bug Burgers 59
Chapter 6: European Farm Revolts 73
Chapter 7: Personal Liberty or Globalist Food Control? 97
Chapter 8: Reclaiming Food Sovereignty for All 109
Chapter 9: Restoring Healthy, Local Food Supplies 133
Chapter 10: Preventing Famine and Finding Unity 155

Resources *171*
Acknowledgments *175*
Notes *177*
Index *213*

Foreword

The hardest thing in life is making decisions.

My Dad, who flew in the Navy in World War II, was concerned enough about the direction and opportunities for US farming that he headed to Venezuela in 1948, eventually buying 1,000 acres of upland bordered by a wide river. With two industrious boys coming along, our family began raising chickens and quickly cornered the local market due to their health. You can tell a lot more about a chicken's health when you buy it live.

In 1960, however, a *junta* struck and amid the lawlessness and score-settling, we fled through the back door as machine guns entered the front door. Dad's decision to emigrate to Venezuela was foundational to our family's future because we saw firsthand how anarchy, corruption, and government ineptitude could plunge a seemingly peaceful and fruitful opportunity into life-threatening chaos.

In hindsight, of course, our family is grateful that we left in the embryonic stages of our farming endeavors and not after building a larger business. Returning stateside, Dad's love for Venezuela made him decide to not go to the Midwest, where both my parents' roots were, but to start over within a few hours' drive of Washington, DC, to enable fast visa stamps to return to our farm in Venezuela. Settling on a worn out gullied rockpile of property in Virginia's historic Shenandoah Valley was a decision that has yielded countless benefits since 1961, when I was a wide-eyed four-year-old. When we fled Venezuela, Dad was 39 and lost the farm, and all equity—everything.

The most common human response to anything is indecisiveness. We don't want to be impulsive. But dilly-dallying can be just as bad. Making the right decision at the right time for the right reason is perhaps the single most important attribute signifying leadership and wisdom.

Confronted with unseemly information or a problem, our tendency is to hope it will all go away. Confronted with our own hypocrisies and intellectual schizophrenia, we'd rather turn on the TV and watch football. History is full of tragedies created due to indecisiveness. Most of us can look back on our own personal stories and name instances where failure to act decisively cost us an opportunity, a relationship, or a positive outcome.

One of the defining maladies of our day is the notion that we can either lollygag along with life as usual without having to make a decision, or its cousin: we won't have to suffer the consequences of our decisions. We've been promised safety nets from government agencies, health care providers, and insurance companies to insulate us from the consequences of our decisions. Eat junk? Don't worry, a drug will fix you at 50. Don't show up to work? Don't worry, welfare is there to pick up the slack. Fail to save for old age? Don't worry, Social Security and Medicaid will carry you to the end. Assuming that society's safety nets will pick us up from every calamity is foolish. What has this century-old safety net produced? The sickest culture on earth. Nutrient-deficient food. Nearly twice as many prisoners as farmers. Young people looking at 50-year mortgages in order to buy a house. Rampant autism, child leukemia, and teen suicide.

The safety net track record is not good. After arriving on our new farm property in the spring of 1961, my Dad consulted with many agriculture experts, both public and private, asking "how do I make a living on this small farm?" The unanimous advice was "plant corn, buy chemical fertilizer, plow the fields, build silos, borrow money, graze the forest."

Dad made a decision to *not* follow their advice. This was the conventional mindset, the key to success in agriculture. But he decided it was the complete opposite of what we should do. Instead, he began reading the lunatic fringe of agriculture: Sir Albert Howard, Ed Faulkner, Louis Bromfield, Robert Rodale, Andre Voisin. These giants, who each had to make a decision about their own life's path, became virtual mentors as we took "the road less traveled."

Truly, that has, in the words of Robert Frost, "made all the difference." Every day each of us must wake up and decide whether we will just go with the flow or examine the flow to figure out if it's going the right way. Do we follow the herd, or in the words of Kit Pharo, become a "herd quitter?" Among people with whom I spend most of my time, the most common vocalized yearning is this phrase: "I just want to disentangle."

Anyone with their ear to the ground today and a head on their shoulders understands we seem to be living at an inflection point as an American nation and probably the whole world. In my lifetime, I've seen autism go from 1 in 10,000 to 1 in 25. I've learned a brand new pathogen lexicon of Latin words: *camphylobacter, lysteria, E. coli, salmonella.* None of these was in common usage when I was a kid. I never knew anyone with diabetes. The term "food allergy" did not exist and neither did "auto-immune disease." I knew a total of two fat people. Period. Cancer was so rare it was associated only with smokers.

Children routinely delivered newspapers and stocked store shelves. Nearly everyone had a backyard garden and canned homegrown produce. Church potlucks all contained dishes cooked from scratch; KFC and McDonald's didn't exist. A farmer could buy his property from the production of the farm. You couldn't buy "boneless, skinless breast" in the grocery store—it was the whole chicken or nothing. You could carve it at home in your own kitchen. Teens carried their rifles to high school so they could stop at a friend's and go deer hunting on the way home from school.

When I look at the changes in my lifetime, I—and many others—sense an unraveling. We can't afford to care for the number of unhealthy people entering the system. We can't head off the school shooters and fentanyl users. And especially since COVID, a majority no longer trusts the venerable institutions that historically offered a safety net for the few folks who needed it. Now, nearly everyone needs it, wants it, demands it, and feels entitled. The safety net has turned into a prison.

Added up and articulated in one place, it makes us fearful for where we're headed. Fear makes us run, which is a good thing. If a lion is chasing you in the jungle, you probably should run. But you can't run forever. What makes you stop? Faith. Faith in something worth doing or building. At some point, you need to make a decision: "I'm going to run away from that, but I'm going to embrace this."

In this fantastic book, prophet (that's what I call him) John Klar dares to articulate the lion chasing us, in all its fury, but in the end brings us to a gentle landing. In hard-hitting, punchy writing that's like reading a tornado, this post-Lyme suffering Vermont attorney lays out why all of us have something big to fear. In his own words, this book is about "toxic food dependence and a loss of self-reliance." Some may call him sensational, but in the words of Del Bigtree, I would argue that "when it's pouring rain and I've built an ark, I don't have time to argue with you about whether or not it's raining."

In that moment, my decision is to head to the ark. Klar is refreshingly candid about the various intellectual schizophrenias plaguing both liberals and conservatives. Like me, he jabs across the political spectrum, enjoying the mantra "I can irritate everyone." He couldn't be more prescient and more right. The conservatives who think Monsanto's concoctions are God's gift to dominion are as much of the problem as the liberals who think "phony baloney" and exterminating cows will save the planet.

Where it all comes together is in the solution. For all the vituperative diatribe against the devouring lion, Klar brings us to safety with chemical-free intentional food buying and production. We can outrun this lion. But we're going to have to make a decision about whether the lion might eat us. Klar makes it clear that the world food system, the oligarchy, the chemical cabal—whatever phraseology you want to us—will devour us. The stage is set. Whether by accident, negligence, or impropriety, the stage is set for some life-altering calamities.

This is a rallying cry to awaken people to action; it's a clarion call to each of us to make a decision about the trajectory of our food and farming systems. The challenge is clear: "get informed." Anyone who reads this book will be informed. And then you have to make a decision. If you're too namby-pamby to make a decision, buy this book and give it to someone who has enough courage to make a decision.

Anyone who reads this book will see with new open eyes. I'm deeply grateful *The Coming Food Crisis* articulates aggressively and precisely the breadth and depth of America's crises. This is a wake-up call. Will you decide to be part of the problem, or part of the solution? We can bring security, stability, and safety back to our food, our farms, and our families. Make a decision today about whose side you're on. Thank you.

—Joel Salatin, farmer, author, food freedom advocate

Preface

In 1978, as a high school sophomore in a semi-urban Connecticut community, I was encouraged to join the school's hiking club by my microbiology teacher. I had always been an avid hiker and spent much of my childhood exploring the forests of Connecticut and Vermont (where my mother's family lived and we often visited). But those were day hikes. The school's hiking club was for backpacking: saddling up with packs to trek for several days or longer, like mules.

Our backpacking trips were invariably along the Appalachian Trail in northwestern Connecticut, occasionally crossing into southwestern Massachusetts. I bought a clunky backpack and a sleeping bag patterned inside with mallard ducks in flight that didn't work too well at temperatures below 40 degrees F. The cheap leather hiking boots in those days were as clunky as the rest of 1970s gear: red-laced "Herman's Survivors" were popular, but clumsy.

These hiking forays matured into a passion for me. In 1983, I took a job in Maine as a summer camp counselor at Camp Samoset II along Lake Casco. At the end of the camping season, I arranged to be dropped off solo on the east side of New Hampshire's White Mountains with my hiking gear so I could take my first hiking journey there.

I spent the next nine days traversing the White Mountains by myself. Back then, there was little foot traffic in the Whites, and I avoided the Presidential Range, seeking the remote wilderness trails. I ran out of water on a hot day and had to summit a mountain with a dry canteen, permanently ingraining in me a deep passion for water over soft drinks—or any other beverage.

When I finally left the woods on the western verge of the White Mountains, I was picked up by my cousin Melanie to retrieve my nonessential belongings before heading back to Connecticut to resume college. As I left the trail and stepped onto the first paved road I had seen in days, a subcompact red car came speeding by. It looked like a spaceship crashing through the idyllic scenery I had been immersed in for more than a week. I had never seen a car this way: it was almost shocking in its contrast with my sojourn in the rugged terrain of the Whites. The car was loud, obnoxiously so. But it was also bizarre, alien to the habitat its driver was obliviously zooming through.

I had carried all my food for nine days, made my own fires and shelter, and collected water from springs or streams. The car was unusual because it was so utterly foreign to the self-reliance I had been learning through backpacking for years. Later, I hiked extensively in Yellowstone National Park, where I took a summer job cooking at the Old Faithful Inn (for $3.65/hour). My three-day weekends became tramps through the Rocky Mountains, usually alone. I still slept in that duck-patterned sleeping bag.

I quit my job in Yellowstone early and spent several weeks backpacking in truly wild grizzly country. I stopped applying for the required hiking permits and spent weeks bushwacking in the northwest corner of the park, using the Madison River as my boundary, seeking trout small enough to fit in my frying pan. I saw moose and bears in their pristine habitat and climbed seventy feet into a fir tree to visit the nest of a bald eagle. I bathed in the Madison and washed my clothes by grinding them into the gravel, then drying them over an open fire. I was "into the wild."

It was 1982, before most of Yellowstone Park burned to the ground in 1988. I took a job cooking pizzas in West Yellowstone, Montana (at $3.50/hour) for a couple of months before hitchhiking back to Connecticut, curling up in my tent and duck-adorned sleeping bag in wooded copses near the highway or on the edges of truck stops along the way.

We humans learn by contrasts. Most Americans have never really been thirsty, let alone truly hungry. The contrast of that White Mountains experience of intense, desperate thirst created a permanent craving for fresh, clean water, the most precious of earthly elixirs. The contrast of the noisy little red car imprinted a keen, heightened awareness of the heedless, utter dependency of most modern humans on technology and infrastructure for their most basic necessities. We don't fully realize our dependence until we have been truly *in*dependent, and most people today have never been.

An additional inspiration for this book stems from my urban journey in high-rise skyscrapers in big cities. After college, I attended the University of Connecticut School of Law, where I focused on tax law and policy, aligning with my plans to return to the United Kingdom to work and live. My first wife was British. We met when I was studying for my junior year abroad at the University of Essex. The only way to work as a lawyer in the UK was to be a tax attorney; otherwise, I would have to recertify as a British barrister or solicitor.

This excursion into tax and finance led me into the wilderness of money supply, inflation, interest rates, debt ratios, and the alienation that came with working eighty-five-hour weeks on the sixteenth floor of a Hartford, Connecticut, office building for two years before the move to England. I served for a year in the city of Birmingham, England, at a Big Six accounting firm. I felt trapped in a confined space and a narrowed intellectual pursuit, out of place. I loved England and its culture, but I missed Vermont and the American wilderness. The contrast again—having tasted the woods, I yearned for them like fresh water and air.

Yet my training in money supply and inflation, like that physical thirst and that rattling little car, didn't leave me. I watched the reckless debt of the mortgage derivative markets spiraling into chaos in the early 2000s. I vocally complained to anyone who would listen that a collapse of financial markets was inevitable, only to be roundly dismissed and ignored, powerless to warn.

By this time, I was on the third leg of my life's journey relevant to this book—I had become a Vermont farmer. After returning to America in 1992, I hung out my shingle as a country attorney and litigator. My first marriage failed, and then so did my health. At thirty-four, with a booming law practice, I became devastatingly ill with what turned out to be Lyme disease. My second wife, Jacqui, and our three children moved to Vermont's remote Northeast Kingdom, buying a 160-acre former dairy farm in January 1999 for $115,000. I believed I had to stay moving to combat the muscle-cramping fibromyalgia that had been accompanied by a bout with Lyme, and at that time, there were no ticks in northern Vermont—we didn't want our young children to be infected with Lyme.

Jacqui has had sheep and horses since she was a child and already had a foundation of farming knowledge that I lacked. She knew what quality hay looked like and how to make it. I had never made a bale of hay or milked a cow. Our Barton, Vermont, farm was where I learned how to make hay and raise livestock, which was the topic of my first book, *Small Farm Republic*.

In 2007, the stock market imploded as I had predicted. We had sold the farm just prior—I was convinced the real estate market would collapse because of reckless lending in the subprime mortgage derivatives market, which it did. We rented another former dairy farm in Irasburg for the next thirteen years, still raising grass-fed cows and sheep, and learning to an ever-greater degree how vulnerable the US food supply has become. It was the little red car again, at scale.

I was born and raised in Connecticut, but most of my family is from Vermont, and many of them still reside there. I grew up with tales of the Great

Depression and the hardships of farming. I knew how impoverished Vermont farmers had been for decades as agriculture declined, but I also knew that those farmers fared better than most city people during that arduous economic slump. The government didn't bail out Vermonters in the 1930s or 1940s the way it bailed out Wall Street in the early 2000s. People fended for themselves: they were more like backpackers than little red car drivers.

These three triangulations of my life—woodsman, financier, and livestock farmer—have unintentionally conditioned me to become acutely aware of the unprecedented threats to the modern American techno-dependent food supply. The little red cars don't run when there is no gas at the pump. The grocery store shelves don't get magically refilled when the industrial food supply system is disrupted. The COVID-19 pandemic was a mere shadow of a glimpse of the threat that still looms over this nation: the supply "crisis" by and large only affected toilet paper. Imagine the chaos and human suffering in a greater crisis that emptied grocery store shelves of essential food supplies.

This book is about those risks. On a deeper level, it is about reconnecting humans to the soil and earth from which they have so recently stepped away, into dependency on an intangible (and inedible) "currency" called money. Paper bills, debt, and gold bars are an illusion of value that can never replace the actual value of healthy soils, well-cared-for farm animals, and agricultural communities that have vanished from most American landscapes in a relative instant. This is where nutritious food ultimately comes from, including Cup-a-Soup and Mountain Meals, popular with backpackers. No hourly wage can replace that connection.

Over two centuries ago, my great-great-great-great-grandfather, Solomon Stoddard, moved to the Vermont hillside where I now reside. He may have had an ox. Family legend claims he lived in a roofed stone foundation for the first five years, which still exists near where I sit—I have taken my children there to pass on that history. A piece of the farm he bought circa 1805 is in the name of my children. Our grandchildren are the ninth generation to know this Green Mountain.

C. S. Lewis observed:

> Tolkien once remarked to me that the feeling about home must have been quite different in the days when the family had fed on the produce of the same few miles of country for six generations, and that perhaps this was why they saw nymphs in the fountains and dryads in the wood—they were not mistaken for there was in a sense a real (not

> metaphorical) connection between them and the countryside. What had been earth and air & later corn, and later still bread, really was in them. We of course who live on a standardized international diet . . . are really artificial beings and have no connection (save in sentiment) with any place on earth. We are synthetic men, uprooted. The strength of the hills is not ours.[1]

How much more synthetic and artificial are we moderns a century after Lewis? Globalism has expanded exponentially, and our foods are more processed and unrecognizable as traditional. And though I have returned to my familial grounds in Vermont, it is more like a haunting, and my own attachment is more sentimental than experiential.

However, I have been raising animals of various kinds for over two decades, and my experiences have taught me that we are connected to the soil more than we realize. I've also learned the hard way that there are powerful government and industry forces that seek to pry us inexorably away from that connection for the sake of power and profit. "Control the food, control the people."

As I emphasize throughout this book, the disconnect of most consumers and policymakers from humanity's fundamental dependency on soil, livestock, and local food system infrastructures has created an unprecedented vulnerability, particularly in America. The US led the technological innovations that increased agricultural productivity and efficiency through the so-called "Green Revolution." The USA thus occupies the front seat on the techno-dependent Magic Bus that is headed directly for a catastrophic cliff of food supply interruption or hyperinflation (likely both). Yet, this book is not a mere jeremiad—it is a call to action and increased awareness for a society that has abandoned rural agriculture in a false belief that small farms are expendable.

In his 1969 techno-thriller *The Andromeda Strain*, author Michael Crichton quoted fictitious scientific geniuses for the proposition that "every crisis has its beginnings long before the actual onset" and that " characteristic of all crises is their predictability, in retrospect." Crichton quotes a fictionalized theoretician as observing: "crisis is a situation in which a previously tolerable set of circumstances is suddenly, by the addition of another factor, rendered wholly intolerable. Whether the additional factor is political, economic, or scientific hardly matters. . . ."[2]

Americans (and most of the industrialized world) today are bookended between Tolkien's idyllic agrarian connection and a technological nightmare in which the current "tolerable set of circumstances" in the industrial food supply and its seemingly magical distribution system is "rendered wholly intolerable" by any number of unanticipated but very real threats. If a noisy little red car breaks down, a tow truck can be called. However, if the American food and distribution system collapses, there is no quick fix, and this is not a society that knows how to backpack, let alone survive off the land.

My grandparents knew how to raise and preserve food. Today's survivalists, or "preppers," delude themselves that they can withstand a sustained shock to the economy with canisters of beef jerky or buckets of dried macaroni and cheese. The widespread chaos that would quickly spread under such a techno-horrific reality would overrun every corner of the country. This book educates readers about these risks, not to persuade humanity to become doomsday preppers or buy backpacks to head into the woods, but to increase awareness so that stopgaps are embraced as public policy. Those stopgaps entail something that should be desirable and uncontroversial in any event: preserve and rebuild local farms and rural communities that have been decimated by technological "efficiencies" and industries geared toward profit above human and environmental health. The modern situation has become "rendered wholly intolerable" and carries risks of an unprecedented crisis that could prove more destructive than a space pathogen or a gain-of-function virus.

The push to consolidate food production has been accomplished by an industry eager to eliminate farmers and livestock from the rural landscape, aided by government agencies, university researchers, and a complacent consuming population migrating to perceived urban and suburban comforts. Wendell Berry, Wes Jackson, Aldo Leopold, and other writers referenced herein have raised alarms for decades to no avail—does it require a crisis *worse* than a pandemic to teach humanity a lesson that will make the Great Depression look comparatively mild?

The current reliance on this illusion of cheap plenty, evident in chock-full grocery store shelves, has obscured hidden costs that are now becoming visible. Any grocery store clerk can explain how quickly the whole illusion can dissolve like vapor. Any money supply scholar can explain how rapidly a fiat currency can become worthless—even the beloved greenback. Any farmer can relate how little most consumers comprehend about the complexities and risks to agriculture posed by modern industrial consolidation and long-distance distribution. Any long-trail hiker can understand the dangers of complete dependency on automobiles and telephones. Any half-competent attorney can make the case for this modern peril of famine within this hubris of progress and the trust of non-farmer "experts." Elon Musk can dream of Mars, but he can't milk a cow.

I have attempted in these pages to examine how the increasingly globalized food supply system threatens to crack, collapse, or be deliberately subverted by globalist or government entities, political or ideological movements, or just plain human folly. I advocate for sensible policies to support the local agriculture that Americans say they want to nurture, while they blindly allow regulatory and market forces to continue choking it into a whimsical memory. It is not just farmers I advocate for, but the deracinated denizens of cities who are unaware of their own connections to soil and countryside, much like mighty Rome just before its fall.

It is not country bumpkins, but all of society, that must become aware of the foundational importance of agriculture and support America's farmers before they become extinct. The Make America Healthy Again (MAHA) movement offers hope. The MAHA movement is both bipartisan and cultural. It represents a deep, almost subconscious, anxiety that there are profound threats to Americans' food supplies, distribution systems, and production methods. These concerns are not confined to one political, racial, or class identity, though there are powers that would seek to divide people along those lines to maintain the toxic status quo.

Introduction

The most joyful times of my childhood were spent in Brookfield, Vermont, where my mother's family have lived for generations. There were no stores to visit or video games to play—the forests, fields, and farms were our playground. I loved being around the farm animals. My great-uncle George Bradshaw milked Jersey cows in neighboring Chelsea, Vermont, and allowed me to help herd the cows with a little stick when I was five years old. My great-uncle Harold Taylor also milked Jerseys, in nearby Williamstown, Vermont, where I would visit the calves in the barn and let them suck on my thumb or lick my hair.

Perhaps the most influential person in my life was my maternal grandmother, Cesarine Stoddard. Grammie was born and raised on the dairy farm operated by the Taylors. Her mother died during the Spanish flu, when Gram was just eight years old. Grammie was very popular in the region, having been a schoolteacher in a one-room schoolhouse for decades. She was extremely frugal, having endured the Great Depression. She indulged us grandchildren in ice cream and big meals, but she didn't take sass and could be a sharp disciplinarian.

Because my parents divorced when I was young, I would often stay in Vermont for weeks at a time to spare my mother babysitting fees. I loved staying on the old Vermont family farm and never wanted to go back to Connecticut when the brief time was up. I played with my many cousins in the woods, poked around in the barn or woodshed, picked apples or blackberries, or searched through the family dump in the steep ravine across the road.

Grammie was a teacher not merely of books but of origins. She described the Vermont landscape by family histories, and could recount who lived where and when, what they did for work, who they married or cheated on, family tragedies, or where they moved off to. Directions always began with something like, "You go past Sadie and Harold's and then turn left where the Browns' place is" or "past Cosset's and the old schoolhouse." Grammie was an encyclopedia of mountainside history. Her identity was bound tightly with her community on that Brookfield hill where she had lived her entire life.

My first regular job was in Chelsea, Vermont, stocking shelves at my Uncle Don's Chelsea Country Store. I worked from 8 a.m. to 5 p.m. each day for one dollar an hour. Don was a butcher and processed pigs and cows from the store cooler for the locals. I operated a pricing gun that printed the cost of groceries on little stickers that I attached to each product before restocking the shelves. Hank Williams and various classic country music singers echoed through the ancient maple-floored building from Don's stack of 8-track cassettes behind the meat counter. Grammie drove me to the store each morning and picked me up at five. At age twelve, I thus began learning about food distribution.

At age sixteen (in 1979), I worked at a Stop & Shop grocery store for $2.90 per hour, stocking shelves and bagging groceries. The store manager, a thick-mustached, thin-framed fellow named Mr. Fortin, was a crusty, cranky overseer who would spy on us to ensure we were working swiftly. I came to appreciate the effort he made to teach me a work ethic: he wasn't just cracking the whip but had a real passion for the business and for imparting a work ethic to us young part-timers.

Similarly, one of the stock clerks took a liking to me and invested in my learning curve in a way that has always resonated with me. Like store clerks today, we rolled carts out stacked high with an assortment of brown boxes slotted for unloading in their appropriate aisles, and we were alternately ignored or disdained by shoppers as they busily bypassed us to make their purchases.

As we sliced open boxes with utility knives and transferred cartons of breakfast cereal or cans of soup onto the designated shelves, the elderly stock clerk often lectured me about the obliviousness of the people who milled past us, not just to our labors but to the magic of the modern grocery store. Sweeping a hand past the ever-full shelves, Dave would say, "All it takes is a snowstorm or an electricity outage, and all the milk and bread are gone in a day! If it weren't for us, this entire store would be empty in three or four days."

I've never been able to shop for groceries without that awareness. Modern food distribution is truly astonishing, but lurking behind it is a delicate supply chain of which shelf-stocking laborers are but tiny cogs. Since 1979, wages and food prices have increased, but that hidden dependency has become both more obscured from "consumers" who take it for granted and more vulnerable due to just-in-time inventories, which are shipped from faraway factories, warehouses, and distribution centers, supplied from Chinese shipping containers or tractor-trailer trucks from Mexico.

Behind the illusion of plenty is a lurking threat to the American food shopper and small family farm alike. The average age of a farmer in the US is about sixty. Within the next fifteen years, approximately half of all farms and farmland will change hands. Such a dramatic handing over of the reins to food supplies is unheard of except in wartime (or perhaps revolution—Mao, Pol Pot, and Stalin effected comparable rapid shifts, with devastating results.) Younger generations eschew the long days and unstable incomes of farming; hedge funds, foreign nations, and billionaires, however, are readily available to buy up farmland and further concentrate their control of these vital resources.

This book is for people interested in understanding the magnitude of these threats and fighting back. Fewer chemicals in agriculture, reduced corporate capture of regulatory agencies, improved testing of food additives, and regulatory and fiscal support for rural and regenerative agriculture are vitally essential policies that must be adopted by both political parties as soon as possible. Bipartisan corporate favoritism has created this crisis; bipartisan bridgebuilding is required to reverse it.

The potential for Americans' grocery stores to become empty overnight has increased dramatically since a shelf-stocking teenager learned of such threats in 1979. The COVID-19 pandemic offered a glimpse as meats and eggs were rationed at many stores, and toilet paper shortages became a headlining crisis. Americans face a tipping point as millions of acres of prime farmland are absorbed into the corporate colossus of industrial consolidation. It is imperative that citizens become informed and united to protect the foundation of their health, economy, and liberties from globalist corporate domination. Time is running out fast. A storm is on the horizon.

CHAPTER 1

It's Living Soil, Not Dead Dirt!

> Culture is a state of awareness of the land's collective functioning. A culture premised on the destructive dominance of a single species can have but short duration.[1]
>
> —Aldo Leopold

Life begins and ends with soil. In humankind's embrace of technological marvels, that foundational aspect of life has been taken for granted, even abused. Scientific reductionism has limited the essentially limitless diversity of microbial life to a "substrate" labeled "dirt." This simplistic oversight may have been the greatest miscalculation of the scientific age, contributing to illness through nutrient depletion and the use of agricultural chemicals. It equally threatens the entire food supply at its deepest foundations.

Following nearly a century of technological advances that increased agricultural yields and efficiencies through the use of machinery and synthetic fertilizers, human scientists are only recently revisiting the false assumptions made about soil. Soil science reveals that humans are directly connected to the soil: their gut microbiomes are literally formed, fueled, and fed by the soil's microbiome. This directly impacts human health, particularly concerning allergies,[2] autism,[3] and autoimmune disorders.[4] Industrial agricultural processes have profound implications for soil health. Erosion and water loss, aggravated by practices that degrade soil health, now threaten to inflict steady losses of productivity and eventually lead to the desertification of America's most fertile farmlands.

Humanity has thus been on an unusual journey in its quest to harness the world's natural forces, often sacrificing good health in a drive to conquer death and disease. Modern humans have divorced themselves from that soil, creating a unique modern predicament that now threatens to harm the soil upon which

American food production depends, depleting vital minerals while increasing water usage and soil erosion. The same antimicrobial forces that are wiping out the American gut are steadily killing the soil biome that ultimately feeds it.

The looming threat of an extraordinary collapse of the entire modern food production and distribution system will further separate human families from the bacterial colonies that nurture them. Quietly, behind the gradual shift away from human microbial refueling by invisible microorganisms, without which we would quickly perish, humanity has also become separated from food itself. Not just food lacking microbial and nutritional health, or packed with chemicals, but what food itself *is*: what it serves, how it is produced, harvested, processed, and distributed, and how much it "costs," not just in fiat currency but in microbial action, soil health, water use, human labor, chemical contamination, fossil fuel use, etc. This alienation has allowed the steady degradation of the nation's healthiest soils to go unnoticed.

The Green Revolution: The Good, the Bad, and the Ugly

The so-called "Green Revolution" of the twentieth century refers to the global proliferation of industrial agriculture following World War II. Agricultural production underwent a rapid and widespread shift from traditional methods to reliance on new hybrid crop strains, mechanization, expanded irrigation infrastructure, and the use of chemical fertilizers, herbicides, and pesticides. These shifts profoundly increased crop yields in the short term. They lifted millions of people out of poverty, but over time, productivity has declined as the hidden environmental and health costs of these practices have become evident.

The benefits of industrial food production were soon visible—increased yields of cereal crops supplied meals to millions and allowed many nations to become net food exporters rather than importers, thereby boosting their economies and food security simultaneously. Poverty was widely eradicated, real incomes rose, infant mortality rates declined, and more food was grown on less land. The putative "father" of the Green Revolution, Norman Borlaug, was awarded the Nobel Peace Prize in 1970, credited with saving over a billion human lives.

The modern world of agricultural technology is truly astounding. Genetic engineering, hormones, antibiotics, and other scientific advances have joined a fossil-fuel-powered array of mechanical marvels that surpass the wildest imaginings of science fiction. Magnificent computer-guided tractors with sophisticated attachments plow the ground, seed vast regions, spray fertilizers, insecticides, and specially formulated chemicals, and harvest a bounty unimaginable a century ago. Specialty machines have been designed for harvesting corn, wheat, berries, watermelons, and greens—a world of technology nearly as varied as the crops available to grow. Irrigation, processing, and distribution networks similarly impress the human imagination.

But this fantastic bounty comes with a tremendous cost. Industrially tilled soils are sickly and eroding. Precious underground water aquifers have been slurped up in dry regions, evaporating rapidly on dying soils. Chemical applications have sickened the soil microbiome, depleted vital minerals, and killed pollinators.[5] Human health is deteriorating as man-made food products tainted with chemicals and deprived of nutritional value have replaced natural provisions.

As is so often the case with technological innovation, the downsides of this revolution were not immediately evident. Because the chief motivation of agricultural conversion was to fill empty stomachs, food quality and ecosystem health were not prioritized. Modern crops, especially those reliant on GMO-dependent monocultures, including tens of millions of acres of corn and soy, rely heavily on synthetic fertilizers, which deplete soils and water resources. The chemical applications (especially pesticides, glyphosate, and herbicides) upon which they are dependent inflict ecological destruction.

The ugly truth of the Green Revolution is that seemingly miraculous productivity gains have masked numerous problems that far outweigh the supposed benefits. Compacted soils reduce tilth and yield;[6] chemical applications weaken soils, accelerating erosion and necessitating ever-greater applications of fertilizers and other chemicals. Roughly half of the world's food production is now dependent on synthetic nitrogen fertilizer use.[7]

Genetic modifications permitted an even greater extension of these perceived production benefits, adding glyphosate as a chemical dependency to the supposedly salvific industrial food production system. America industry, university researchers, and government agencies all pushed US food production toward greater "efficiency" and yields, sacrificing crop biodiversity and local agrarian cultures on the altars of profit and technological progress. Large-scale agricultural production increased farm consolidation. Only larger enterprises had access to credit (often from foreign investors) and could take advantage of bulk purchasing power.

The consolidation of food production, processing, and distribution into an ever-shrinking club of enormously powerful corporations or massive farms diminishes local food supplies and local food security. It also centralizes food production, creating a dependency on fossil fuel energy—diesel and gasoline to power tractors and equipment, and natural gas to manufacture synthetic fertilizers.

This arrangement worked economically as long as oil and other fuels remained cost-effective. Rising fertilizer costs (which spiked sharply during the COVID-19 pandemic) have already begun to reverse those favorable economics. Over the decades, industrial crop yields have declined, necessitating ever-higher applications of fertilizers and other inputs to maintain yields. Pesticides, herbicides, and defoliants, as well as agricultural machinery and irrigation systems, are all derived from and dependent upon crude oil for their manufacture.

Industrial fertilizers have dramatically exacerbated environmental problems, especially from synthetic urea—excess urea results in emissions of nitrous oxide, which is considered by the greenhouse gas metric to be 265 times more potent than carbon dioxide. Water quality and quantity have both suffered significantly from the Green Revolution, as chemicals pollute drinking water and aquifers are depleted far more quickly than nature can replenish them.

Corporations profited tremendously from the Green Revolution, but human and environmental health have been dangerously compromised. Commodity output and economic growth increased at the expense of soil, water, food wholesomeness, and food security. Long-standing regenerative farming practices were abandoned, chemicals were spewed recklessly, and water supplies were gobbled up shortsightedly. Unsurprisingly, yield rates have steadily declined, necessitating the use of more land, chemicals, and fossil fuels.

Inexpensive, plentiful food supplies are thus a short-term illusion, constructed atop a fragile dependency on finite energy sources that are steadily becoming more costly. The system is both economically and environmentally unsustainable, as well as unhealthy for humans and the ecosystem. Yet, this unnatural production model is enthusiastically embraced by the cadre of corporate profiteers who have led the charge to "save the world" with gimmicks and deceptions about agriculture. These same forces now conspire to pressure the entire world's agricultural production into this toxic, food-dominating model in the name of mitigating climate change and averting global famine. This consolidation increases the long-term risks of famine.

The greatest cost of this seemingly wondrous industrial transition remains concealed from most people's awareness: dependency on these technologies, replacing the once-universal local connection between humans and soil. When God evicted Adam and Eve from the Garden of Eden, He left them an umbilical cord to the life-giving Earth. That nurturing connection has been effectively severed by the radical modern shift from a direct relationship with soil, plants, and animals to a dependency on cheap oil pumped from deserts or ocean floors far away, on computer chips manufactured in Taiwan, on distant, impersonal supply lines, and on processing and preservatives.

Writer and environmental activist Wendell Berry prophetically observed:

> The food industrialists have by now persuaded millions of consumers to prefer food that is already prepared. They will grow, deliver, and cook your food for you and (just like your mother) beg you to eat it. That they do not yet offer to insert it, pre-chewed, into your mouth is only because they have found no profitable way to do so. We may rest assured that they would be glad to find such a way. The ideal industrial food consumer would be strapped to a table with a tube running from the factory directly into his or her stomach.[8]

Corporate America, now sitting at the table of the World Economic Forum in partnership with the United Nations and the World Health Organization, seeks to make the final connection of that tube from its New World Order factories to our human navels. Dazzled by the technology and ease promised, humanity has taken the proverbial bait at great peril.

Once disconnected from rich soils and nutrient-dense foods, humans become not only physically ill but also alienated from other vital connections. Wendell Berry correctly observes that "As industrial technology advances and enlarges, and in the process assumes greater social, economic, and political force, it carries people away from where they belong by history, culture, deeds, association, and affection."[9] This severance unmoors modern human populations from their ability to reclaim their own food production, including cultural knowledge, community, rural lands, livestock, seed genetics, and the tools and other resources required to grow their own food.

The journey to rediscover the primacy of food in human health is a homecoming to agri*culture*, its rich history, complex economics, vibrant community, and profound meaning. It is not just food that has set modern Americans adrift: it is the alienation from farming and food culture, the loss of rural communities and economic sustenance, and the abandonment of agrarian life in favor of techno-urban alienation and confinement. Most importantly, it is an utter surrender of self-determination and liberty to corporate-government domination.

The Loss of Seeds

The US lost an estimated 93 percent of its heirloom seed varieties between 1903 and 1983.[10] Heirloom, or heritage, varieties of fruits and vegetables are cultivars that have been preserved and handed down through local farmers and communities, and which are not used in modern commercial agriculture. For instance, the US planted nearly five hundred varieties of lettuce in 1903, reduced to just thirty-six by 1983.[11] These additional food reserves, along with the biodiversity they offered as protection against future blight or other plant diseases, are now lost forever.

The impact of this decline, repeated in most vegetable crops including radishes, peas, and beets, is more than merely a loss of biodiversity. The fate of heirloom seed diversity demonstrates the broader industrial shift in modern agriculture to a dangerous focus on profits and yields at the expense of the health of plants, soils, and humans. Moreover, hidden within the short-term illusion of plenty are seeds of destruction: food crops are concentrated in a few large producers instead of being stewarded by millions of small households that once saved their own seeds. These industrial crops are then transported huge distances to consumers who have become geographically, biologically, and culturally disconnected from their food supplies. This is a disaster waiting to unfold, repeated in the industrial consolidation of the nation's livestock industry.

The theological concept of an "idol" contemplates a fixation by which the human focus is so absorbed that God (in this case, God or Nature's provision of food) becomes obscured to the point of invisibility or irrelevance. Humanity's modern techno-mystical faith in industrial technologies' ability to guarantee a perpetual food supply is a misplaced idolatry. The only things that human technology has created that last forever are the more than twelve thousand "forever chemicals" (per- and polyfluoroalkyl substances, known as PFAS) that never break down in the ecosystem and accumulate in the human body.[12]

Obscuring the human connection to the land is a panoply of uniquely modern idols. Grocery stores present an illusion of plenty, and yet a busy hive of workers constantly replenishes those shelves daily with provisions trucked long distances from faraway factories, many overseas. The tractor-trailer trucks that deliver most of these "goods" are modern technological marvels, dependent on deteriorating highway infrastructure, microchips not manufactured in America, and diesel exhaust fluid (DEF) primarily imported from China.[13] Massive barges stacked with countless containers ferry many of these foods through international waters. Magnificent tractors, combines, sprayers, and harvesters move about sowing, tending, and reaping the crops packed for transport, which are then processed and packaged in sprawling, gleaming factories using yet more technological specialization—all dependent on cheap fossil fuels.

Throughout history, this dramatic shift in food production has been fleeting, dependent on cheap energy for its brief existence. The techno-idolatry of modern man is, in turn, utterly reliant on the steady and plentiful supply of low-cost energy, without which food prices would quickly spiral out of the reach of affordability for most consumers.

Concurrent with this dependency is another idolatrous folly: fiat currencies are themselves a human creation, not nearly as clever as the current state of the world suggests. Americans worship the US dollar, but gargantuan debt and reckless bipartisan money-printing threaten to unmoor the mighty greenback from any actual underlying value. This means that, aside from oil and gas supplies, humanity has staked its ability to continue procuring affordable food on an illusion of a reliable currency.

This dependency of farming, food production, and food distribution on cheap energy and fiat money extends, of course, to other areas of modern life. Americans who heated their homes with coal or firewood a century ago now employ "efficient" gas or oil heat or perhaps wood pellets manufactured in a factory. The heavily subsidized push to convert all heating systems to electric heat pumps is a final drive toward complete grid dependency: homes will be utterly reliant on both stable fuel prices and a stable currency to stave off the cold.

The wonders of modern travel and farming have occluded the collective memory of human dependency on horses and oxen. In a few decades of technological transformation that began a mere century ago, man's long-standing symbiotic relationship with horses for work and pleasure vanished, replaced by cars and trucks that have become far more technical, computerized, and microchipped than when the Model A Ford became popular. Cars, tractors, and trucks pollute; horses and oxen gifted humans with their manure, *locally*.

Refrigeration transformed the ability to store food, enabling larger purchases, fewer trips to the store, reductions in foodborne disease, and unprecedented liberty to enjoy fresher, more diverse foods. Combining refrigeration with transportation permitted the sale of perishables over longer distances with less loss, loosening societal bonds yet further. The United States in 2025 imports more than half of its lamb from faraway Australia and New Zealand,[14] a market inconceivable on such a scale in 1930—not very environmentally sound, and vulnerable to disruption.

Companion to these stunning advances has been globalization itself. Wendell Berry has characterized globalization as the greatest weapon of mass destruction ever created by humanity, referring to its culture-leveling, economy-destroying tendency to reduce all issues to profitability, efficiency, and market share. In the short term, consumers have benefited from lower costs for goods and a broader selection. However, globalization has favored the sizeable corporate entity over the less competitive local merchant or manufacturer, leading to consolidation and elimination of diversity in production. This has fostered yet greater dependency under the illusion of endless plenty. Additionally, globalization exponentially amplifies the risks of invasive species, disease spread, and supply chain disruptions, while also increasing pollution through long-distance shipping.

With all this abundance has come unprecedented waste. Americans discard nearly 40 percent of their food supplies annually, most of it into overflowing landfills, where it comprises 22 percent of municipal solid waste.[15] This profligacy further damages the ecosystem, not just in terms of carbon dioxide or methane, but also in the chemicals superfluously poured over soil and water.

This steady destruction and depletion is masked by an illusion of affordable plenty, which itself encourages yet more consolidation and dependency. This vicious cycle of detachment from the local and simple in favor of dependency on the complex and distant has "developed" humanity into ever greater peril, even as the pursuit of digital entertainment, online gaming, and other technological diversions distracts from the historical necessity of being aware of food and self-reliance.

Eclipsing Vulnerability

This partial list of technological dependencies that have interrupted the natural order of human interdependence with plant, soil, and animals is a reflection of the dark warnings of Isaiah about humanity's worship of idols it has created with its own hands.[16] The push by globalists to reverse anthropogenic climate change by converting humanity to a diet of bugs, processed plants, and synthetic meats further increases food dependency on multinational corporations and a globalized food production and distribution system. Instead of moving mankind further over that industrial cliff, a return to a focus on natural soil and nutritional processes is the solution to environmental degradation and will improve human health outcomes while reclaiming food security.[17]

The world, and America in particular, face an inevitable contraction and correction of their food supplies driven by economic, social, and geographical realities. Inflation, technological dependency, and fragile distribution systems threaten a starvation never witnessed in world history, let alone in America.

The soil and earth are sufficient to provide food for all humans, albeit with hard work and distributism, so that the cultural, economic, and environmental interconnectedness of humans and food is nurtured. Modern mankind has tried to slip the surly bonds of toil in dirt, replacing that life-giving association with a sterilizing, alienating, toxifying technological imposter system that destroys soil, water, animal, and human health. The consequence of an abrupt disruption of that impressive but illusory usurpation of the natural order of life will inflict unprecedented food insecurity, food price inflation, social and political upheaval, widespread malnutrition, and even starvation in what has long been regarded as "the breadbasket of the world."

There is only one way out of this perilous plight: revitalizing America's rural communities by supporting existing farms and encouraging more young people to homestead or start an agricultural venture.

CHAPTER 2

From Soil to Computer Chip

> It is a well-understood principle in business that any organization like agricultural research . . . stands in need of a periodical critical examination to ascertain whether the results obtained correspond with the cost and whether any modifications are needed in the light of new knowledge and experience.[1]
>
> —Sir Albert Howard, *An Agricultural Testament* (1940)

The technological achievements of modern society are genuinely amazing, and this awe extends to advances in agricultural science and production. Unfortunately, the "Green Revolution" was presented by industry and government as profitable to farmers, but it more often led to farm debt, input dependency, and the destruction of farmlands. At the same time, profits flowed to fertilizer and grain companies, tractor and equipment manufacturers, and university salaries for "studies" of agricultural productivity. The number of farms steadily declined. Consumers didn't notice or care much about farm families as their grocery bills dropped. The modern miracle of industrial agriculture was praised as a great wonder of the world, saving humankind from famine forever.

Even before this explosion of plenty, wise voices prophesied doom. Aldo Leopold and others warned of the life-giving centrality of healthy soils for human health and explained that humanity was destroying soils: "The effort to control the health of land has not been very successful. It is now generally understood that when soil loses fertility, or washes away faster than it forms, and when water systems exhibit abnormal floods and shortages, the land is sick."[2] Sir Albert Howard, another strident voice on soil proved correct today, told farmers more in 1940 than all the modern universities and gene-splicing laboratories combined. Citing multiple studies demonstrating that artificial fertilizers caused "a continuous increase in disease, both in crops and in livestock,"[3] Sir Albert held that "transforming wastes into humus" was "the key to prosperity."[4] His essential work, *An Agricultural Testament,* influenced many great agrarians, including Wendell Berry, who similarly warned of the dire threat that soil erosion and urbanization posed to America.

Sir Albert grew up on a Shropshire (England) farm and excelled in botany at Cambridge before working in India for twenty-six years, directing several agricultural research centers. Reminiscent of American colonists abducted by Native Americans who then chose to remain in tribal cultures, Howard traveled to India to teach that nation about modern agricultural methods but was instead converted by their agri-*culture* to understand the primacy of soil microbes and natural manures in composting and humus creation, calling the Indian peasant farmers and the pests in their soil his "two professors."

Food consumers today are essentially being asked to choose between two professors—one says junk food is fine, and plants and animals can be raised like a laboratory recipe using nutrients and chemicals; the other says the entire food system depends not on the chemicals but the microbes teeming in a sensitive network of organisms that must not be disrupted with artificial chemical adjuncts. Howard became that second professor for farmers willing to listen, forging the organic food movement while rebelling against a growing scientific view that plants could be grown effectively simply by spraying three basic chemicals on them: nitrogen, phosphorus, and potassium (NPK).

Howard's premise, outlined in his book *Farming and Gardening for Health or Disease,* was that plant and animal diseases arose from unhealthy soils, and that rebuilding and nurturing these soils would enrich the health of plants, animals, and humans. In this, Howard was combating NPK professors: Justus von Liebig and others argued a reductionist (Cartesian) chemical viewpoint, dubbed the Sprengel-Liebig Law of the Minimum, in which plants do not depend on soil microbes but on a few crucial elements, arguing that they "find new nutritive material only in inorganic substances."

Howard became increasingly distrustful of industrial forces that were more interested in profiting from humans than making them healthier. Biased profiteers sought to discredit his theories, and university "science" has been polluted ever since.[5] Farmers were told by industrialists that all they needed was magical (often government-subsidized) chemicals to bloom their fields; their destruction and debt enslavement—along with the loss of their farms, livestock, and soils—ensued.

Howard's view of modern industrial agriculture was summed up ominously in *An Agricultural Testament,* wherein he compared modern practices to the folly of ancient Rome:

> The farmers of the West are repeating the mistakes made by ancient Rome. The soils of the Roman Empire, however, were only called upon to assuage the hunger of a relatively small population. The demands of the machine were then almost non-existent. In the West there are relatively more stomachs to fill while the growing hunger of the machine is an additional burden on the soil. . . . Can mankind regulate its affairs so that its chief possession—the fertility of the soil—is preserved? On the answer to this question the future of civilization depends.[6]

That future is here, and Albert Howard is a much better authority on farming and soil science than Klaus Schwab, Bill Gates, or the World Health Organization's Tedros Adhanom Ghebreyesus.

The United States has witnessed monopolistic efforts to consolidate control of food supplies for profit throughout its history. Industrial consolidation in the early twenty-first century accelerated during World War I as America increased food production to feed a starving Europe. Following the war, US crop prices plummeted as Europe resumed growing its own foods. Abusive practices by entrenched monopolies ensured that equipment, fertilizer, and other farm inputs remained high in cost. During the Great Depression, Americans struggled to afford food while 750,000 family farms failed between 1930 and 1935—a quarter of all the nation's farms.

By the 1990s, the EPA, FDA, and USDA were all clearly captured by pharmaceutical, chemical, agricultural, and food corporations. Pretending to protect the American consumer while running interference for the planet's worst corporate polluters, the flow of chemicals was turned on full spigot. Some offending substances were rightly targeted, but atrazine, glyphosate, and a long list of highly profitable chemical compounds banned around the world are still poured copiously over Americans' soils and food crops.

The issue of agricultural pollution may not immediately appear relevant to food security, but implicit in the study of soil science is the threat of desertification, irreversible erosion, and the loss of precious water resources forever. The toxins and practices now standard to agricultural production harm human health, undermine economic productivity, and destroy rural American culture and community. They also create food (chemical) addictions,[7] anxiety,[8] depression,[9] and lower IQs[10] and otherwise weaken the human ability to liberate itself. These chemicals and industrial methods are the silent killers of the entire industrial agricultural system. Industrial agriculture is in its environmental death throes: this is what "unsustainable" means.

Into this mix entered the sudden propaganda that it is not chemicals that are destroying human health, or industrial farming that is destroying human connection, culture, economies, and cultures—the great threat to the planet and its humanoid denizens became an urgent "inconvenient truth" overnight, as Al Gore's book and movie launch ushered in a diversion to war on life-giving carbon dioxide. The resulting climate change crusade shifted the entire environmental movement's focus from known anthropogenic *toxic carcinogens and endocrine disruptors* to less provable assertions that nontoxic carbon dioxide and other "greenhouse gases" cause planetary warming.

The immediate consequences of this political shift were twofold. Voters were told to focus on greenhouse gas "pollution," and a massive new industry was born to manufacture supposed solutions to "carbon toxicity." The truth that this was a corporate scam is visible in the toxic *chemical* pollution resulting from this response. Despite propaganda relentlessly advocating for their salvific urgency, the deleterious environmental impacts of these heavily subsidized "clean" technologies are apocalyptic in their effect.

The debate about whether humans are adversely impacting the climate with carbon dioxide (and cows are suddenly enemy number one in the environmental crosshairs) is a red herring. As chronicled here and well-documented in the death of birds, insects, amphibians, and just about everything else in the early twenty-first century, it is abundantly clear and beyond rational argument that whether or not humankind is spiking the globe's temperatures, it is *most certainly* destroying the Earth with ecotoxins at an accelerating rate.

Today's "inconvenient truth" is that the rate of toxification has now gone into overdrive, aided and abetted by a short-term, regressively leveraged spending spree on "renewables" manufacturing processes that spew phthalates, PFAS, and a list of thousands of forever chemicals into the air, soils, water, oceans—and children's bodies. How quickly humanity could agree that toxic chemicals are bad if not embroiled in conflict over carbon dioxide!

Environmentalism's priority shift from human health to climate change inverted the consumer conscience from "What might these products I use do to harm me?" to "How do these products harm the planet?" Consumers transformed from humans to be protected, to shameful polluters who should feel guilty—not for flat-screen TVs, mobile phones, or a hundred polluting recreational activities, but for eating meat, driving cars, and warming their homes. Not the nonessential pleasures but the vital fundamentals in the human hierarchy of needs. Not the carcinogens and endocrine disruptors, but carbon dioxide.

There is a difference, then, between "climate science" and "climate politics," and within environmentalism, a natural enough divergence between carbon dioxide that allegedly causes climate change and man-made chemical poisons that most certainly do cause death and disease. Theory versus law; nontoxic versus toxic. The solution to the climate problem proposed by globalists and environmentalists was to *generate more ecotoxins than ever before to mitigate the flow of carbon dioxide.*

EVs and solar panels are the shiny new thing—buying one's way out of consumption but consuming *more* instead of less. EVs pose planet-toxifying threats by virtue of their lithium and tire rubber requirements alone, no matter how much carbon dioxide they do or do not "save." They are new pollution in old bottles: they all end up in landfills beside the solar panels, fiberglass wind turbines, and heat pumps being churned out like techno-hotcakes "to save the world." This frenzy of industrial activity is not saving the world—its demise is instead being hastened for corporate profit and globalist domination.

Industrial agriculture, facing increasing scrutiny for its endless chemical applications to America's farmlands and food, was rescued by the perfect environmental scapegoat in the pivot to "carbon pollution." The push for organic foods free from agricultural toxins and for labeling that would alert consumers, thereby undermining profitability, posed a serious threat to the quarterly earnings reports of Big Ag and Big Chem. Instead of allowing small rural farms to reclaim their market share, these companies could perpetuate their existing processes—and even create new ones—in the name of mitigating climate change.

Plant-based and synthetic meats have attracted many billions of dollars in venture capital and corporate investments. These are dependent on the current chemical earth-soaking required for (often patented) monoculture GMO soybean, corn, and other plant crops. Global organizations and national governments are advocating for a plant-based diet, greater agricultural centralization, and reduced livestock numbers—increasing dependence on synthetic fertilizers, pesticides, fungicides, and herbicides while removing manure-producing cows from agricultural systems.

Much carbon sequestration is attributed to forest regrowth (called "rewilding"). Forests sequester carbon dioxide until the trees die or burn; unless harvested, the carbon is eventually rereleased back into the air. Grasslands, especially rotationally grazed farmland, sequester far more CO_2 than forests, *indefinitely*.[11] This is why well-managed livestock, rotationally grazed and fed grass instead of grains, are the *solution* to the carbon lost to the atmosphere due to industrial agricultural processes.

Carbon credits pitched as beneficial to the environment are a scam. Soil health is not measured by carbon content alone, any more than plant growth is governed solely by three NPK elements. Carbon credits (even if accurately measured and administered) are only marketable "at scale." They will thus favor large operators over small ones, allocating yet more subsidization to Big Ag at the expense of small or start-up farms. Carbon credits do not reward farms that have already been good stewards of the soil, and they are exploited by large polluters who purchase them to "offset" discharges from industrial smokestacks with illusory carbon sequestration by forest owners and farmers.

Another type of carbon sequestration is underground storage of liquefied carbon dioxide. This method is scientifically dubious. An entire industry has evolved with taxpayer subsidies and tax credits to launch this mad scheme that likely doesn't work at all: the ground-stored carbon dioxide seeps back out, as reflected in IRS recapture rules for 45Q tax credits that claw back payments when the liquified CO_2 escapes through a complex scheme.[12]

Big Tech money has flowed copiously to "rescue" humanity from carbon dioxide while spewing forever chemicals and cell-damaging toxins in this devilish bargain. NASA has developed satellite technology to "help" farmers track warming and crop health—while claiming Americans' lawns are a net carbon sink (ignoring fossil fuel and manufacturing inputs entirely) that need not be monitored or curtailed.

Routinely, these new technocratic "solutions" to the supposed problem of cow-induced climate change are touted as world-saving and game-changing, even characterizing toxic chemical pollution as "green" or "sustainable." EVs are presented as "net-zero" regarding carbon, but they are anything but "net-ecotoxins." Neither are solar panels, heat pumps, or wind turbines. Yet the shameless industrial overlords who have lulled humanity into ever greater dependence on the processes that are sickening them are constantly devising new ways to deceive.

The climate-change "industry" cannot profit from peasant farming, let alone monopolize, control, and maximize profit margins for food, the way it can with proprietary processed foods. Therefore, the new sales pitch is that scientific technology will "cure" the climate crisis by increasing crop yields using the same soil-destroying chemicals and methods that *caused* the agricultural crisis.

How the world ever fed itself before Big Tech arrived is a long story: how the world will feed itself after Big Tech implodes is the issue addressed in these pages. Consider the stealthy sales pitch for microbe-destroying synthetic fertilizers (as opposed to ubiquitous animal manures) being "refashioned" to rescue agriculture from the damage those applications have inflicted. Scientists claim they are developing a "new" version of synthetic products for the industry's existing manure substitutes:

> Changing how ammonia is produced has environmental and economic benefits and enhances food security. This can be achieved by lowering the energy requirements and carbon emissions associated with traditional ammonia production. . . .
>
> Several key areas that the research focuses on are reducing environmental impact, advancing green chemistry, promoting energy security and catalyzing technological innovation.[13]

Industrialism's pied piper is playing its misleading flute to itching consumer ears—the solution is at hand, and humanity will be rescued from its industrial folly by yet more of the same. "Catalyzing technological innovation" is quasi-religious rhetoric: such catalysts have *created* the crisis that Albert Howard rightly warned would threaten mass famine and the fall of Western civilization.

These scientists claim they are "promoting a healthier planet" by reducing, but not eliminating, the ecotoxic discharges from a destructive industrial system that converts fracked natural gas (methane) into synthetic urea fertilizer, ostensibly to "save" the soil. This is sugarcoated with climate cult terminology that tortures the English language: synthetic fertilizers now will "enhance food security" using "green chemistry" for "environmental benefits." Synthetic fertilizers sustain magnificent wealth for corporate players, but they compromise food security and soil health.

Microbe-rich livestock manures rebuild deteriorating soils, like those of the bison herds of old, improve soil nutrients for both plant and human health, and enhance water retention. No laboratory will ever improve on that method, no matter how silk-tongued its researchers. The very terms "green chemistry" and "greener alternative" are misnomers and deceptions. There is nothing green about synthetic fertilizers, and the most that can be honestly said about proposed "improvements" to these destructive processes is that they are "less toxic" while remaining highly damaging.

Examples abound of the industrial ag and food processing industries striving to reinvent themselves as consumer-concerned environmental gurus. They have long proven themselves to be as profit-driven and consumer-callous as cigarette manufacturers (who once also owned most of the nation's food processing enterprises).

A key focus to reverse this grand deception is to educate Americans about the "real" science of genetically modified organisms (GMOs). To hear the techno-mystical industrialists promoting their food wares, GMOs are the greatest invention ever to hit the Earth.

Most GMO crops have not been developed to increase yields or grow crops in new frontiers—they have been explicitly developed for proprietary profitability. GMO corn and soy, for instance, consist mainly of plant species designed to grow in the presence of a plant-killing chemical called glyphosate, popularly known in a proprietary mixture by the (patented) brand name Roundup.

The technology is admittedly impressive—Roundup kills virtually every green thing it touches, inhibiting the ability to grow by interfering with the vital shikimate pathway, but not the corn, soy, or other crops that have been genetically altered to withstand it. The glyphosate and its residues remain in the soil, in food, and in American women's breast milk,[14] and the EPA battle continues over whether that is a good thing—especially when glyphosate is employed not as a weed killer but as a crop desiccant (sprayed directly on the plants just days before harvest) for wheat, oats, sugar beets, barley, sugarcane, buckwheat, millet, and potato crops.[15]

Glyphosate is banned or restricted in many nations, but continues to be approved by the US EPA despite tens of thousands of lawsuits alleging glyphosate is a carcinogen that causes non-Hodgkin's lymphoma.[16] Bayer, which acquired Monsanto and its patent rights in 2018, has paid out more than $10 billion in settlements[17] of claims by plaintiffs alleging that the proprietary Roundup product caused their cancers. The chemical was discovered by Monsanto Corporation in 1970; non-Hodgkin's lymphoma cases have increased 168 percent since 1975.[18]

The World Health Organization in 2015 identified glyphosate as "probably carcinogenic to humans," but the US EPA has repeatedly approved its use. The contentious battle over the safety of this chemical continues as EPA faces ongoing challenges to its determination.[19] Mexico has been fighting against

GMOs for years, seeking to ban them for human consumption pending further research into their impacts on human and animal health.

After the North American Free Trade Agreement opened Mexico's markets to US GMO corn, Indigenous maize farming was severely impacted: Mexico now imports 45 percent of its food, making cheap processed foods more prevalent than ever and displacing traditional diets. Mexicans eat far more corn than most societies, and by 2013, the nation grew concerned about a profound obesity epidemic.[20] Mexico lost some 900,000 farming jobs in the first decade of NAFTA as US corn poured over the border, prompting the nation to "insist . . . that GM corn threatens human health, and that modified seeds threaten Mexico's agricultural traditions and cultural identity."[21]

In December 2020, Mexican president Andrés Manuel López Obrador issued a presidential decree calling for the phaseout of both GE corn for human consumption and glyphosate no later than January 31, 2024.[22] The nation prohibits domestic commercial production of GE corn,[23] and battled the US and Canada to amend NAFTA, claiming

> [I]ts restrictions are indeed based on peer-reviewed science documenting the risks of consuming GM corn with glyphosate residues. These risks are particularly elevated for Mexicans, who consume more than 10 times the corn consumed in the U.S. and do so in minimally processed preparations, such as tortillas.[24]

While EPA claims glyphosate's benefits outweigh its environmental harms, this is far from clear—especially regarding impacts on varying soils and their diverse microbial communities. An ancillary question to the human health impacts of glyphosate (and the additional undisclosed chemical ingredients in Roundup) is whether the widespread applications of these products adversely impact the soil microbiome. This raises the specter of potential harm to soils and the human gut,[25] in addition to lymphoma or other cancer risks.

The issue of glyphosate toxicity, coupled with the impacts on water, soil, and air from the manufacture and application of synthetic fertilizers, is directly related to food security. If these chemical potions damage soils and microbes, their continued use will accelerate erosion, and destroy humanity's agricultural lands, and crop yields will decline inexorably. If they are discontinued suddenly, crop yields are likely to plummet, leading to vicious food price inflation and shortages. Should glyphosate prove innocuous, the issue of soil degradation and pollution attributable to synthetic fertilizers will remain a threat.

However, regardless of whether glyphosate is carcinogenic to humans, it is unquestionably cancerous to food security and liberty. The majority of traditional vegetable varieties are lost forever; the scant remaining genetics are being patented into GMO creations that are not found in nature, which are dependent on their growth for proprietary chemicals, including glyphosate, without which they will not thrive. GMOs permit private corporate ownership of every morsel of food, a fishy prospect under any circumstances.

The story of how GMO seeds came to be protected by patent illustrates the commercial influence wielded by large chemical and agricultural companies. Having developed its Roundup Ready soybeans for the commercial market, Monsanto Company faced a legal challenge from an Indiana farmer named Vernon Hugh Bowman, who planted held-back seeds that possessed the company's patented genetic resistance to glyphosate but bypassed Monsanto's licensing contracts. Mr. Bowman was somewhat boastful about his achievement, leading to a lawsuit that ultimately reached the United States Supreme Court.

In 2013, the Supreme Court, in a unanimous decision in *Bowman v. Monsanto,* applied US patent law to Monsanto's genetically modified soybean seeds. Justice Elena Kagan recounted Bowman's agrarian sin against the "owner" of the genetics of future plant generations grown from its seeds:

> [Bowman] purchased beans from a grain elevator anticipating that many would be Roundup Ready; applied a glyphosate-based herbicide in a way that culled any plants without the patented trait; and saved beans from the rest for the next season. He then planted those Roundup Ready beans at a chosen time; tended and treated them, including by exploiting their patented glyphosate-resistance; and harvested many more seeds, which he either marketed or saved to begin the next cycle. . . . Monsanto still held its patent, but received no gain from Bowman's annual production and sale of Roundup Ready soybeans.[26]

The Court recounted what would happen if Bowman were not stopped, and other farmers simply planted future generations of the seeds they purchased from Monsanto:

> And farmers themselves need only buy the seed once, whether from Monsanto, a competitor, or (as here) a grain elevator. The grower could

> multiply his initial purchase, and then multiply that new creation, *ad infinitum*—each time profiting from the patented seed without compensating its inventor.[27]

That sounds like *traditional farming*—creating seeds and replanting them, over and over again. But this is verboten for patented crops unless a fee is paid. Imagine buying a puppy and raising it, only to be told that all its progeny will forever not be your own. This is the proprietary monopolization enabled by GMO seeds and their patented companion potions.

Intangible property rights must be protected to encourage research and development. However, the tale of GMO seeds raises novel issues for humanity. If heirloom seeds disappear and only patented seeds dependent on patented chemicals are available, the US Supreme Court's *Monsanto* decision is a condemnation of humanity to market servitude. Corporations must not be permitted a monopoly on seeds and food any more than oxygen or water.

The more GMO crops predominate, the more challenging it becomes for farmers or home gardeners to raise crops untainted by chemicals or protect organic genetics from drifting pollen. Pesticides and herbicides often "drift" into neighboring fields of organic crops, tainting not just the plants but also the soil and water. With GMO crops, the genetically modified pollen is airborne and can cross-pollinate organic, non-GMO, or heirloom plant varieties, compromising their seed genetics.[28]

The pattern of legal shields for glyphosate-dependent GMO crops extended to Australia, where organic farmer Steve Marsh sued a neighboring farmer for cross-pollination of Marsh's organic canola crops with wind-blown seeds. Marsh claimed 70 percent of his crop was denied organic certification as a result, and that he suffered yearly losses that threatened his livelihood and ability to keep his farm. Australia's highest court affirmed a lower decision denying Marsh's complaint and ordering him to pay $804,000 AU in legal fees.[29]

The messaging that glyphosate is the sine qua non of food production and that the chemical is "sustainable" despite mixed scientific evidence about its potential impacts on animal and microbial life is a common refrain that mirrors assertions that man-made renewable energy products that emit forever chemicals are "necessary" to save the world from carbon dioxide (and cows and other natural processes). In both cases, the profit bias must be weighed against the potential implications for long-term planetary and human health. When corporations claim humanity cannot survive without their patented technologies, perhaps the transition of humans from living animals to industrially enslaved chattels is reaching Huxleian fruition.

American states are paving the way for the preeminence of chemical-dependent GMO crops, overtly favoring them over organic seeds, heirloom genetics, or non-GMO hybrids. Georgia and North Dakota have enacted state laws that shield pesticide manufacturers from liability for illnesses caused by their products, provided they follow deficient federal labeling requirements. Many developing nations, meanwhile, including India, have taken the opposite route—GMO crops and their seeds are banned there. The stakes are high for consumers and corporate "stakeholders" alike: technological battle lines are being drawn.

Syngenta, Bayer, Dow AgroScience, DuPont Pioneer, BASF, and other GMO seed sellers jostle for market dominance, yet all GMO seeds and the chemicals upon which they are dependent increase a food oligopoly slowly choking off traditional self-reliance for American farmers. As Food & Water Watch has warned, "Genetically modified foods—GMOs—are another tool industrial agriculture uses to control our food system. GMOs aren't about feeding the world, they're about corporate profits."[30]

The clues to this effort to steadily expand market share while preventing a return to traditional farming are implicit in technologies developed not to improve the ecosystem or soil health, but to secure proprietary power. Even after GMO patents expire, these crops remain dependent on glyphosate, mostly sprayed as Roundup. This secret, proprietary concoction will maintain its market dominance due to that fact.

Other clues are exhibited by the industry's "Terminator"[31] technologies, which involve genetic alterations of plants to ensure they will not grow or reproduce without patented chemical applications, requiring the repurchase of seeds annually. The International Union for the Protection of New Varieties of Plants has served for fifty years to protect new plant varieties with intellectual property laws, even as unpatentable heirloom seeds have diminished and disappeared. The ancient practice of seed-saving has been steadily eroded by cheap, colorful commercial packets—increasingly, for the Western world, there is no going back.

It is easy to see why such efforts to control all food-plant seeds eternally with "genetic use restrictions" are viewed with trepidation by many farmers and agricultural regulatory agencies worldwide. Seed-saving is still widely practiced in developing nations, but the introduction of GMO crops has had a devastating impact on local agriculture, soils, and economies around the world. This includes India, but also US-neighboring Mexico, where the NAFTA onslaught of GMO corn decimated peasant maize agriculture, pushing many farmers to grow marijuana and later opium poppies—Mexico is now the world's leading grower and exporter of "China White" heroin.[32]

GMO crops inevitably contaminate organic or hybrid neighbor crops through the natural process of cross-pollination, rendering their neighbor's seeds worthless for replanting. Corn is particularly susceptible to this transgenic contamination due to its open-pollinated nature: each corn tassel produces up to 25 million pollen grains that can be carried thousands of feet by insects, humans, and wind.[33]

As a 2020 law review article explains, this "death by cross-pollination" is well underway: "American farmers are under attack by uncontrollable technology. . . . Crosspollination can lead to catastrophic ends for owners of small, organic farms in the era of patented GMOs."[34] That "catastrophic end" of traditional farming is the end game of corporate designs for eternal dependency.

Traditional farming has its hands legally and biologically tied. Organic crops cannot harm GMO crops—GMO seeds are not kept back for replanting, and there is no "genetic contamination" that will undermine their marketability or yield. Conversely, GMO pollen (and herbicides and other chemicals from GMO crops) routinely compromises organic crops, polluting their DNA and preventing reuse for seed, as well as tainting them to the point of unacceptability for sale as organically certified. Organic growers face higher overheads to maintain clean soils and water—this commercial imbalance ensures the long-term destruction of non-GMO crops and precious natural resources.

Controlling markets increases profits, as does capturing regulatory agencies such as the USDA, FDA, and EPA to approve profitable chemicals that may not be suitable for use in food *or* soil. The snake oil sales pitch that "only GMOs can feed the world" and that GMOs will save humanity from its death by carbon dioxide[35] ensures an ever-expanding bottom line for a long list of polluting corporate profiteers. Increasingly, Big Ag proponents claim that GMO crops create more environmental benefits than organic or conventional cropping. Their chief argument is that GMO genetics are more productive (a claim that is itself controversial) and will thus use less land area and reduce carbon emissions. A typical claim is that "genetically modified crops support climate change mitigation."[36]

This is patently false. Even if glyphosate and the scores of pesticides and synthetic fertilizers employed in GMO-cropping are not harmful to human or environmental health, the argument that this cropping system is more efficient and improves yields (thus sparing the ecosystem) is simply untrue. Over time, the application of these human-made chemicals breaks down soils and kills vital microbial life, increasing erosion while reducing the capacity of soils to hold water. To achieve the same production returns requires ever more application.

Aldo Leopold warned about exactly this biological reality in his 1939 essay, "A Biotic View of Land." Leopold depicted the plant and animal community through a "biotic pyramid" as an energy circuit, with soil as its foundation. Farming extracts energy from soil, which must be recharged naturally. Leopold explained:

> The process of altering the pyramid for human occupation releases stored energy, and this often gives rise, during the pioneering period, to a deceptive exuberance of plant and animal life, both wild and tame. These releases of biotic capital tend to becloud or delay the penalties of violence.[37]

Many modern studies affirm Leopold's prescient analysis, yet industrial advocates continue to falsely claim that GMO monocropping is beneficial to the world's climate because it is more productive. Corporations cannot monopolize markets and agricultural inputs if peasant humans are allowed to farm freely. The Green New Deal, a road map for big-government control, was never enacted as law but encompasses every social issue under the social justice umbrella, including Indigenous rights, labor unions—and free incomes, clean water, and food (and education and housing) for all. It is a fantasy of platitudinous nothingness, but within the climate jargon is the blueprint for complete food domination while the earth is rapaciously plundered. The Green New Deal envisions a frenzied gold rush of industrial manufacturing activity that is a fox-in-the-henhouse scenario, with corporate profiteers cashing in while toxifying the planet.

The Green New Deal represents the ultimate greenwashing of entire madly polluting industries. It proposes to subsidize manufacturing "industries" that construct buildings and fabricate gleaming stainless-steel vats or powerful engines and novel technologies to "save the planet" from carbon dioxide while churning out chemicals that pollute air, water, soil, *and* food. Investing this much money in regenerative farming incentives would sequester far more carbon dioxide in weakened soils than is "saved" by these industrial manufacturing subsidies, thereby reducing chemical pollution in the ecosystem rather than increasing it. The investment in soils would bear healthier long-term returns than the list of fancy not-so-renewable doodads that will accumulate in landfills in twenty to thirty years (if they work at all).

The transition to complete dependency on industrial food systems and "renewable energy" manufacturing that pollutes soil, food, and water conjures Wendell Berry's eerie prediction in 2012: "The two great aims of industrialism—replacement of people by technology and concentration of wealth into the hands of a small plutocracy—seem close to fulfillment."[38] This noose is closing as the currency wobbles and these technologies create ever more substantial threats that could disrupt the world's food supply overnight.

CHAPTER 3

The Uniquely Modern Threat of Famine

The frailty of everything revealed at last.[1]
—Cormac McCarthy

During my summer stays in Vermont as a boy, I spent time with my Uncle Don Jacques, who would often take me with him and his oldest son (my cousin Louis) around the Green Mountain hills hunting for woodchucks. Woodchuck hunting requires mowed pastures so the varmints and their holes can be seen, and so we toured the remaining pastures and hayfields of the nearby mountains, sneaking up silently to get a long-distance shot at these wary tunnellers.

Almost every field we hunted in the 1970s is now grown in with pasture pine, weeds, and scrub brush. Others have been developed into residential lots. Many fields are completely reforested, including a family pasture in which I learned to drive in my cousin's 1963 Plymouth Valiant—I have recently harvested mature trees from the ground I once drove across like a golf course.

As dairy and other farming in Vermont has declined, the state has sourced more and more of its food from other jurisdictions. We didn't buy avocados from Mexico in Vermont stores in 1975, but the decline of small, local farms was already well underway.

I regularly drive past one field where Uncle Don used to take us hunting. I forget the farm family's name, but their farmhouse and outbuildings were already reduced to stone foundations and field rubble when we scoured the fields for woodchucks. By the 1980s, development in Vermont had yielded a massive custom log cabin, poised dominantly at the entrance to the front pasture of this old homestead, which was later sold at auction to newcomers who did not farm. The fields are growing back, large pastures now dotted with residential landscaping shrubs that impede farm equipment and mowing, the woodchucks thriving in the absence of predators or hunters.

This former farm that has become a seasonal vacation home is emblematic of the economic and cultural shift that has swept through America since the end of World War II. Millions of acres of erstwhile farmland have been gobbled up and chopped into parcels for commercial development, suburban sprawl, private vacation residences, hedge-fund investments, or forestry (aided by favorable tax provisions and funding for reforestation). Such lands cannot be easily reverted back to productive agricultural use.

At the same time, operating farmlands are increasingly consolidated into ever larger ventures. This shift has been accelerating as farmers age—a dramatic transfer of farmland is unfolding as aging farmers seek to retire while their children decline to follow in their paths. High agricultural land and equipment prices deter new entrants, whether they are growing crops or livestock. This fuels further consolidation, industrialization, and dependence on GMO monocultures.

This national trend is amplified in large cropping regions, where large-scale facilities dwarf small operators. The number of Iowa farms exceeding two thousand acres has tripled over the last twenty-five years, mirroring a national trend. Iowa lost nearly 9,800 farms since 1997; nationally, the number of lost businesses exceeds 300,000. About 20 million of Iowa's 30 million acres of farmland is owned by people over age sixty-five; 40 percent by people over seventy-five.[2]

This pattern of small-farm decline is evident nationwide. Here in Vermont, I no longer make my own hay but buy it from a short list of farmers in their seventies who will soon retire. Who will grow and make hay for horse and livestock owners when this generation retires? Equipment, land, and input costs have escalated rapidly in recent years, and the learning curve for new farmers is steep—these old-timers possess generations of knowledge not available in schools or colleges. The future of Iowa, like that of Vermont, portends non-farm transfers that harm rural economies, or consolidation of vast tracts of land by hedge funds, large farms, or others (Bill Gates is one of Iowa's largest landowners).

The consequences of this transition toward ever-greater centralization, mechanization, and long-distance distribution are profound. Americans have become steadily more separated from their food supply through physical distance, a decline in accumulated agricultural knowledge, a reduction in healthy farmlands, a loss of local plant and livestock biodiversity, and the disappearance of the former suppliers, equipment, and infrastructure that once served the abandoned agrarian way of life.

Like reclaiming fallow farmlands and cutting them into unfarmable residences, preserving agricultural knowledge faces a similar cultural extinction. The average age of an American farmer is approximately sixty, with few young entrepreneurs taking up the reins of land stewardship. A study of USDA statistics reveals that midsize American farms have taken the most significant blow: most farms in America in 2025 are either huge or consist of selling some corn and cukes at a roadside stand.

The slow decline of the farming culture, as well-documented by Wendell Berry in his seminal book, *The Unsettling of America*, has continued unabated for over 100 years, coinciding with the increasing corporate hegemony and consolidation of the food supply. The vertical and horizontal integration of the meat industry has steadily pushed animal husbandry into Concentrated Animal Feeding Operations (CAFOs), where profits are maximized at the expense of animal, human, and ecological health. Slaughter and processing facilities have been similarly concentrated, at the loss of hundreds of small-scale local facilities that once served rural communities. Such practices have seeded unprecedented risks of disease and supply disruption.

The array of potential disruptions to this fragile food procurement system is daunting, concealing multiple threats that have grown with this unprecedented technological transition. The threats posed are not merely to available agricultural land but also extend to newly discovered vulnerabilities in food production, distribution, processing, and storage. Any substantial interruption of any of those three areas threatens the entire food supply system, and each area presents unique exposures to sustained disruption.

Modern agricultural food production relies on affordable energy supplies, including synthetic fertilizers, pesticides, herbicides, and glyphosate, which are derived directly or indirectly from fossil fuels. It also relies on patented seed supplies of genetically modified monoculture crops that deplete the soil, weakening its ability to retain precious water. Tractors and specialized farming equipment are manufactured in fewer and fewer locations, dependent on microchips and specialty parts that are not widely available and often must be shipped long distances, or from overseas. In contrast, the popular Ford 8N tractor of the 1940s was easy to work on, and replacement parts were plentiful.

Fossil fuel dependency for food production creates two disparate threats: fuel supply interruption and energy price inflation. An OPEC-style embargo, war affecting oil-producing nations, or conflict near key strategic choke points for oil tankers could create oil shortages. Such crises would likely spike oil and other fuel prices internationally. Runaway domestic inflation, overregulation, natural disasters, domestic or foreign social unrest, and other potential disruptions could also cause energy price inflation. Because food production involves layers of energy inputs from tilling to fertilizing to harvesting, the impact of energy inflation on food prices compounds exponentially. (This was seen in the COVID-19 pandemic, when most US fertilizer prices roughly tripled, and grocery store prices jumped 20 percent in a single year.)

Gargantuan US crops are processed at an equally mammoth scale to convert them into products for consumption. Factories run on electricity (dependent on fossil fuels) and employ large-scale industrial technologies that depend on routine maintenance, specialized industrial equipment and knowledge, and substantial capital outlays. Vast amounts of food are gathered and channeled into these processing facilities, a miraculous technological accomplishment that carries unique threats of disruption not present in local, small-scale farming.

America's awe-inspiring distribution system requires road and infrastructure maintenance, an enormous fleet of 4.5 million[3] constantly bustling semi-trailer trucks, containers loaded on barges and processed through key ports, retail stores supplied with a steady flow of goods, and the ability of consumers to travel freely to various food retailers and restaurants. It is an admirable accomplishment in efficiency but is under growing threat of indefinite or permanent disruption.

To comprehend the lurking threat to future food supplies posed by these advances in technology and inventory management, a brief survey of the potential impacts of various possible adverse events presents an unfolding picture of potential doom. Those tractors, semis, and international barges depend on microchips, affordable fuels, market and social stability, various specialized inputs, and sophisticated maintenance.

Consider the impact on each aspect of this system of food supply—production, processing, and distribution—of an oil crisis, electromagnetic pulse (EMP), asteroid, earthquake, volcano, world or regional war, currency collapse, terrorist assault, social disorder, cyberattack, pandemic, sustained labor strike, or globalist (or domestic) coup. This partial list of possible future cataclysms exposes a much longer list of dire consequences: crops unplanted or unharvested, container ships backed up at sea, tractor-trailer trucks stalled on highways, factories idle, grocery store shelves and residential pantries bare.

More Americans are waking up to their tenuous food dependency and what it portends for the future. It is not a matter of whether the food supply system is punctured; the question is *when*, and for how long. Considering just a handful of potential consequences to food production and distribution during a sustained crisis reveals the dire and profound nature of the situation, and why food supplies are a national security issue not to be taken lightly.

The avalanche of consumer goods, including food, that arrives daily via containers from foreign lands presents a daunting flow of commerce. Most containers are unloaded at one of America's larger maritime ports. The United States witnessed a short-term surge in container traffic during COVID-19, increasing from roughly 46 million twenty-foot equivalent units (TEUs, the volume of a standard shipping container) in the top twelve US seaports from 2018 to 2020, to 53 million TEUs during 2021 and 2022.[4] Although shipping has returned to pre-pandemic levels, the capacity limitations of this logistical marvel were tested during the pandemic, and their vulnerabilities were starkly revealed. US maritime gateways handled 40 percent of the international freight value in 2022. Tractor-trailer trucks transported about 72.6 percent of all US freight by weight in 2021.[5]

As scale has been pushed, new risks have been created. Colossal container ships now pose an unprecedented threat to US bridges and infrastructure, which were not designed or constructed to withstand the impact of heavy collisions. The March 2024 Key Bridge collapse in Baltimore followed decades of warnings by a maritime safety committee that it was at risk of precisely the kind of tragedy that occurred.[6] The danger includes failure to deliver goods—the Baltimore Bridge carried an estimated 30,800 vehicles daily over its arches before the barge struck, and the central East Coast shipping hub of the Port of Baltimore was debilitated by the bridge's collapse for months or perhaps years.[7]

Highway Infrastructure

Federal mandates require commercial tractor-trailer trucks to use diesel exhaust fluid (DEF) and electronic logging devices (ELDs) in their operation. Each presents serious, unprecedented threats to food and goods distribution. DEF is an emissions control liquid the EPA requires in diesel engines manufactured after 2010 as an "after-treatment technology" to reduce vehicle emissions. This additive is mandated for most modern diesel truck fleets. Without it, many trucks cannot exceed five miles per hour in speed, or be operated at all.

However, EPA mandates for DEF in diesel engines were not matched by increases in domestic DEF production, and China manufactures much of the world's DEF. US truckers, who consume some 37.6 million tons of DEF annually, faced DEF shortages around the nation when China reduced production during COVID-19. Because DEF is produced from natural gas, its pricing can be volatile. Its production is influenced in tandem with urea fertilizers, also manufactured from natural gas, further exposing food supplies to inflation. A widely used but inflation-sensitive substance, urea has created a dangerous dependency in modern industrial globalization and "too big *not* to fail" distribution systems.

ELDs have been highlighted as an additional Achilles' heel for US trucking. A 2024 study concluded that more than 14 million medium- and heavy-duty trucks could be vulnerable to security breaches from these devices. Mandated by the federal government for most heavy-duty trucks, electronic logging devices track driving hours and log data on engine operation, vehicle movement, and distances driven. The study determined that these devices, of which only a small number of models are used for most trucks, are susceptible to co-option or control by hostile interests, creating a potential for sabotage or terrorism.

One concern is that ELDs can be manipulated as "truck-to-truck" viral worms that can be wirelessly controlled by other vehicles to pull over to the side of the road, crash into a bridge abutment, or plow into oncoming traffic. They can also be used to manipulate data or spread malware from truck to truck in a cascading chaos. The researchers warned that

> [V]ulnerabilities in commercial trucking systems could allow hackers to take control of, steal data from, or even disrupt entire fleets by spreading malware unnoticed between vehicles. . . . Such an attack could lead to widespread disruptions of entire fleets, with severe safety and operational implications.[8]

Water Aquifers

The human assault against underground water aquifers is global, with US aquifers under particular strain. The industrial capacity to produce bumper crops with advanced irrigation technologies has steadily depleted primary US water resources from both surface waters[9] and vital underground aquifers. While recent droughts have highlighted this slow-moving disaster, the loss of water is so astronomical that wet years do not make up for the drawdowns—US water supplies for agricultural and residential uses are under profound threat throughout most of the country.[10]

Precious aquifers are the future of Americans' food supplies. At current rates of depletion, the time will arrive when there is no water to pump from the ground to fill Midwestern swimming pools, sprinkle over sprawling lawns, or nurture life-giving crops.[11] This is a consequence of sloppy agricultural policies that subsidize the overproduction of food and thus overuse of water.[12]

A robust shift in agricultural policy, focusing on water usage and practices, could help reverse the disastrous destruction of America's aquifers. Yet, that shift is not likely to occur anytime soon, as long-standing battles over water rights, farming subsidies,[13] and access to limited resources continue to thwart efforts to respond comprehensively. In the absence of aggressive countermeasures, the trickling away of the means to grow US food crops will continue.

Soil Erosion

America is contributing to the desertification of its fertile agricultural lands. One study found that Midwestern erosion is happening ten to a thousand times faster than in preagricultural times.[14] Another study[15] concluded that the midwestern US has lost 57.6 trillion metric tons of topsoil in the past 160 years due to agricultural practices, equivalent to a loss of approximately two millimeters of soil annually. This loss of soil is due not to cows or climate change, but to large-scale plowing. The result is that fertile topsoil has vanished from approximately "one-third of all the land devoted to growing crops across the upper Midwest."[16]

No number of EVs or solar panels will reverse this soil loss, nor will carbon credit trading or trees grown to "sequester" carbon dioxide. This steady destruction of life-giving soils means that industrial agriculture is slowly killing the soil and soil microbiome in America's most fertile lands. Soil erosion presents a measurable and imminent threat to food supplies (and nutrient content) that is being widely ignored. America faces a future Dust Bowl if remedial steps are not promptly implemented.

As with water rights, however, competing interests threaten a continuing Tragedy of the Commons regarding soil health. Government incentives to plow weak soils and expand crops pressure farmers to exploit soils to stay economically viable. The more soils are washed away or depleted, the more fertilizers and other adjuncts are required to maintain crop yields, and more irrigation is needed to moisten sickly soils that are losing their capacity to retain water.

This vicious cycle is killing soils and soil microbiomes, necessitating ever more chemicals, wider swaths of tillage, and increasing volumes of water to maintain existing crop yields. The policies of the World Health Organization, World Economic Forum, and United Nations to compel humans to eat more plant diets and fewer cows exacerbate these problems exponentially by increasing reliance on tilled land using mostly GMO monoculture crops rather than returning livestock to the land where they rebuild soils and feed microbes without the artificial infusion of destructive synthetic fertilizers and ubiquitous herbicides.

Flooding

Americans have been conditioned to view every flood event as a consequence of climate change. If so, then the risk of a dramatic interruption of American agriculture must be perceived as a tandem threat—but one that exists regardless of global warming claims. Long before anthropological activity is alleged to have contributed to global warming, flood threats to the American food supply were genuine. Industrial agriculture compounds these threats.

Most Americans are unfamiliar with the Great Flood of 1862 in California, which swept away much of the region's livestock and agriculture overnight. California's agricultural production in 1862 was a tiny fraction of what is produced today. The San Joaquin Valley yields some 40 percent of all US nuts and fruits on a mere 1 percent of the nation's land.[17] This area had subsided an estimated twenty-eight feet by 1970, and drops an additional foot every year, mainly attributable to water drawdowns from underground aquifers for residential and agricultural uses.[18] A repeat flood would be more dramatic than the 1862 episode, which is estimated to have destroyed one quarter of California's taxable real estate, and extended into Nevada, Utah, and the Southwestern states.[19]

A repeat of the 1862 California flood is probable. Climate scientists claim the potential for far more rain due to human greenhouse gases threatens to aggravate the event exponentially.[20] The land on which that forgotten flood occurred is now populated with far more food production and is more than thirty feet lower in elevation than in 1862.

The threat of flooding to food crops and their distribution is not limited to California. The United States loses billions of dollars in crops annually due to flooding, excessive precipitation, and hurricane events. The more the ground subsides due to water drawdowns for residences and irrigation, and the more soil is destroyed due to chemical applications and over-tilling, the more likely and severe the risk of cataclysmic flood events becomes.

Drought Risks

Drought has been pressing the nation for several years, if not decades. Climate change allegedly will compound drought risks, but as with flood and erosion, no climate crisis is needed to sound this alarm.[21] The bounty of US crops is constructed on a fragile reed of depleted soils, depleted aquifers, and long-distance supply lines. Vermonters, with their abundant water resources, are dependent on midwestern growers for their grains and produce: no one is exempt from this national dependency. The highly concentrated agricultural production of the nation has foolishly centered the lion's share of food crop production in the vulnerable Midwest and California.

Drought is the most significant crop killer worldwide and in the United States. The Food and Agriculture Organization of the United Nations labels drought as "the single greatest culprit of agricultural production loss," costing the sector some $37 billion US annually. Agriculture incurs 82 percent of all drought impacts.[22]

In the United States in 2023, Texas alone suffered nearly $5 billion in drought-caused crop losses, Kansas over $3 billion (including over $1 billion in wheat, $780 million in soybeans, and $605 million in corn), and Nebraska some $900 million in crop losses linked to drought.[23] Droughts are becoming more common and intense around the world, including in the US.

The impacts of drought on food supplies extend to livestock feeds and livestock health, and contribute to long-term aquifer losses as well as soil deterioration, forest fires, and desertification, all of which increase agricultural vulnerability in future seasons. These threats to food supplies are aggravated by suburban sprawl and residential water demands, particularly in the crop-producing states of Arizona and Nevada, where many Californians are emigrating for retirement or improved living standards. Expanding conventional crop production for humans or animals compounds these pressures, including making synthetic meats (from GMO crops) or vegan foods. The entire world's food supplies—especially grains—confront risks that escalate yearly.

Pollinators

Numerous studies suggest the world's pollinator insects are disappearing. Vital crop pollinators include not just honeybees but wasps, beetles, ants, flies, and butterflies. Pollinators are not essential to many of the world's largest crops, which ironically means that massive corn and GMO monoculture crops are harming other agricultural sectors in lower-income countries that rely on pollinator-dependent crops, such as cocoa, coffee, palm oil, and avocados.

Pollinator loss is caused by drought, habitat loss, and the application of herbicides, pesticides, and other chemicals. Agriculture is not the sole culprit, as habitat loss is also attributable to roadways, residential and commercial development, lawns, and non-native gardening practices. Residential activities also contribute to a long list of man-made chemicals used in household products, recreation, entertainment, and lawn care. Humanity produces a substantial amount of toxins without understanding their impact on pollinators.

The loss of pollinators does not portend a sudden collapse of food supplies, but it does threaten steady declines in productivity. Lost crop productivity pressures farmers to expand into more areas (further restricting pollinator habitat and depleting water and soils) or apply yet more chemicals and fertilizers to maintain yields. This vicious cycle will, in turn, further compromise pollinators and thus many crop yields.

Hyperinflation or Currency Failure

The United States is heavily indebted. The interest payments on its national debt now approach one trillion US dollars annually, and the nation has been increasing the national debt by $1 trillion every 100 days. This is hardly sustainable. Printing more and more money to stave off economic hardship ultimately seeds inflation, especially in food, housing, and fuel prices. Debt-fueled inflation is unlikely to disappear and is likely to compound rapidly.

Hyperinflation has devastated the currencies of many nations, with recent examples including Venezuela and Zimbabwe. The US dollar is not immune to these threats and has steadily inched toward a dangerous cliff of over-leveraging. The rapid weakening, or utter failure, of the greenback is essentially baked into America's future now: the question is when, and how quickly, the currency will unravel. The next question then becomes: will the federal government replace the paper dollar with an electronic/digital fiat currency that will monitor every transaction undertaken, and how will that impact food prices and availability?

Foreign (BRICS) nations are conspiring to undermine and sidestep the US dollar, adding to other potential fiscal pitfalls. The specific vulnerability of US food supplies to currency depreciation is thus considered in detail in Chapter 8: Reclaiming Food Sovereignty for All.

An Energy Crisis or War

Turbulent conflicts in the Middle East and Eastern Europe threaten to disrupt or spike oil and gasoline prices and interrupt international trade in food and technological necessities. China and Russia have both issued bellicose threats against the United States. Israel and Iran trade missiles in a sensitive oil shipping region where various extremist terrorist groups could target any number of choke points.

Oil prices directly impact farming overheads and the costs of processing and distributing food. Due to consolidation, expanded supply lines, and just-in-time inventory systems, American agriculture is exponentially more vulnerable to these price spikes than it was during the 1970s OPEC oil embargo. Everything that has made food cheaper and more plentiful has made it more vulnerable and susceptible to disruption by an energy crisis or trade interruption.

Much like the fragility of a fiat currency, the impact of rising energy costs on food production and distribution is an inevitable crisis. Cheap food depends on cheap energy, which is a finite resource subject to production and distribution risks. Energy costs are compounded throughout the US food production system, so any persistent increases in energy costs, even if modest, will accumulate rapidly in retail food pricing.

This unavoidable economic pressure[24] will reverse the illusion of cheap food that has been artificially sustained throughout most of the last century, compelling farmers and consumers to seek new pathways to affordability. Much of the unwinding of traditional agriculture will be thrust into reverse—at some point, it will be more economically viable to again farm with horses and horse-drawn equipment rather than oil.[25] Because this pressure is inevitable, energy scarcity and its impacts on long-term food prices and availability are addressed at length in Chapter 4: Food Inflation: Thousand-Dollar Gallons of Milk?

EMPs or Cyberattacks

The threat of a large-scale cyberattack or EMP has evolved from a vague science fiction theory to a real-life menace, together with threats from artificial intelligence (AI) turned to malicious purposes. China and Russia, in particular, have demonstrated a capacity to inflict digital harm. Russia disrupted Elon Musk's Starlink satellite service in Ukraine and routinely assaults US and NATO resources.[26]

Security Magazine summarized the growing threat of cyberattacks, noting that by 2025, cyberattackers are expected to have "weaponized operational technology environments to successfully harm or kill humans" including "disruption to food suppliers causing shortages":

> Cyberattacks in critical infrastructure and healthcare sectors don't just affect data—they can also wreak havoc in the physical world. . . . The wave of recent cyberattacks has impacted everything from oil pipelines to hospitals and shows no sign of stopping. Even worse than that, they

> may soon turn deadly. The cyber battlefield has expanded, and the stakes are higher than ever before.[27]

A century ago, such scary weaponry would be far less scary—a power disruption in 1925 would not have eviscerated Americans' food supplies the way it would today. Moreover, heating, travel, health care, and refrigeration are now all techno-dependent and grid-reliant in ways unimaginable to humans of the past. Evolving technologies have been accompanied by evolving new threats, for which the current food system has taken zero precautions.

Predicting Famine

Malnutrition and famine had increased globally before COVID-19, including in the United States. One recent study concluded that "between 2005 and 2020, the number of children facing simultaneous water and food insecurity in the United States more than doubled."[28] This was greatly exacerbated by the pandemic's disruption of supply lines, food processing, and farming. Worldwide, this led to an increase in the number of people facing hunger by tens of millions—according to some reports, over 122 million more people are facing hunger since 2019 due to the pandemic, the war in Ukraine, and repeated weather shocks.[29]

A recurrent problem in addressing famine events is allocating resources to impacted areas in a timely manner. This requires reliable prediction methodologies for drought, war, disease outbreaks, economic shocks, political upheaval, and significant weather events, but even with such technology, many events are simply unforeseeable. Though climate alarmists claim modeling predicts weather events decades into the future, drought modeling lacks any such precision. It is not like predicting the weather for Memorial Day: "Forecasting drought months into the future is even harder. Weather forecasts stretch out only a few weeks. Moving beyond that requires an understanding of large-scale climate patterns that influence weather over months or years."[30]

Predicting famine requires a sensitivity to pestilence, political turmoil, economic shocks, hostile conflicts, ethnic tensions, and other variables that can cause crop failure or food supply disruption. No mechanism exists to accurately predict these future calamities or the other alarms raised by this book. The fact that timely prediction of famine events is a difficult challenge is an additional cause for concern about US food supplies, exposing false comfort that American food supplies are somehow immune.

From Fields to Lawns

In less than a century, most Americans divorced themselves from the land and became dependent on industrial food. This transition was marked by a seismic exodus of rural Americans into cities and suburbs, a gut-transforming shift in diet, and a conversion of the entire world's economy to dependence on fossil fuels to replace horses and oxen.

The population of the United States in 1925 approximated 116 million people,[31] and 16.4 million horses (and 5.7 million mules and burros).[32] By 1959 the nation had largely abandoned the trusty horse: a mere 3 million remained. Today there are approximately 6.65 million[33] horses (and 292,000 mules or burros in 2012) in a nation of 340 million people.[34] That's an increased human-to-horse/mule ratio from 5.25 to 49, and most of these animals today are used for pleasure rather than primarily for work.

The concept of returning to dependency on horse or ox power may seem anachronistic in light of modern technological advances, but even AI needs (a lot of!) energy to operate. The point here is not a horse endorsement, but a call to awareness—Americans who just a few decades ago nurtured extensive vegetable gardens, bought meat from their neighbors, or kept a calf or lamb on pasture are now hemmed in by a crowded network of food-sterile lawns, suburban sprawl, and paved commercial developments. Much of this decorative land has been doused with chemical lawn fertilizers, pesticides, or herbicides.

This is a dystopian vision of a doomed, unsustainable way of life. It is a picture repeated across the nation and the developed world. Consider that Vermont boasted 27,000 dairy farms in 1927,[35] reduced to a mere 529 by 2023.[36] A nation of 116 million agriculturally connected Americans has devolved into a nation of 340 million mostly urbanite industrial food dependents. This is not desirable, beneficial, or sustainable.

Most people are utterly oblivious to this reality or dismiss the problem in cavalier techno-mystical ignorance. Here in Vermont, I am surrounded by parcels of former farmland acquired by out-of-staters. The farmhouse we rent was once part of a larger parcel where my cousin and I would regularly hunt woodchucks back in the 1970s. The farm was last used as a dairy in 1959; the fields have not been hayed since the early 1980s. When I asked the current (now neighboring) owner of the fields that once belonged to this parcel if we could keep some cows or sheep on his pastures, he declined, saying, "We want to let the land grow back naturally." Nearby are two other former dairy farms that are similarly fallow. People have forgotten where their food comes from, and how much work it takes to clear and maintain fertile farmlands. This exhibits an enormous, misplaced faith that the Walmart food system will always prove reliable.

Globalists

Globalist designs must now be added to this litany of potential threats to control all food supplies in the name of rescuing humanity from its climate-warming plight. European farmers in revolt represent rumblings of dissent against this globalist takeover. Businesses making profits do not like losing market share, and food is Big Business: this food battle is heating up far more than the planet.

Corporations have long demonstrated their prioritization of profits over human health. Food and cigarettes have a similar pattern in product creation and rollout. When consumers began questioning the health issues related to cigarettes (despite advertisements using doctors and athletes to claim cigarettes were healthy and "refreshing"), tobacco companies responded with "light" cigarettes that offered an illusion of healthfulness but were no better than regular cigarettes.

Similarly, when soda was demonstrated to cause obesity, "diet" soda sprang up—making people even sicker and fatter in the name of improved health outcomes.[37] Margarine was peddled as healthier than butter. Baby formula was sold as an improvement over human breast milk, followed by prepared baby foods (tainted with heavy metals, according to recent studies).[38] Fake meats and bug burgers are paraded as healthier than grass-fed steaks. State GMO labeling requirements were displaced by federal labeling that is inscrutable and difficult for consumers to understand.

Thus, the globalist push to eliminate cows and create more technological dependencies via lab-cultured meats and plant-based meat substitutes. The same corporations that tilled the soils into erosion, drained the aquifers into depletion, and soaked the nation's farmlands with glyphosate, atrazine, and neonicotinoids now claim that only giving those same companies even greater domination of human food supplies will avert the disaster they seeded.

And so, Americans are told that cows are a problem for the climate, when in fact, cows sequester carbon in the soil when properly managed and produce manure that replaces destructive synthetic fertilizers. Those plant-based diets that are supposed to replace cows pose substantial threats of their own: they are mostly derived directly or indirectly from GMO monocultures that depend on chemical applications for growth. Grass blades are God's solar panels, but the World Economic Forum (WEF) and others counsel growing trees instead of pastures, amplifying human dependence on the same chemicals, technologies, unhealthy processing, and cheap fuels that have engendered the current dependency.

This scam is visible to Dutch and Irish farmers, but it is lost on most US consumers. Those claiming that cows must be eradicated to save the world from methane are the would-be rulers of mankind, proposing to control all food production, financing, technology, and distribution using counterproductive methods, favoring corporate "stakeholders," and intensifying food control to the point of total hegemony. Indeed, this is the closing of the noose—control the food, control the people, the profits, the media, and everything else.

The World Bank recently laid out this plan plainly in a report titled "Recipe for a Livable Planet." Leveraging the food production crisis it has created to justify totalitarian food control is precisely what the corporate "partners" of the WEF desire. The list of partners includes Bayer (formerly Monsanto), JBS Foods, Syngenta, Dow, BASF, and many other major players in the food, fertilizer, and chemical businesses. Notably absent from the WEF are food rights activist Vandana Shiva, libertarian farmer Joel Salatin, or any small-scale or peasant farmers.

Ironically, the argument for handing over all human food production to a unified globalist cabal is framed as one of preparation against growing food system vulnerabilities. The World Bank's report proclaims:

> The global food system's reliance on just-in-time international commodity supply chains, or supply chains that make food and input materials available just when they are needed, makes it susceptible to systemic shocks and high price volatility, as there is no time or redundancy buffer to account for potential supply-chain disruptions. . . . The COVID-19 pandemic and its consequences on the entire food value chain highlighted the vulnerability of the food system. . . . Also, the globalized nature of the agrifood system can lead to food price volatility.[39]

Overlapping Threats and Risks

Like the chemicals that infect Americans' food supplies, these potential threats may be compounded. An EMP might be discharged in conjunction with cyberattacks. A pandemic may unfold during an oil crisis or war in the Middle East. Severe drought could coincide with a nuclear assault by China or Russia, or a domestic terrorist attack by extremists. Global economic turmoil or tariff wars could spark runaway inflation while floods ravage productive agricultural areas.

In turn, such events would impact sown fields, energy supply costs, processing facilities, trucking and distribution systems, grocery stores, and consumers seeking food, all concurrently. Tractors may be stopped in their rutted tracks, container ships or tractor-trailer trucks sit idle, or factories closed down (as occurred with US meat processing during COVID-19), all concurrently and disparately, across the nation and around the world. To presume none of these threats will ever materialize is to continue throwing dice as the odds grow worse. It is only a question of *when* these risks materialize, and how severe they will be.

A Recipe to Avoid Famine?

This book echoes many of the same concerns as the World Bank's "Recipe for a Livable World" report but offers an entirely different prescription. The solution to humanity's foolish dependency on cheap, ultra-processed, environmentally destructive food production is not a grand global hegemony controlling every aspect of farming and food production, but the *exact opposite.*

A return to less destructive, smaller-scale, and local agricultural production, using technology sparingly but wisely, will counter these threats directly and immediately. Cows and other livestock, properly husbanded, reverse soil and water loss, improve fertility, reduce the need for synthetic fertilizer applications, decrease dependence on monocultures and GMOs, and help heal what industrial agriculture has damaged. Ethanol production is an expensive, inefficient, soil-destroying corporate boondoggle: these lands can be grazed by cows instead.

Beneath most all these potential vulnerabilities is a dubious bargain with technology, which promises ease and comfort but threatens sickness and starvation. Humanity must be rescued from industrial agriculture, not plunged more deeply into dependency. The source of humanity's unique modern plight is the abandonment of personal responsibility for food production or even knowing where one's family's food comes from. Reclaiming that awareness and connection to the earth is the sole path to a return to human and environmental health. Globalists claim that only further corporate empowerment and technological innovation can address these issues, ultimately serving corporate profiteers at the expense of human and ecological health, as well as long-term food security. The way out of industrial enslavement for humanity is not to double down on industrial chemicals and methodologies; it is to end them.

CHAPTER 4

Food Inflation: Thousand-Dollar Gallons of Milk?

> The first panacea for a mismanaged nation is inflation of the currency; the second is war. Both bring a temporary prosperity; both bring a permanent ruin. But both are the refuge of political and economic opportunists.[1]
>
> —Ernest Hemingway

Like much of the global industrial food "system" that it has pioneered, the entire American food production and distribution arrangement is increasingly dependent on chemical fertilizers and pest-killers, massive, specialized equipment, and automated CAFOs to produce grist for a Dickensian industrial processing labyrinth. Beneath this dangerous reliance on technology and mechanization that replaced centuries of human self-reliance lurks a steadily growing, volatile dependence on cheap energy, and an unstable currency. Perhaps the most predictably likely threat to this system is old-fashioned inflation.

Inflation is driven by money supply, and both American political parties have demonstrated a capacity for spending borrowed money. Food prices are additionally pressured by commodity price fluctuations for fossil fuels, especially diesel fuels used in agriculture and natural gas used to manufacture synthetic fertilizers. If these underlying energy inputs escalate in price, a cascading "knock-on" effect will compress broader inflation pressures into exponentially more substantial leaps in grocery store prices.

Markets, math, and interest rates care little about equity, social justice, or whether poor people eat anything at all, let alone eat healthily. This dog-eat-dog of market capitalism is not held at bay by socialist economic models—Venezuela was economically decimated when its well-intended socialist spending programs collapsed in tandem with plummeting international oil prices. Americans (and their banking institutions) appear to have forgotten or abandoned basic monetary precepts that impact inflation and economic growth. The consequences of unethical, shortisghted monetary supply will dramatically impact Americans' grocery store shelves.

Whether or not Americans witness an imminent currency collapse, inflation pressures in oil and other agricultural inputs promise to inflict future rises in food prices, amplified for products shipped long distances. Despite technological advances such as fracking, oil and natural gas are limited natural resources that will gradually become more costly to extract. This will cause steady and irreversible price rises in food products, almost all of which are directly or indirectly dependent on the industrial production of these energy staples.

"Cheap" food is an illusion: humanity has been splurging on a cheap energy binge that has despoiled the environment while allowing modern consumers to (literally) grow fat off that petroleum hog. History will one day perceive this energy binge as a mere momentary blip in the arc of human "progress"—perhaps the most destructive activity humans have ever "progressed" to.[2]

US monetary policy has followed the same shortsighted, profit-driven course as its food production and healthcare systems. Even if the nation produces the healthiest food in the world, it will become unaffordable and unavailable if hyperinflation unravels the entire economy. Like industrial food production, current US monetary policy is unsustainable and will ultimately implode. Both are Ponzi schemes: one pyramids debt; the other, chemical contaminants.

A loaf of bread will one day cost more than $1,000 in America, and a gallon of gas will one day cost the same—it is just a matter of *when*. Currency inflation is an attendant reality of money supply, exacerbated exponentially as a risk when that money supply is not linked to any tangible underlying assets but is merely a symbolic piece of paper: a "fiat currency." An American family could purchase a modest new home for $15,000 and a functional new car for $2,000 in 1960—the houses and cars have grown in size and amenities, but the greenback has withered in purchase power. A meatball sandwich that cost $2.50 in 1975 is now $12.50—and *smaller* (and less healthy).

When the price of diesel hits $40.00 in this ever-inflating monetary system, the price of tractors, food packaging (made from fossil fuels), processing, seeds, distribution, and every other input will rise. The cost of raising livestock in Concentrated Animal Feeding Operations (CAFOs), which are currently profitable despite tight margins, will rapidly escalate. In contrast, cows raised on pastures will not see any monetary inflation in the cost of their renewable solar panel grass blades,[3] though the price of industrially raised hamburger will shoot to the moon in the wake of its diesel-fuel dependency.

Forecasting or guarding against inevitable food price inflation necessitates an understanding of industrial food production and its energy dependence. If natural gas were to encounter a production or inflation crisis, the nation's entire industrial food system would be threatened: synthetic fertilizers, especially nitrogen-rich urea, are manufactured from natural gas. Farmers who simply spread manure on their fields (often employing cow power, as the girls are happy to disperse their solid and liquid soil supplements while dining) will see no increase in fertilizer overheads as they are self-reliant for their soil improvements on the timeless methods that feed instead of destroy soil and microbial health.[4]

A sharp or sustained increase in fuel prices, whether driven by natural market forces such as supply interruptions, spikes in demand, or artificial human intermeddling in dubious fiat currencies, would quickly distress the entire US industrial agricultural system. Whenever the death of industrial agriculture unfolds, and by whatever cause, the shock will seismically transform modern agriculture from a wondrous worldly achievement into an inefficient economic calamity. The accelerating dilution of the real value of the US dollar is already unfolding.

The higher the prices for oil-dependent, ultra-processed foods climb, the more consumers will be growing gardens and swapping food in barter—rescuing themselves from toxins while striving to make economic ends meet. This transition is inevitable: America has too much debt, the world is racing to unseat the primacy of the almighty dollar, and the unpopularity of government spending reductions or tight monetary policy will likely continue to fuel undisciplined spending. It ends badly, in something far worse than a recession and potentially more devastating than any war the United States has ever waged: it ends in hyperinflation.

US National Debt

It is no secret that the United States has embarked on a borrowing binge. The national debt increased from about $1.5 trillion[5] in Ronald Reagan's 1984 to $37 trillion in 2025 (about $108,500 for every person in America as of August 2025), a multiplier of nearly twenty-five over forty years. If the US continues on this fiscal trajectory at the same rate, in 2064 it will be carrying $864 trillion in national debt. This conservatively assumes a linear debt expansion: the rate of debt increase has not been linear over the past four decades, accelerating steadily with growing entitlement spending and debt service. (Thus, the projected cost of $1,000 for a gallon of gas or loaf of bread, without Peak Oil or natural disaster to exacerbate inflation.)

The statistical machinations of American banks and regulatory agencies have become deliberately opaque: unemployment, inflation, jobs reports, and money supply data have become as much of an adversarial game of hide-and-seek caveat emptor as grocery store ingredient labels. Even accepting the trustworthiness of federal government data, America is in dire fiscal peril.

Several measures of debt load are screaming fiscal fire alarms: the pure number of $37+ trillion is beyond the human mind to comprehend. The national debt has been employed as a communal credit card. Faced with higher inflation that outpaces wages, American consumers are struggling with climbing credit card balances subject to unprecedented interest rates. Congress has been pleasing constituents with spending intended to woo votes for a very long time, and it's a hard habit to crack. Voters have often supported this exact monetary mismanagement: short-term payoffs traded for long-term economic drag. (How about those student loan payoffs, proposed trillions in slavery reparations, or monthly COVID-19 checks?)

That national debt is still being carried, at ever higher interest, absorbing the savings and loan crisis, wars in Iraq and Afghanistan, 2007–2008 Wall Street collapse, military spending, and a massive, multitrillion-dollar spending spree for "renewable" energy products and COVID-19 pandemic relief. *All* this spending is still carried at interest on the national credit card. The moral hazard in unaccountable expenditures is compounded by the complacency this seemingly unlimited tab has enabled. The debt road for America is reaching its inevitable dead end.

No nation in history has been more enamored with its currency. People around the world have long idolized the American fiat bills (once upon a time backed with gold and silver bullion; now backed by the increasingly dubious "full faith and credit" of a spendthrift federal bureaucratic behemoth.) This love affair has deceived people into a delusion that the mighty greenback is immune from math and economics.

Surely the greatest currency in human history, issued by the greatest economic powerhouse, with the greatest military and the most revered national flag ever flown by humanity, is immortal and can never fail to dazzle the eyes? Yet all these things are tarnished and declining—the currency will likely falter and fail in hyperinflation.

A standard measure employed by economists is the ratio between a nation's total debt and its underlying economy measured in gross domestic product (GDP). The United States may in hubris perceive that it can exceed debt-to-GDP danger zones with impunity, but rising interest rates are already pummeling real economic growth, and no fiat currency can escape the disciplined boundaries of mathematics.

Still, not all debt is the same. A young woman buying a machine shop on credit, or a young man opening a hairdressing salon, incurs debt for an income-earning capital asset that itself provides the means for repayment. Similarly, government spending that funds national productivity feeds GDP growth, reducing that important debt-to-GDP ratio and perhaps even yielding taxable returns that replenish coffers depleted by mountainous social programs and entitlement spending.

Regardless of who bears political blame (or fault) for inflation, this growing threat will continue to rise unless repaid. The illusion that central bankers can stave off inflation and bolster a sinking economy simply by tweaking interest rates or printing more cash is dissolving. America's debt load is unsustainable. Its economy is destined to go entirely off the fiscal rails, absent a profound (and unlikely) shift in fiscal policy.

America's debt-to-GDP ratio is slightly higher than the country's previous record in 1946. World War II's industrial boom created the foundations for decades of unprecedented economic growth and technological advances in the United States. The nation's blistering economic expansion, including the explosive Green Revolution, yielded tax revenues that reduced the national tab to a mere 30 percent of GDP in 1981.

At 120 percent of GDP and climbing, the United States is now shouldering a peacetime debt load that rivals most of the developed world. A Penn Wharton Budget Model conducted in 2023 warned:

- We estimate that the US debt held by the public cannot exceed about 200 percent of GDP even under today's generally favorable market conditions.
- Under current policy, the United States has about twenty years for corrective action after which no amount of future tax increases or spending cuts could avoid the government defaulting on its debt whether explicitly or implicitly (i.e., debt monetization producing significant inflation). Unlike technical defaults where payments are merely delayed, this default would be much larger and would reverberate across the US and world economies.

- This time frame is the "best case" scenario for the United States, under market conditions where participants believe that corrective fiscal actions will happen ahead of time. If, instead, they started to believe otherwise, debt dynamics would make the time window for corrective action even shorter.[6]

Over the past forty-five years, neither political party has genuinely expressed the will to tackle this reckless pork-spending spree.[7] The national debt is projected (absent extraordinary needs such as an economic downturn, pandemic, natural wildfire or hurricane tragedy, or military conflict) to reach 133.9 percent of GDP by 2029.[8] The "best-case" scenario is not even on a make-believe wish list of fiscal directives, and the time frame for averting collapse shortens the longer action is delayed.

Some money-watchers are not so sanguine about a ten- or twenty-year window for corrective action. Former Indiana governor Mitch Daniels has issued a strident alarm:

> With debts already about to surpass the nation's entire GDP, and adding close to $2 trillion more this year, only a dwindling number of denialists doubt that a cataclysmic reckoning, including double-digit damage to Americans' income growth, lies ahead. It's past time to prepare.
>
> The sense of social betrayal that the debt crisis will stir might require actions the nation has rarely contemplated. An accompanying economic collapse could unleash violent reactions in a country that has become grimly familiar or even inured to such conduct.[9]

International markets and monetary systems aggravate this domestic fiscal weakness. A worldwide economic recession, interest rate spike, or banking crisis could puncture the American economy and currency simultaneously, sparking stubborn "stagflation" such as the country battled in the late 1970s when the nation's debt hovered around 30 percent of GDP, not the 120 percent[10] of 2024. The United States had ample flexibility to incur debt in 1980 to jump-start a stagnant economy; it has little leverage left as the twenty-first century deepens.

The focus here on the US national debt excludes other factors that influence inflation or even, possibly, deflation,[11] despite high debt loads. Economist James Rickards, in his tellingly titled tome *Sold Out: How Broken Supply Chains, Surging Inflation, and Political Instability Will Sink the Global Economy,* identifies "five factors that may cause higher inflation: deficits, demographics, monetary policy, politics, and supply shocks."

The focus of Rickard's analysis in *Sold Out*, though, is supply chain disruption, which itself can seed hyperinflation simultaneously with chaos. Rickards warns that modern distribution systems have become so interconnected and sophisticated that they present an unprecedented threat of utter failure on short notice. He writes:

> [T]he drive for efficiency has led to the frailty at the heart of the current breakdown. The supply chain failure is global and not limited to semiconductors and ships. Anything from champagne to cheesecake might be missing on the shelves. . . . Any system that scales too far will collapse of its own weight. It's just a matter of time.
>
> [I]t's just a matter of time. That's the condition the world faces now. The meta supply chain is collapsing. Data points such as port backlogs, trucker shortages, and bare shelves are symptoms, not the main event.[12]

In his sequel, *MoneyGPT: AI and the Threat to the Global Economy*, Rickards extended the concept of supply chain vulnerability caused by the intricate successes of its innovations to modern AI-driven banking and monetary systems. As more banking institutions, individual investors, investment firms, and hedge funds have embraced highly technical AI algorithms and money management systems, market efficiencies have magnified in efficiency but created unprecedented risk of collapse. Bank runs and market implosions can now be accelerated in ways that regulators and even wary investors cannot foresee or forestall:

> Regulators still have not learned the lessons of 1998 and 2008—the Fed Put, an understanding by investors that the Fed will buy securities in distressed markets, is still alive and well. They've read about AI/GPT but don't understand its power. Bank runs are not about capital ratios and liquidity. They're about confidence and psychology. . . . The banking system, which is intrinsically fragile, is more fragile than ever. We're counting down to a crisis so large even the Fed cannot contain it.[13]

The picture Rickards paints of vulnerabilities to supply chain and market vulnerabilities easily punctured due to the very thing that makes them marvelous—their efficiency—implicates food supplies doubly. Food distribution and the ability to purchase foods are completely dependent on both systems. Yet, food production itself similarly masks the capacity for collapse hidden in its own efficiencies and consequent fragilities.

Is BRICS a Threat?

The dollar has been shielded for decades by its close connection with petroleum prices, earning it the occasional moniker "petro-dollar." International tensions have led an increasing number of countries to challenge this dollar dominance. A movement initially led by the five "BRICS" nations (Brazil, Russia, India, China, and South Africa) and dubbed "de-dollarization" deliberately seeks to dethrone the almighty dollar. This alliance doubled in size in 2024 when Egypt, Ethiopia, Iran, Saudi Arabia, and the UAE joined its ranks.

The stated objective of the BRICS coalition is to restructure the world's currency system away from its dependence on the dollar. Vladimir Putin has thus triumphantly proclaimed that the "irreversible process of de-dollarisation of our economic ties is gaining momentum"[14] as more and more nations join this flight from the US dollar:

> The BRICS challenge poses significant threats to the US dollar. As BRICS nations sell US Treasuries to buy gold, the influx of dollars back into the US economy could lead to increased inflation. Additionally, a weaker dollar makes it cheaper for foreign nations to purchase gold, solidifying the BRICS' leverage.[15]

It is unclear how effective this growing opposition to US dollar supremacy will become, or how long it might take to significantly impact the dollar's primacy. However, these BRICS sentiments are likely to increase as more nations depart from dollar-centric policies, fueling US dollar inflation as the Federal Reserve and the US Treasury Department strive to protect the beloved greenback.

Hyperinflation in America?

"Hyperinflation" is generally understood by economists to refer to a specific monetary condition characterized by rampant, uncontrollable inflation that ruthlessly levels entire economies at 50 percent *per month.* Mainly because the US dollar has always proved to be the most resilient and trustworthy fiat currency of the world, the abandonment of gold and silver bullion in favor of shoddily regulated printing presses poses the threat that this 50 percent threshold of monthly inflation could—and almost surely will—rear its ugly head on America's shores.

Americans' hazy recollection of 1970s inflation—when interest rates hit 21 percent under Paul Volcker[16]—was recalled more clearly following a wealth-destroying inflationary spike during the Biden administration's tenure. But this "transitory" inflation, as it was called, proved sticky enough to stay. This was a 20 percent annual food price increase, a small fraction of the economic destruction that sustained runaway inflation would inflict. Hyperinflation has impacted many nations in the past, often due to factors similar to the pressures currently impacting the US economy and money supply.

Germany and Hungary

Germany and Hungary experienced severe hyperinflation following World War I, fueled by the war reparations imposed on both nations by the Treaty of Versailles. Hyperinflation in Weimar Germany reached rates of more than 30,000 percent per month as prices doubled every few days.[17] Hungary's experience was even worse, regarded as "the worst hyperinflation ever recorded": inflation reached 41.9 quadrillion percent per month as prices doubled every fifteen hours.[18]

Zimbabwe

An example of hyperinflation more similar to current pressures on the US dollar was Zimbabwe, whose daily inflation rate of 98 percent in March 2007 persisted until early 2009. The legacy of this experience remains on Amazon.com and eBay.com, where currency collectors can purchase a $100 trillion Zimbabwe dollar bill for about $175.00 US. The causes of Zimbabwe's hyperinflation are directly traced to overspending, corruption, social justice programs, and fiscal mismanagement.

President Robert Mugabe intervened in Zimbabwe's currency and economy, leading to the nation's precipitous economic decline. Elected on promises to lift citizens from poverty, Mugabe launched his Economic Structural Adjustment Programme (ESAP), which negatively impacted the economy, and then initiated land seizures of white-owned farmland in the name of anticolonialism to be redistributed to blacks (regardless of farming experience). This seeded distrust and uncertainty about future property rights, but also economic implosion and famine—many farms fell into neglect or dramatically reduced production, undermining exports, the national economy, and food supplies. Banks began to fail, and farmers were unable to obtain loans.

Millions of middle-class Zimbabweans fled the nation, taking their wealth with them.

As Zimbabwe began to sink under growing debt and spending, Mugabe involved the nation in a costly war in the Congo and borrowed heavily from the International Monetary Fund to improve living standards and bolster social programs. Then he turned to printing money to pay the rising tab: by November 2008, Zimbabwean inflation reached 79.6 billion percent month-on-month, or an annual rate of *89.7* sextillion percent.[19] The Reserve Bank of Zimbabwe blamed this inflation on US and international economic sanctions.

Venezuela

Venezuela offers a recent example of reckless monetary policy that has led to nation-destroying hyperinflation. Hugo Chávez dramatically escalated social program spending financed by high oil prices; when oil prices subsequently plummeted, the nation rapidly accrued unsustainable debt loads. Nicolás Maduro took over leadership in 2013 with an economic solution: print more money. By 2016, inflation had risen to 800 percent; by 2018, that number had increased to an astounding 80,000 percent.

Venezuela's experience offers other lessons. As public outcry and protests erupted, increasingly authoritarian measures sowed greater distrust and more public unrest. These pressures (also present in Mugabe's reign) undermined public confidence in the government, the economy, and the nation's currency. By 2019, approximately 10 percent of Venezuela's population had fled the country, "the largest human displacement in Latin American history, driven by shortages of everything, including food as well as the Maduro regime's oppressive treatment of dissent."[20]

Venezuela has managed to rein in its cataclysmic hyperinflation by drastically chopping government spending, but this has undercut vital social programs, aggravating human suffering in the short run. Inflation remains quite burdensome at 50 percent annually, but this is a great relief compared to the 130,000 percent that wreaked economic havoc for some four years there.[21]

Of the various threats to Americans' food supply, inflation is perhaps the most guaranteed—a ballooning federal debt, deficits as far as the eye can see, and massive spending on social programs have amplified the risks of inflation until remedial action is implemented. Inflation of 5 percent per month quickly erodes real wealth; hyperinflation, at 50 percent or more per month, is one of the worst catastrophes that can befall any nation and looms menacingly over the United States at the quarter mark of the twenty-first century. (Though, as

James Rickards warns, deflation is also a possible outcome if economic activity plummets. It is quite likely that food prices could spike rapidly while non-essential goods like cellphones, flat-screen TVs, and new cars plummeted in price.)

Consider the parallels with the US in other nations that have ventured down this pathway. In the name of reducing poverty, social programs have seen a significant increase in spending in the United States, particularly during the COVID-19 pandemic. Certainly, alleviating poverty is a noble goal, but putting the costs on the collective credit card of the nation will seed far greater suffering and poverty in the long term.

Frighteningly, "modern monetary theory" (MMT) holds that the United States Treasury can open the printing press spigots full bore:

> MMT proponents argue that governments can spend as necessary on all desirable causes—reducing unemployment, green energy, better healthcare and education—without worrying about paying for it with higher taxes or increased borrowing. Instead, they can pay using new money from their central bank. The only limit, according to this view, is if inflation starts to rise, in which case the solution is to increase taxes.[22]

If it sounds too good to be true, it usually is. As one expert economist has observed:

> The reality is that eventually someone must pay for fiscal deficits. However, the long lags between a massive run-up in debt and the eventual crisis it creates make debt tempting for politicians. I know of no example of a country that has pursued money-financed fiscal deficits and then transitioned back to more-conventional policies once the economy recovered.
>
> Examples abound in which printing money to solve a fiscal debt problem hasn't worked. There are no examples that I am aware of in which MMT has worked. It is a theory with no practical relevance.[23]

Promises of universal income, unlimited spending on social programs, or racial reparations are all tempting offerings by politicians seeking votes. Still, there is no economic track record for the fiscal survival of such reckless folly. However, the track record of hyperinflation is plain to see. Increasingly, prominent economists are raising the alarm that Americans are headed off a fiscal cliff of despair if high debt loads persist. Once unleashed, hyperinflation is impossible to stop without inflicting tremendous economic hardship, usually on the lower and middle classes.

Few voices in political leadership are calling for fiscal sanity. However, the second Donald Trump administration has an opportunity to curtail rather than amplify federal debt and spending (the "One Big, Beautiful Bill" does not bode well, though in theory some of that spending will bolster long-term growth). Time will reveal that so-called "modern" monetary theory is a fantasy likely concocted to rationalize grossly irresponsible spending.

In this regard, Albert Einstein's observation is practical that "Whether you can observe a thing or not depends on the theory which you use. It is the theory which decides what can be observed." Americans wishing to understand their nation's true current plight must consider traditional economic theory and the experiences of previous nations, rather than burying their heads in the fantasy of economic theories with no track record.

Concurrently, Americans are watching their farmland being bought up by ultra-wealthy investors and foreign nations, including Iran, China, and North Korea.[24] Other farmland is being withdrawn from food production in the name of "rewilding" and conservation. The "land back" movement advocates for the reallocation of lands to "historically marginalized" communities; agricultural "equity" calls for allocating farm stewardship not based on ability, but on skin color. Although such efforts are far short of President Mugabe's disastrous policies in Africa, the intention and the potential economic damage of such initiatives reflect similar theories that ignore economic history.

The war in Ukraine and other military spending abroad may not burden the US dollar to the same degree as Zimbabwe's currencies did when Mugabe embarked on the war in Congo, but the compounding effect is pronounced. The US national debt includes decades of foreign military spending that has yet to be paid for by future generations—how much more can the fiat currency take before it fails?

The real culprit here is overspending, regardless of the justification. Massive money printing creates an illusion of wealth and plenty in the short term, followed by a sobering reality when the debt comes due. The temptation to exploit others' future wealth through printing presses is too tempting for many politicians to resist.

John Maynard Keynes, unacquainted with modern monetary fictions, warned that "By a continuing process of inflation, government can confiscate, secretly and unobserved, an important part of the wealth of their citizens."[25] Economist Thomas Sowell agrees: "It is a way to take people's wealth from them without having to raise taxes openly. Inflation is the most universal tax of all."[26]

Milton Friedman warned, "inflation is always and everywhere a monetary phenomenon in the sense that it is and can be produced only by a more rapid increase in the quantity of money than in output. . . ."[27] Walter E. Williams concurs: "Increases in money supply are what constitute inflation, and a general rise in prices is the symptom."[28]

America is quickly approaching the endpoint of its borrowing (and thus money-printing) abilities. Following a debt-ceiling battle in Congress—itself a sort of "Boy who cried wolf" process that inures Americans to what seems a droll ritual—economist Peter Schiff called this a Ponzi scheme running on Monopoly money:

> The U.S. Treas. Sec. has admitted the only way to avoid a default on the National Debt is to raise the #DebtCeiling so the Govt. can borrow from new lenders to repay existing lenders. . . . This amounts to an official admission that the U.S. is running the world's largest Ponzi scheme.
>
> "Why do people willingly participate? It's because they don't realize it's a Ponzi scheme," Schiff says. "They think they're going to get paid back. When they realize they're going to be paid back in monopoly money, they're not going to want to lend.
>
> "In fact, they're not going to want to hold on to these Treasuries and the only buyer is going to be the Federal Reserve. And that's when the printing press is going [in]to overdrive and the dollar is going to fall through the floor.[29]

The point here is not to blame any one individual—the nation's debt has been rising ineluctably since Ronald Reagan's tax cuts were not matched with reductions in spending. The point is to draw attention to the reality of this debt drag on real economic growth, its cumulative impacts as it escapes human regulatory control, and how it morphs into deadly hyperinflation. The potential inflationary effects on food prices, as well as possible interruptions to food supply and production, are apparent once people properly contemplate the monetary implications ahead.

This analysis invites an assessment of current American vulnerabilities as the US dollar's purchasing power deteriorates. Hawaii and Alaska face higher-than-average food costs because both states import most of their food.

Venezuela's economic woes were exacerbated by its concurrent dependence on oil income and food imports: as tax receipts and national income plummeted due to declining oil prices, exchange rate shifts rapidly increased the prices of imports. Food is not a discretionary expenditure.

Below the public radar, the global expansion of industrial food and agriculture has dramatically shifted America's food sources abroad. The same advances that have enabled American consumers to enjoy avocados and bananas in winter have created ever greater US dependency on foreign sources of both raw and processed foods. So long as the fiat dollar remains stable, and absent other disruptions contemplated in these pages, this growing dependency will remain invisible. A shock to the US monetary system would quickly imbalance exchange rates and cause a sudden increase in food prices overnight.

The USDA has quantified the changes in US food exports and imports over the last twenty-five years:

> The United States is the world's second largest agricultural trader, behind the European Union. U.S. agricultural exports and imports increased significantly over the last 25 years due to the economic ascension of many emerging economies, as well as the implementation of foreign and domestic policies that expanded U.S. access to foreign markets. Over the same period, the geographic and product composition of U.S. agricultural trade shifted, as rising incomes and growing supply capacity of emerging economies reshaped global supply and demand for agricultural and food products. . . .
>
> Between 1998 and 2023, total agricultural imports more than quintupled in value, reaching $195 billion in 2023. . . . Consumer-oriented products have dominated U.S. agricultural imports and have grown faster than total agricultural product imports, increasing on average by nearly 7 percent annually since 1998. . . . U.S. agricultural exports have grown steadily over the past 25 years—reaching $174 billion in 2023, up from $57.3 billion in 1998.[30]

The most significant increases in both exports and imports have been of processed foods, but an alarming imbalance is evident in the USDA's figures. US exports of bulk and high-value commodities increased from $34 billion in 1994 to $116 billion in 2023, a factor of 3.41. Over the same period, increases in imports of these categories rose from $27 billion in 1994 to $190 billion in 2023, a growth factor of 7.04.[31] Americans are importing more food than ever, at almost twice the rate of growth in exports. This is a giant sucking sound, not of manufacturing jobs but of agricultural production.

Pastures and fertile lands paved over for malls or residential development cannot be reclaimed for agricultural production; lands rewilded with conifers and hardwoods will not readily replace dependency on foreign processed foods. Overproduction of heavily subsidized corn (including for inefficient ethanol production) and soy leads to depressed markets for these commodities, undermines foreign producers, and diverts fertile farmland from production for vegetable crops or livestock grazing.

The problem is compounded once inflation takes hold. The government will find itself under extraordinary pressure to maintain or increase social benefits as the vise grip of inflation tightens. The only way out of a steep inflationary cycle—let alone an episode of hyperinflation—is to either increase economic growth or slash public spending. A government already tapped out by overspending is left with no monetary tools in its financial war chest.

The abuse by governments of their monetary systems to support social programs becomes a well-intentioned paving of the road to hyperinflationary hell—once unleashed, inflation devastates the real value of social safety nets, such as welfare and social security, simultaneously tying the government's hands to increase benefits without aggravating inflationary pressures. Only austere measures, including substantial cuts to government spending (as successfully employed in Venezuela by the Maduro administration), can counter the ravages of hyperinflation.

Additionally, a weakened US currency becomes more vulnerable to price shocks from commodity inflation, particularly those related to fossil fuels. From the field to the store shelf, cheap energy is the hidden miracle worker of the Green Revolution, and will evaporate overnight if energy markets erupt or encounter long-term volatility. High debt loads and ill-considered monetary policy increase market volatility.

Hyperinflation is a vicious destroyer of wealth and social order. The entire United States economy and social safety net is threatened to its very foundations. In time, it may require more than 1,000 mighty greenbacks to purchase a single gallon of milk. Just ask the Zimbabweans and Venezuelans who fled their homelands.

Waiting on the Federal Reserve or a spendthrift Congress to reform the currency and curtail debt may prove a long haul. Improving food security and insulating the nation from food price inflation does not need to wait: every American can take steps to guard against this potential threat.

CHAPTER 5

Cows, Climate, and Bug Burgers

> Science has never succeeded by burying the manifestations of unintended consequences. It has succeeded when we recognize them and deal with those issues. That's hard to do when you have a belief system that becomes a religion.[1]
>
> —Don Huber

A constant mantra of the climate change movement is that cows are environmentally destructive, that a plant-based diet is better for human health and to prevent global warming, and that synthetic or plant-based meats offer an improved diet to solve these problems. This is essentially false, raising an important question: why is such blatantly ridiculous information being propagated as truth? The agriculture "industry" that has insidiously overtaken farming and food production seeks to cement yet more market share, and globalist entities populated by these same corporations seek to consolidate raw power.

As backdrop to this bovine inquiry, American diners must question why their food supplies (something necessary for life and health) are targeted while less justified energy consumption (and pollution generation) spews from American lawn mowers, flat-screen TVs, cellphones, laptops, golfing, skiing, snowmobiling, and flying to the Caribbean in wintertime? Americans are not being asked to consume less of these activities, which are more easily curtailed, cannot be justified in the name of food or survival, and pollute far more than cows on pasture.

Indeed, NASA claims[2] that lawn mowing is a net carbon sink due to the carbon sequestered by grass clippings—while ignoring the 800 million gallons of gasoline burned and spilled on American soils by gas-powered lawn mowers *each year*! This is propaganda, not science or public health policy. Something is most undoubtedly rotten within this spiel.

The world is being systematically lied to about cows. Believing the Earth is warming due to anthropogenic activities becomes more challenging when the proposed response creates far more greenhouse gases *and toxic pollution* than are eliminated—this is the case with solar panels, EVs, and wind turbines. There is no climate rescue there, but instead a frenzied rush to tear up the Earth for profit, burning coal and fossil fuels at an *accelerated* rate in the name of environmental rescue. This is obviously fraudulent once externalized ecotoxins are evaluated.

The truth about cows easily exposes the falsehood of this globalist propaganda. Consider the following facts, which will be proven here in turn:

- Cows do not only burp and fart. They poop and urinate, feeding the soil microbes with solids and liquids ignored by the gas-focused crowd. These microbes digest methane, sequester carbon and nitrogen, and break down both methane and the ecotoxins generated by manufacturing and other industrial processes.
- Methane and carbon dioxide are very different in their impacts. The "science" used to measure cows' enteric emissions is skewed to favor industrial agriculture and malign pastorally raised cows. Industrially managed cows generate far more carbon dioxide than rotationally-grazed livestock, because they are dependent on industrial equipment to feed them and transport their manure.[3] Additionally, there is no cumulative climate impact caused by cow methane, as levels from cows are relatively stable. Cows are producing methane at close to the same rate as agriculturally generated methane is dissipating.[4]
- Rotationally grazed cows, such as those used in peasant populations, are a very different environmental animal than CAFO-housed animals. Understanding the differing methods of husbandry reveals two very different management systems—it is industrial enslavement of cows, not cow biology, that creates excess waste and generates pollution.
- Efforts to patent cows or cow products that will be genetically crafted to counter methane may well create proprietary intellectual property rights (patents) governing animals themselves. Might it be that the corporations that have patented plants and the chemicals upon which GMOs are dependent would seek to secure similar market control over other food products, including livestock? Will the government prohibit natural cows in favor of these new corporate-owned creatures, or

require that all cows be fed patented food additives to curb methane, in an effort to "save the planet" by imposing absolute food control?

- Most plant-based alternatives to meat are unhealthy and highly processed. Moreover, they are dependent on GMO monocultures that destroy biodiversity as well as soils, and require chemical applications of glyphosate, synthetic fertilizers, and a slew of pesticides and herbicides that end up in these foods while contaminating water supplies.
- Lab-grown or "cultured" meats are also grown from these GMO crops, with all of the attendant soil, water, and environmental destruction chronicled in these pages. The world-saving fake meats are grown in atmospherically controlled, anthropogenic laboratories, gleaming with stainless steel tanks, gauges, and plastic tubing—cows don't generate these. However, they do generate layers of manufacturing profits in tandem with PFAS, phthalates, and other ecological pollutants.
- Animal rights activists claim cows and other livestock must be eliminated from the food supply for ethical reasons. This advocates the slaughter of cows in the name of saving them. Animal husbandry is about stewarding soil, water, and animals in a very close-knit and nurturing relationship. Industrial agriculture perverts these principles. Many animal rights activists seek to abandon tens of thousands of years of human-animal symbiosis, including for the world's Indigenous and marginalized peoples, in their opposition to industrial animal management.

While humans target gentle cows for extermination or genetic mutation in the name of saving the planet, the gargantuan folly of ignoring the rampant non-food consumption by Americans will far outweigh any environmental progress achieved. The globalist NGOs and corporate behemoths who claim that only their patented chemicals and genetically modified creations can save the world are interested in profits, and they surely don't want consumers to stop buying plastic toys, electronic gadgets, or any of the ubiquitous polluting, inedible products not targeted for elimination.

The new "climate science" of methane and its relative warming impact posits that methane is "equivalent" in its warming effect to eight times the impact of carbon dioxide over twenty years.[5] This scientific-sounding analysis of "global warming potential" (GWP) of various gases conceals sketchy arguments employed to eradicate cows. These relative measures of ratio are skewed to favor industrial cows, which emit far more carbon dioxide than free-roaming animals due to their dependence on fossil fuels for feeding and housing. This metric overlooks the substantial benefits of naturally grazed ruminants, including the fact that their manure feeds soil microbes that consume methane.

The climate science argument is that a molecule of methane traps more heat than a molecule of carbon dioxide. However, methane has a short atmospheric lifespan (seven to twelve years) before decomposing into water and carbon dioxide, whereas carbon dioxide persists for centuries. Methane emissions from cows are essentially stable—as new cow farts rise into the air, the ten-year-old farts of past herd members dissipate.

Properly stewarded cows are "net-zero" on both carbon dioxide *and* methane. Industrially confined cows are not: they are dependent on fossil fuels to grow their crop foods and to transport their waste. The climate change modelers do not distinguish between these two dramatically different livestock management systems.

Synthetic fertilizers promoted to replace cow manure do not feed soil microbes, but they do generate the manufacturing byproduct of nitrous oxide, which is rated as 273 times higher in GWP than carbon dioxide.[6] How is it environmentally beneficial to replace cow manure with these man-made pollutants that harm instead of replenishing soils and nourishing the soil microbiome?

Many chemicals not found in cows are far more potent as planet warmers than any of these alleged "pollutants." Tetrafluoromethane has numerous non-agricultural applications, an estimated lifespan of 50,000 years, and a GWP of 5,301 over 20 years and 10,587 over 500 years. Hexafluoroethane is used in semiconductor manufacturing, boasts a 10,000-year atmospheric lifespan, and has a GWP of 8,210 over 20 years and 18,200 over 500 years. Sulfur hexafluoride, used in the semiconductor and electric power industries, has a 3,500-year lifespan and a GWP of 17,500 over 20 years; 32,600 over 500 years. Nitrogen trifluoride, employed in producing DRAM computer memory, flat panel displays, and thin-film solar cells, lasts for an estimated 500 years with a GWP of 12,800 over 20 years; 20,700 over 500 years.

Cows do not emit these chemicals, are not employed in food production, and are not targeted for "net-zero" emissions, let alone eradication. They are hazardous waste materials that are unhealthy for humans and highly detrimental to the planet. Note that they *are* necessary to produce solar technologies, tracking technologies (to reduce carbon emissions) proposed for livestock and food production, and surveillance technologies proposed for "smart cities" to supposedly rescue humanity from climate change.

If greenhouse gases indeed pose an existential threat to life on Earth, why are these and other chemical offenders not public enemy number one, rather than cows? Why aren't American consumers pressured to eliminate semiconductors and flat-screen TVs from their purchases to spare the planet from nasty man-made ecotoxins, which are scientifically rated as tens of thousands of times more planet-warming and thousands of years longer duration than bovine sources of hamburgers and steaks?

British academic Ian Scoones has documented the shoddy climate science employed to malign the world's cows in the name of industrial agriculture's sins. Professor Scoones strives to assess the full range of climate impacts of disparate agricultural systems, claiming "there is much uncertainty around the seemingly authoritative facts and figures about livestock's methane emissions." This contrasts markedly with the oversimplified deception currently embraced by a chattering class of cow-slandering researchers.

In "Livestock, Methane, and Climate Change: The Politics of Global Assessments,"[7] Mr. Scoones analyzed the varied and complex environmental impacts of cows:

> By failing to differentiate between livestock systems, global assessments may mislead. Inappropriate measurement, verification and reporting processes linked to global climate change policy may in turn result in interventions that can undermine the livelihoods of extensive livestock-keepers in marginal areas, including mobile pastoralists. In the politics of global assessments, certain interests promote framings of the livestock-climate challenge in favour of contained, intensive systems, and the conversion of extensive rangelands into conservation investments. Emerging from a narrow, aggregated scientific framing, global assessments therefore can have political consequences. A more disaggregated, nuanced approach is required if the future of food and climate change is to be effectively addressed.
>
> The oft-repeated argument that cows are just as bad as cars in terms of climate impacts misses many important nuances; not least that methane and carbon dioxide have very different impacts in the atmosphere, and the fact that emissions figures for livestock include both direct and indirect emissions (across the whole life cycle), while those for transport cover only direct emissions.[8]

There are two distinct analyses required to accurately measure cows' emissions. The differences in environmental impacts between extensive and intensive agricultural systems are profound—cows in CAFOs may pollute, but cows properly grazed in a rotational system are net-*negative* in terms of carbon dioxide and methane emissions, while generating clean food and feeding microbes that break down chemical toxins in the soil.

Professor Scoones has undertaken a thorough study of cows around the world, noting that large American cows have been used to arrive at unreliable data when applied to cows in the developed world; that substantial bias supporting industrial agriculture pervades most existing bovine climate impact "studies"; that baseline greenhouse gas emissions must be assessed relative to the "additionality" of livestock; and that anti-cow allies to the industrialists are conservation groups which make for strange bedfellows:

> An unlikely coalition of scientists, policy-makers, environmental campaigners, journalists, diet-change activists, and those backing industrial production of protein has emerged, focused on technological solutions to climate mitigation. Inadequate data and inappropriate analysis supports such positions, while condemning and vilifying extensive livestock production. Yet, due to a lack of voice and influence in global assessments, compounded by multiple scientific uncertainties, inappropriate assumptions, and data gaps, injustices arise for extensive livestock producers, particularly pastoralists. This in turn undermines effective global debate on the future of food and climate change.[9]

There currently is very little "effective global debate" about cows because they are being almost universally maligned by propagandists.[10] Well-managed ("extensive") livestock build soils, increase biodiversity, and sequester carbon dioxide. A "per cow" metric is employed that ignores the important differences in herd management, which favors arguments for animal concentration and industrial farming methods. As Scoones rightly points out:

> This argument is presented in terms of improving "efficiency" and "modernizing" production; doing away with what are seen as wasteful and inefficient extensive systems. As we have seen this is a very selective view, failing to look at the full range of both impacts and benefits as required by a more holistic, systems view. But it nevertheless serves certain corporate farming interests that make profits from "big meat

> and dairy," and feeds into a narrative of technological modernization with a narrow view of efficiency at its core. . . .[11]

Professor Scoones's work exposes the market-driven lies of monied interests that seek the techno-mystical industrial domination of the world. These same actors peddle proprietary synthetic meats and plant-based meat substitutes as salvific when, in reality, they are the precise *opposite*—sickening, chemical-dependent, highly processed food frauds that shouldn't be manufactured at all unless it is some sort of perverse effort at biowarfare: Americans and their regeneratively reared cows are under attack.

A profound hidden threat to food liberties is latent within the mad rush to displace existing cow herds with genetically modified or factory-fabricated creations that are supposedly designed to produce less methane over their lifespans. Non-farmer Americans are largely oblivious to the importance of this cow-seizing step toward total food domination by corporate profiteers. Food and farming are a multitrillion-dollar business. Oligopolic domination of 100 percent of the market secures indefinite future profits with no competition.

Currently, these multinational chemical, agriculture, and food processing companies control the vast majority of US plant crops, either directly through patent ownership of GMO corn, soy, and other crops, or indirectly through ownership and production of the chemicals upon which they utterly depend. Even for non-GMO crops, dependency on synthetic factory-made fertilizers means yields will dramatically plummet if farmers do not steadily buy these environmentally destructive industrial applications from Big Chem. Synthetic fertilizers are incredibly inefficient in delivering nutrients to plants.[12] Many modern plant varieties have become dependent on them.[13] Natural manures could more efficiently supply a third of global fertilizer needs.[14]

A conversion of American diets to plant-based meat substitutes or synthetic meats ensures a continued dependency upon faux foods that cannot be replicated in the home garden, even as more and more laws (including local ordinances and zoning regulations) push the backyard chicken farmer or vegetable steward into compliant dependence. The same system is stealthily subsuming the nation's meat production.

A rural American homesteading family with a domestic cow is free from this industrial dependency and can produce milk or meat for themselves and their non-farming or urban neighbors. Cows and sheep can be raised entirely on grass, liberated from questionable grain diets, profit-making chemical concoctions, and the lurking inflation that will drive up food costs. That cow on grass is undeterred by rising natural gas prices, supply disruptions, or conflict in the Middle East. The corporate overlords of food find such liberties intolerable. They are implementing a plan to eliminate such independent farming methods in the name of climate rescue and "efficiency."

These companies already control (or directly own) most of the chickens and pigs housed in industrial operations. If they have not already consolidated these animals into dystopian CAFO operations, where animals are treated like commodities and every input is market-driven, they possess the means to do so at any time. Unlike cows, pigs and chickens are already dependent on factory feeds; no alternative production at scale of these meats is available.

Corporate profiteers are very jealous of their earnings reports and market share, and understandably resentful of cows. If grain or other prices skyrocket, grass-fed cow farmers can readily adapt. CAFOs depend on fossil fuel, fertilizer, and chemical companies, which are their true masters. The "extensive" traditional livestock agriculture of the small-scale or family farmer stands in the way of utter and total food control: patenting cows (for lower methane in enteric fermentation), eliminating cows (as proposed in Holland, France, and Ireland), slandering cows, taxing cows (as Denmark is already doing),[15] and creating (eventually mandated?) synthetic meat or plant-based substitutions are a path by which to bring cows and their stewards into corporate/government enslavement. The effect will be much like the loss of heirloom seed varieties—once humanity becomes dependent on industrial methods, there is no turning back.

All of these supposedly world-saving "advances" create unprecedented dependencies. The propaganda that the world must go vegetarian to avoid catastrophe is patently false, constructed upon fabrications about cows and their supposed methane production. The astronomical profits involved in manufacturing synthetic fertilizers explain why they would be favored by the corporations that manufacture them over animal manures that have served humanity for eons. This also explains why cow gases are emphasized while cow solids and liquids are systematically ignored by those who call for cow culling.

The global fertilizer industry was valued at $384.37 billion in 2024, projected to exceed $543 billion by 2030.[16] Rice, wheat, and corn comprise the world's chief field crops and cover 38 percent of the world's land. Chemical fertilizers are the most widely used products in the agricultural sector, with a 72 percent market share; the agricultural sector accounts for approximately 33 percent of the global fertilizer market. US synthetic fertilizer production has continued to grow steadily but relies on imports of all three key components of "NPK" fertilizers: nitrogen, phosphorus, and potash. America imports 93 percent of its potash from Canada.[17]

The USDA reports that commercial fertilizer production peaked at 23.7 million nutrient short tons in 1981.[18] This dependency on synthetics for food production is more than just damaging to soils and water. It exposes American food prices to volatile shifts in input costs.[19] Farmers and consumers alike experienced price volatility during the COVID-19 pandemic, as the price of most synthetic fertilizers *tripled*.

The EU initiated a different kind of fertilizer policy through its "Farm to Fork" strategy, which called for a 20 percent reduction in commercial fertilizer use by 2030, although this plan has since been withdrawn, largely due to industry pushback.[20] The United States proposes an industrial-centric model of doubling down on the follies of the past:

> The European approach stands in stark contrast to the U.S.'s vision for cutting emissions from the agricultural sector, which relies on high-tech fixes and data-driven "precision agriculture," which would help farmers apply fertilizers more efficiently but doesn't set targets for reducing their use. The U.S. strategy does not promote organic farming, which precludes the use of synthetic fertilizers. Less than 1 percent of U.S. farmland is farmed organically.[21]

The common refrain from those embracing chemical-based agriculture is that it is "the only way to feed the world."[22] However, if the "only way" leads to steady soil erosion, water pollution, and depletion, as well as the loss of precious nutrients and microbes, then that path inevitably leads to environmental Armageddon and mass starvation—this is the very definition of "unsustainable." A 2018 report determined that synthetic fertilizers warm the planet more than the commercial aviation industry and cause substantial environmental harms.[23]

Technologically, replacing synthetic fertilizers is more practicable than banning commercial flights. Bill Gates famously observed that his jet touring was environmentally honorable because he purchases "offsetting" carbon credits,[24] a perverse modern quasi-religious "indulgence" that does not eliminate the ecotoxins generated by jets. If Bill opposed synthetic fertilizers (he does not) or bought "offsets" that were not harmless CO_2 but rather chemical toxins, there might at least be some sanity or reason behind his trade-off shenanigans. Sadly, both sanity and reason have been abandoned in pursuit of an unjustified fearmongering used to manipulate people into greater subjugation by the corporatocracy of which people like Bill Gates are profiteering ringleaders.

Bill Gates's greenwashing is common among those wealthy enough to afford jets, expensive EVs, and carbon credits. Studies show rich virtue-signalers generally pollute more, and "that despite buying and driving an EV, the average purchaser of an EV still had a higher carbon footprint than people who did not buy such vehicles."[25]

Such studies reveal the folly of so-called "renewable" energy manufacturing—*all* of these supposedly carbon-sparing technologies emit toxins, conceal their full environmental impacts, and lull humanity into continued consumption using an illusion of effectiveness. It is not the EV drivers who are at fault—it is the industry and the Bill Gateses who have beguiled them with false advertising.

Similar compassion must be extended to vegans and vegetarians striving to be mindful of their impact on the ecosystem, who have been misled into believing that all animal husbandry is inherently pernicious and that a plant-based diet is healthy and beneficial for the planet. Both of these beliefs are simply fallacious. Not only are most plant-based diets unhealthy and even toxic (unless organic), they contribute to the deaths of animals: "It has been estimated that producing wheat and other grains results in at least twenty-five times more sentient animals being killed per kilo of usable protein when compared to meat production."[26] The cows and other livestock these people are clamoring to exterminate in the name of liberation have long been the providers of nutrients for soils in which to grow nutrient-rich plants, and life for humanity by their conversion of grasses into healthy meats. Without cows, these diners will be surrendering themselves to a diet dependent on synthetic fertilizers, often blended with a long list of pesticide, fungicide and herbicide residues used to "increase productivity and efficiency" at the expense of environmental and human health.

Such salesmanship boosts profits by preying on people's good intentions. The push in 1990 for McDonald's and other fast-food chains to convert from beef tallow to hydrogenated plant oils was assisted, if not entirely accomplished, by animal rights activists who were allied with the food corporations, for whom hydrogenated fats were far more profitable. Increasingly, the public is becoming aware of this scam as the "real science" weighs in. A large-scale study published by *The Lancet Regional Health - Europe* concluded that "health benefits from a plant-based diet can potentially disappear when these foods are ultra processed":

> . . . ultra-processed plant-sourced foods (think: French fries) can increase the risk of cardiovascular disease.
>
> "These findings advance current knowledge by highlighting that a higher intake of plant-sourced foods may only bring about better cardiovascular health outcomes when largely based on minimally processed foods while a higher intake of plant-sourced UPF may have detrimental effects on health," the authors write.[27]

Like cows, not all plant-based foods are the same. However, most plant-based meat substitutes and so-called synthetic, or "cultured," meats *are* the same in their use of GMO monoculture crops to "grow" or imitate meat.[28] They are the creations of the same scorched-earth "Green Revolution" machinations that are methodically destroying America's soils and waters: "Meanwhile, around the globe farming operations are being consolidated and switched to commodity monocultures, and management is falling to a generation groomed to use chemical inputs as traditional know-how fades into the past."[29]

Synthetic meats were touted initially to corporate America and venture capitalists for their profitability. Long proud of its ability to eliminate human workers from its production chain, Big Ag envisioned a technological fantasy in which it could convert cheap corn, soy, or beans into delicious tenderloin steaks and chicken fillets, leaving animal husbandry and reliance on farmers in the dumpster. In "theory," it all sounds grand (like perpetual motion machines or lead-to-gold alchemy of bygone days). In reality, the billions of dollars thus far frittered away on these technologies have yielded disappointments—production of cultured meats cost-effectively at scale is proving not just problematic but impossible.[30]

Even if they were technologically feasible, fake meats would still pose profound environmental problems. The full extent of externalized costs of production (as witnessed with renewable energy manufacturing and Bill Gates's plane rides) for cultured meats includes plastics, rows of stainless-steel vats, heated (or cooled) buildings, computers, and monitoring equipment. These cow-replacing factories generate a long list of *chemical* pollution that far exceeds anything cows could ever emit while quietly chewing their cud composed of renewable grass blades.

Cell-cultured meats plugged as replacements for cows are fantastical. Venture capitalists and a climate-anxious public have been lured to believe synthetic animal meat substitutes will solve environmental problems while liberating farm animals. The war on cows is not an effort to preserve the planet but to amplify growing food hegemony by chemical-pushing oligopolies. Those who claim they have created an economically viable and ecologically friendly synthetic meat product are peddling phony baloney for self-interest.

Bug Burgers and Cricket Crunchies?

The slim smile that crosses Americans' faces when bug burgers are broached is much like the cow fart amusement—they can't be serious, right? Yet, just like synthetic meats and plant-based meat substitutes, there's big money in growing, processing, and peddling bugs.

A 2020 report projected that the insect farming industry would grow 27.8 percent annually (to $8 billion by 2030), "providing cheap, sustainable animal feed—and even protein for human consumption."[31] The industry has far outpaced those predictions: a more recent study found that "the North American insect protein market was valued at nearly $48 billion in 2023 [and is] projected to reach over $274 billion by 2031."[32]

China boasts big CAFOs that harvest six billion cockroaches a year,[33] and France hosts one of the largest insect farms in the world, producing fifteen thousand tons of protein annually.[34] A similar facility was opened by the same French company (InnovaFeed) in Decatur, Illinois, in 2024.[35]

Insect farming may prove viable for pet foods, livestock feed, and humans as well—it is appealing from an environmental perspective to employ cockroaches to divert human food scraps from the waste stream, although perhaps not so appealing for humans to eat. Bugs are still not as effective as cows at building soils, though—and all these facilities require construction, electric lighting, heating and/or cooling systems, paved lots, etc., which are not necessary for the eons-old traditions of animal husbandry.

In contrast to the pesticide residues routinely detected in many fruits and vegetables, cows fed organic grass (rather than grains grown with GMO technology) are free of these sickening contaminations. Yet still, the lies about cows persist. One discussion of utilizing controversial CRISPR technology (and garlic) to reduce enteric emissions in cows noted:

> On average, a cow emits approximately 220 pounds of methane annually, which is about half the emissions produced by a typical car. According to the Food and Agriculture Organization, cows are responsible for around 4% of global warming.
>
> If the researchers' efforts are successful, they could potentially eliminate the largest human-made source of methane and significantly impact global warming trends.[36]

This needs to be corrected. Cows are the *most significant* "human-made source" of methane? Cow methane is *cow*-made and is more than offset by other cow assets that sequester carbon and break down methane—no CRISPR gene editing required. Also, beef and dairy cows raised in CAFOs generate far more methane than rotationally grazed cows because of the additional methane generated in noisome fecal lagoons.[37] This blame-shifting perversion is reduced to the false claim that "avoiding meat and dairy is the single biggest way to reduce your impact on earth."[38]

Here again a pattern is revealed. The consumer goods targeted by those claiming they are driven by a desire to spare the world from carbon dioxide and methane are narrowed to necessities (food, transportation, heat, and energy) as priorities of the globalist rescue plan. Consumer goods that are discretionary or even luxurious, including an almost unending array of electronic gadgets, fireworks displays, and speedboats are among the first things humanity could live without, yet they are merely ignored. Concurrently, the ecotoxins generated by these nonnecessities (and EVs, solar panels, heat pumps, and wind turbines) during their manufacture and disposal are often disregarded in favor of the tiresome distraction of greenhouse gases.

For instance, the Environmental Protection Agency states that even when the costs of battery manufacturing are factored in, EVs are cleaner for the planet because they create fewer greenhouse gases:

> Myth: Electric vehicles are worse for the climate than gasoline cars because of battery manufacturing.
>
> Some studies have shown that making a typical EV can create more carbon pollution than making a gasoline car. This is because of the additional energy required to manufacture an EV's battery. Still, over the lifetime of the vehicle, total GHG emissions associated with manufacturing, charging, and driving an EV are typically lower than the total GHGs associated with a gasoline car. That's because EVs have zero tailpipe emissions and are typically responsible for significantly fewer GHGs during operation. . . .[39]

Apparently, the EPA is unconcerned or unfamiliar with the lithium and cobalt mining slurry contaminating the crops, water, and farmland of the people of Congo,[40] the coal plants being constructed in China to smelt aluminum for EVs,[41] the dramatic increase in rubber particulate pollution created by EVs,[42] or the eventual processing and disposal of EV batteries.[43] But, like NASA with lawn mowers, and industrialists claiming that CAFO cows emit less methane than grass-fed cows, the EPA simply sidesteps discussion of toxic chemical pollution by using the sole metric of carbon dioxide, which warms, rather than focusing on the forever toxins that kill.

Cows and other livestock play a central role in sustainable food production, soil restoration, water preservation, and reversal of the toxification and loss of precious soils and water. To focus global resources to eliminate, genetically alter, or tax cows while synthetic fertilizers, GMOs, glyphosate, and a host of chemical toxins are touted as planet-saving alternatives and the only way to feed the world, is to con humanity into dependency and ecoterrorism for short-term profits.

Whether or not it is the intention of these industrial forces to enslave, sicken, and wipe out humanity is irrelevant. This way lies the path of genocide by bovicide, whether deliberate, greedy, or just plain ignorant.

CHAPTER 6

European Farm Revolts

> Since the farmers' movement in Holland, which started two years ago, the farmers are starting to say, "You can't do this, we can't make a living, we can't continue our jobs,"—it will be the end of farming in Europe if we let Brussels implement what it wants to implement.[1]
>
> —Patricia Chagnon, Member of European Parliament (2022–2024)

Efforts to shutter farms and reduce livestock numbers in Europe to remediate climate change have made international headlines as farmer protests have rocked the social and political foundations of many countries there. Dutch and Irish farmer revolts have evolved into powerful political movements aimed at protecting and defending farmers, their culture, and local food production. Concurrently, Ukraine, the vast "breadbasket of Europe," has witnessed its organic grain harvests overtaken by GMOs and foreign ownership, destroying its fertile farms as a condition for war loans.

It may be difficult for Americans to perceive how these European battles relate to US agriculture. The justification for closing down three thousand Dutch farms and culling tens of thousands of Irish cows was climate change, but much like coal plants are constructed in China to satisfy US demand for solar panels, shifting food production outside of Europe does nothing to reduce net carbon (or net ecotoxins) unless *methods* are changed. Indeed, such abrupt disruptions are economically and environmentally inefficient: food will be transported over longer distances, often from nations with few, if any, environmental or labor regulations, and will require more significant refrigeration or other energy inputs than if produced locally. Longer transport distances also increase threats of supply disruptions and food shortages.

Similar pressures are coming to bear on American farmlands. Climate ideology embraces "rewilding"[2] of much existing farmland, which is double folly:

as discussed in the previous chapter, well-stewarded grazing lands sequester far more carbon dioxide than trees, indefinitely;[3] food supplies displaced by (government subsidized) rewilding projects must then be supplied from farther and farther away. Dependence on China for solar panels and semiconductors is a different matter than dependence on Chinese-grown and processed foods.

The Biden administration announced a unilateral Executive Order to force implementation of government conservation of 30 percent of all the nation's lands by 2030; 50 percent by 2050.[4] President Donald Trump has suspended these plans, but this rewilding policy continues to dominate in globalist prescriptions to counter climate change. Restricting private landownership would not enhance food supplies. President Biden's innocuous-sounding rescue plan, bringing the entire federal government[5] to bear not on preserving healthy foods but prioritizing "climate change," is indistinguishable from the ideological justifications for farmer warfare in Europe.

The high-sounding climate goals are strongly influenced by the powerful "stakeholders" of GMO patents, synthetic fertilizers, and chemical concoctions. The Biden administration and USDA Commissioner Tom Vilsack endorsed synthetic fertilizers and GMO crops even as the EU tried to clamp down on both. These policies parallel what was done to agriculture in Ukraine, and what has been done to India, Mexico, and Iraq in the name of rescue. The effort has now been unleashed across Europe, prompting farmer revolts.

Hints at the stealth corporate GMO takeover of the world's farmlands are offered by US "climate czar" John Kerry:

> "We can't get to net zero—we don't get this job done—unless agriculture is front and center as part of the solution," he said. "This sector needs innovation now more than ever.
>
> "A 2-degree future could result in an additional 600 million people not getting enough to eat," he said. "And you just can't continue to warm the planet while also expecting to feed it."[6]

The opposite is the case—you can't expect to feed the world if you undermine healthy soils and food production in the name of global warming. The Green Revolution's industrial "innovation" in agriculture inflicted destruction on small farms, soils, water, and food supplies by big businesses partnered with universities and technological "experts." Novel equipment and chemicals that undermined human and environmental health and traditional farming were peddled as beneficial, reaping massive profits for a small group of corporate behemoths. The Green Deal in Europe and the Green New Deal in the US are extensions of the same forces of industrialization.

The fields of Ukraine fed 400 million people organically—does the forced conversion of these fertile lands to corporate ownership, GMO crops, and chemical saturation "feed the world" and save the climate? Rotationally grazed cows and other regenerative farming methods are the "innovation" that will reverse environmental harms to soils and waterways while sequestering massive amounts of carbon dioxide.[7]

An evaluation of the relative health merits of plant- versus meat-based diets, or the "right" of people to choose unhealthy (for themselves or the climate) diets, is not undertaken here. "Reducing farm animals" eliminates humanity's crucial source of organic (manure) fertilizer, which is needed to halt the destruction of the climate, health, soil, and water caused by synthetic fertilizers. The argument that humans must eat plants, bugs, or synthetic meats to "save the environment" parallels the destruction wrought by fraudulently named "renewables" manufacturing that spews forever chemicals. Initiatives to shift from cows to GMO crops increase pollution, dependency, and corporate profits at the *expense* of human health and environmental sustainability.

The United Nations and the World Economic Forum have weighed in against cows, favoring technological innovation and digital interconnectivity, and calling for a global transition away from cows in the name of climate rescue, equity, and human health. Both also appeal to increased government and NGO control, investments in technologies, "incentives" to encourage people to abandon cow and meat diets, and further genetic modifications of cows that will likely yield proprietary powers for corporate market dominance. These two organizations conspicuously display a long history of pushing toward a global totalitarian "solution" falsely presented as necessary to save the world (from humanity?).

There are significant differences, as well as similarities, between European and American farming that offer essential lessons for agricultural policy. Many of the pressures on European farmers are familiar to Americans—conflicting regulatory frameworks, vague and costly environmental and wildlife regulations, inequitable farming subsidies that favor large operations at the expense of small, conservation and animal rights groups allied with mega-corporations and NGOs, input price inflation (especially for fertilizers), and skyrocketing farmland costs exacerbated by speculation. Differences include disparate farmer demographics between the EU and US, divergent policy priorities regarding synthetic fertilizers and GMO cropping,[8] and market disruptions and future uncertainty in Europe caused by Ukraine's massive agricultural production.

The Dutch Farmer Revolt

Holland is one of the world's most farming-intensive nations, a direct consequence of the Dutch struggle against Nazi Germany in World War II. Following the Netherlands' cooperation with Allied forces in Operation Market Garden (a failed Allied effort to pierce a line into Germany through Dutch territory) in September 1944, Germany retaliated with a brutal blockade of the tiny nation. Aggravated by a freezing winter and shortages of fuel and equipment, the blockade was devastating to the Dutch people, leading to tens of thousands of deaths by famine.[9] Thousands of urban children were sent to the countryside to live.

The Dutch response was to rebuild their agricultural economy robustly, so that they would "never again" suffer such misery, death, and privation. The resulting farm focus and flourishing of the nation has been as much a marvel as its fantastic system of levees and idyllic windmills. This intensification of food production formed the backbone of the Dutch economy and provided food for much of Europe.

The "attack" on Dutch farmers originated through the combined impact of EU laws regarding climate change, wildlife protection, and widespread tropes about cows being the preeminent culprits in pollution. Claims that bird populations in the Netherlands were threatened by nitrates and other agricultural pollution evolved into demands for drastic reductions in overall cow numbers, with little attention paid to differentiating between farming operations based on regenerative versus CAFO farming.

Instead of being praised for its agricultural marvels, Holland and its passionate farmers have been shamed and denigrated. The UK's *Guardian* newspaper howled that "The country has the highest density of livestock in Europe—more than four times that of the UK or France—with more than 100 million cattle, chickens and pigs in total."[10] During World War II, this agricultural productivity would have been praised as a good thing. Instead, the EU and climate alarmists began pressuring the Netherlands to eliminate cows posthaste. As in all individual European states, the pressure to change emanates from the European Union:

> The highest Dutch administrative court found in 2019 that the government was breaking EU law by not doing enough to reduce excess nitrogen in vulnerable natural areas, due to farming and industrial activities. . . . The 13-year multibillion-euro plan . . . includes paying some Dutch livestock farmers to relocate or exit the industry, and

> helping others transition to more extensive (as opposed to intensive) methods of farming, with fewer animals and a bigger area of land. . . . The end result is expected to be close to a one-third reduction in the numbers of pigs, cows and chickens in the country.[11]

Dutch farmers and consumers united in a massive revolt. The core idea of improving extensive methods of farming over industrial systems is laudable. Still, numerous problems with fairness immediately arose: many Dutch families have farmed "intensively" for generations, constantly encouraged by the same government now seeking to close them down (as in Ireland). Furthermore, numerous nonfood industries have *increased* their pollution (especially of ecotoxins rather than comparatively innocuous greenhouse gases) while Dutch and other European farmers have leveled off or even reduced emissions and have made numerous environmental improvements for decades.

A general problem with grand regulatory schemes is that they are fostered by sprawling government bureaucracies disconnected from on-the-ground realities. Food, like pollution, is generated at the local level. Government proposals to "fix" local agricultural problems are inefficient, susceptible to corruption by industry and political actors, and add layers of additional costs for farmers already reeling from plummeting commodity prices while fertilizer, fuel, and land prices head to the moon. Dutch farmers, like their US counterparts, are stuck in the middle.

An additional complaint was that lost food production would mean not just lost GDP for the Netherlands and livelihoods for many citizens but would shift production yet farther away to potentially unregulated regions (like China or the global south) where net pollution would be *increased*, food would be shipped longer distances, and food security would be compromised. (The Dutch are understandably a tad intent on this last point—the Nazi blockade is not forgotten there, even if the EU and climate activists are oblivious.)

The Nazis lifted their 1944 blockade of the Dutch when conditions became so severe that a complete breakdown was unfolding, but multiple hardships still ensued. The damage could not be undone during that brutal winter. Similarly, shutting down a third of the nation's livestock in the name of reducing carbon dioxide risks disrupting food supplies irrevocably and unleashing waves of future suffering. Many European countries depend on the Netherlands for their food imports (directly from Holland or from its imports, reexported across Europe, especially of grains and animal feeds imported from Paraguay, Argentina, Uruguay, and Brazil).

Increased Russian exports and instability in Ukraine also roiled agricultural markets in Europe and threatened economic viability for many farmers. Grand bureaucratic plans from on high threaten innumerable economic and environmental harms, aggravated when the globalist solutions of GMOs and synthetic fertilizers are proffered as the solution. Such prescriptions pose a significant threat to long-term food security for Europe and the world.

Ireland's Farmer Revolt

Ireland's livestock farming is deeply ingrained in the nation's cultural identity and economy. The infamous Potato Famine occurred much earlier than the 1944–1945 Dutch famine caused by the Nazi blockade, but it lasted far longer (1845–1852) and was exponentially more severe. More than one million Irish perished in the famine; another million fled the nation in a mass exodus.[12] The famine (aggravated by British prejudices,[13] not dissimilar in some ways from the victimizing of the Netherlands by foreigners) permanently altered the Irish social conscience as well as Ireland's demographic, political, and economic landscape.

This defining episode in Irish history explains the modern Irish passion for domestic food production and security. This in part explains the predominant agricultural landscape of the land of Éire: 72 percent of the little island's land area is used in agriculture, of which more than 50 percent of all farms operate specialist livestock farming.[14] The Irish government has for decades encouraged its farmers to produce food, including regeneratively. Many Americans purchase grass-fed cheddar cheese from Ireland on a daily basis. In 2021, "data on organic markets . . . show[ed] an annual overall growth rate of 9% within Ireland" and a 56 percent growth rate in the UK and EU between 2015 and 2019.[15] Irish consumers and farmers have been shifting toward more sustainable "extensive" systems for years with government encouragement. However, the EU then decided to target the nation's cows.

Before the EU's Irish cow culling was announced, Ireland pushed farmers there to microchip their cows with identifying ear tags. Effective July 1, 2022, the Irish Ministry of Agriculture, Food, and Marine (DAFM) implemented "a legal requirement on herd keepers to officially identify all newborn calves with a tag set containing an EID tag" in the name of "helping" farmers.[16]

No mention was made of using electronic ear tags for cow confiscation.[17] Government publications emphasized the system's benefits for herd management, tracking individual animals, and filing information online—but not tracking cows for elimination.[18] Shortly following the implementation of this tracking system, it was announced that Ireland was to eliminate two hundred thousand of its 7.1 million cows because it supposedly has "the worst methane emissions per capita in the [EU] bloc" and the second-highest rate of greenhouse gas emissions.[19]

The economic cost of herd reduction was estimated at $640 million. The government proposed to cull sixty-five thousand cows annually using voluntary options as a "retirement exit scheme."[20] Skeptics suspected a different scheme entirely. US Congresswoman Harriet Hageman cried foul play:

> In Ireland, she said a mandatory EID served a nefarious purpose and was used to track inventories. The government ordered 41,000 head of livestock be sent to slaughter to combat global warming. . . . Hageman said the agencies lack the ability to order a slaughter or cull order unless they know where the cattle are located. . . . "They're not trying to solve a problem," she said. "It's just another way for our government to manipulate the process, manipulate the market, and attempt to impose a social agenda on private industry."[21]

The Bulletin of Atomic Scientists unwittingly reinforced Hageman's allegations in an article titled "Ireland Isn't Culling Cows for Climate. But Maybe It Should Be?," claiming "cows alone are responsible for about one-fifth of Ireland's total contribution to anthropogenic climate change" and "cows do present a possibly insurmountable obstacle to the country's decarbonization policies":

> The country simply has too many cows and too few avenues for reducing their emissions enough to meet targets.
>
> The case of Irish cattle underscores the core problem of emissions-reduction policies. Eventually, such policies simply must restrict profitable business, choosing planetary health over the economic performance of a given industry. This includes restricting or phasing out highly polluting machines, be they coal power plants or cows.[22]

Critically assessing these claims reveals that atomic scientists are not bovine brainiacs. The article claims "the country has too many cows" (a dubious, political statement), inviting the question of whether Ireland has instead too many cats and dogs—pets aren't food. Their manure ends up in landfills, generating methane without fertilizing food crops.

The writer then claims that food and profitability must be sacrificed because "such [emissions-reduction] policies simply must restrict profitable business, choosing planetary health over the economic performance of a given industry." That is a myopic but revealing claim: the government that is clueless about cows, readers are told, *must* kill cows. The author compares bovines to polluting machines and coal power plants that spew ecotoxins, then claims it is "undoubtedly true" that governments will also have to impose laws to restrict consumers from eating meat.

The piece closes by projecting the problem of "complex state bureaucracies, pushed back against by organized special interests, and complicated by a polarized society in thrall to social-media-driven agitation" onto farmers defending their lands, cows, and livelihoods. The opposite is demonstrably true: the EU is a complex mega-bureaucracy that overlaps with those of individual nation-states. The organized special interests of Big Ag, globalist food conglomerates, and wildlife and animal rights NGOs have conspired to circulate false propaganda against vitally important cows.

Farming Changes in France

France, too, has seen its cows assaulted by the bureaucratic machine that thinks cows are worse than coal-fired plants and cars. Though the nation has been reducing overall herd numbers for years, a court there ordered the government to cull yet more cows.[23]

Critics condemned the court's decision as "simplistic," and France's Minister of Agriculture and Food Security, Marc Fesneau, "pointed to the environmental benefits of farming and concluded that "we need livestock farmers more than ever."[24] The Court went even further, however, speculating about future food supplies and the availability of meat after cows are extinct (presumably replaced with fields of solar panels from China):

> It also added that France would still be able to produce enough meat to feed its population without imports if the public stuck to guidelines which recommend eating no more than 500g a week. . . . The French Interprofessional Association for Cattle and Meat, Interbev, said in a statement that the fields in which cows graze help capture carbon and protect biodiversity. . . . It also claimed that the continued reduction in cattle herds would "accentuate the increase in imported meat" asking "Are we really ready to sacrifice our sustainable farming model and food sovereignty?"
>
> "This is why Interbev deplores the fact that the climate issue is too often reduced to carbon issues alone," the association added.[25]

The pattern repeats: falsehoods, deafness, more falsehoods. France already reduced its cow herds from 20.3 million cows in 2000 to 19.1 million in 2011 and 17.3 million in 2021. The country's agriculture ministry projects those numbers to drop further at current rates to 15 million by 2035, and 13 million by 2050.[26] Apparently, that is not fast enough for the burp-obsessed, and so government bureaucracies are throttling farmers aggressively while promising no one will have to give up meat so long as they (for now) consume less than 500 grams (1.1 pounds) a week. That's one steak and one burger.

Yet even this assurance is a deception—the government will eventually close that meat intake down to zero, as the mayor of Lyon, France, did during the COVID-19 pandemic. Red meat was removed from that city's school menus in the name of social distance protocols. *Vox* called the switch "environmentally friendly" and belittled opposition: "The response from the French agricultural establishment was hysterical."[27]

Still, atomic scientists and others, including the WHO, WEF, and UN, persist that the only way to save the planet is for all of humanity to give up meat and eat only the GMO chemical-dependent plants saturated with pesticides they control. Something smells rotten not just in Denmark, but across every nation victim in the EU. The French Court's assurance that meats will remain on French tables is a shallow faith, at best. (Presumably, the judges and EU leadership will still enjoy fillet mignon without limitation.)

In 2020, approximately 93 percent of the EU's farms were "classed as being family farms, defined as being farms on which 50 percent or more of the agricultural labour force is provided by family members." Larger farms (over 50 hectares, or about 123.5 acres) were more common in France (46 percent) than in most EU states; France generated 17.2 percent of standard output for all of the EU, surpassed only by Italy.[28] Reducing France's cow numbers will quickly "save the planet" by eliminating a foundational agricultural resource of food, and herds of animals that can be grass-fed and sequester carbon: the Court made no distinction between industrially versus regeneratively husbanded cows, just as in the US.

French MEP (Member of the European Parliament) Patricia Chagnon was asked her opinion as to whether Brussels was guilty of "excessive overreach in climate policy and agricultural matters." Her response insightfully summarized the European farming battles the world has watched with fascination:

> There are individual triggers in individual member states because of national legislation. But it all goes back to Brussels and three essential

> issues. . . . It is first of all the unfair competition that is being imposed on our farmers through free trade agreements, driving prices down. . . . Second, there are numerous, complicated legislation, regulation, and administrative burdens that are also imposed by Brussels. . . . Third, there is an overall philosophy of degrowth in the European technocratic elites here in Brussels. . . . When you put all that together and you add the "agri-bashing," you have the ingredients of these European-wide agricultural protests. . . .
>
> Over the past 20–30 years in the EU, there have been constant small attacks on agriculture. It started with sort of shaming them for being dirty for using filthy products, for being polluters, coming from the extreme Left ecologist wing basically. . . . So these ultra-liberal, globalist, capitalist, multinational companies—they want to be able to shop worldwide and just feed us with produce on which they can make the biggest profits. . . .
>
> So, this globalist Right and this ecological extremist Left have found a common enemy: European agriculture. This is why their attacks on farmers have been so efficient, because they've been attacked by both sides.[29]

The political pressures on French farmers from non-farmers, including animal rights activists, climate alarmists, and industrial lobbyists, are compounding the loss of farmers and consolidation of farms there. French farmer Etienne Compagnon explains that most French farms still depend on grain crops and imported fodder:

> [The] vast majority of animals for milk production have grain or corn silage for energy and soya from Brazil for protein. For beef, it depends from region to region. In the mountains, grass still represents a big part of the diet in summer, but in more productive areas more intensive production methods are used. In all cases, grain is used to finish animals.

Converting livestock to more regenerative systems is underway and possible, but Etienne warned that the greatest threat to French farming, whether conventional or regenerative, arises from the steady loss of people willing to farm:

> [As for] the decrease of the overall herd, the main driver has been the decline in the number of farmers in activity. As in many countries,

> farmers are aging and not enough new farmers are replacing them. Of course this phenomenon has many roots and facts, however access to land is a huge issue. It is very hard for a young farmer to get started if you are not taking over a family farm (which is my case) and in parallel many farmers are retiring without their children wanting to take over.[30]

This phenomenon is repeated worldwide, exacerbated by a century of policies and economics that favor large, "efficient" farms over widely dispersed smaller ones, while not protecting farm families from rising commercial and residential land prices. Farm incomes will never achieve the per-acre earnings of factories or commercial/residential leasing. Yet, factory workers and suburban residents will always need the fuel of healthy food to function. It is a crisis that has steadily worsened across the "developed" world.

Implications for US Agriculture

American agriculture differs from that of the European Union, but as recounted above, numerous US and global leaders have called upon the United States to initiate changes to farming methods and dietary choices in the name of addressing climate change, promoting equity, and supporting biodiversity. However, the US diverged from the EU's green plans for agriculture, which called for 20 percent reductions in synthetic fertilizers and 50 percent reductions in pesticide use—the USDA does not want to turn off that chemical spigot, instead claiming synthetic fertilizers and GMO technologies are the solution to climate change and world hunger.

American farming demographics differ significantly from those of European farmers, with implications for US policies and the potential for political resistance, as seen in Europe. Without consumers rallying at their side, America's farmers are unlikely to have the same impact on the nation as they have in Europe. America is losing farmland at an alarming rate, and the number of US farmers is steadily shrinking—there won't be thousands of tractors descending on Washington, D.C., anytime soon.

The complex labyrinth of state and federal regulations confronting American farmers has added to food costs, favored destructive industrial practices, and contributed to the decline of small and midsize US farms. Something as innocuous-sounding as expanding EPA water regulations to regulate toxins from chicken and meat processors becomes profoundly impactful when the sins of Tyson Foods are cast upon small- and midsize processors.[31] Compliance costs are prohibitive for many facilities, threatening existing small-scale processors at a time when many areas are desperate for more. "Get big or get out" is alive and well, throwing out small-scale meat and poultry processors with the mega-industrial bathwater.

Similarly, USDA regulations that dispense farmer disaster relief with priority to people of color and women[32] may be well-intentioned, but violating the Equal Protection Clause in the name of "equity" threatens to reduce food supplies for *all* genders and races. Race- and gender-based disaster relief for farmers overlooks issues of "merit" related to the causes of losses, years of experience, size of operation, the importance of market products to the economy or food supply, or other practical agricultural measures of performance relevant to an effective disaster response.

Another destructive regulatory bullet was narrowly dodged by small farmers when a burdensome initiative to compel them to report staggering volumes of supposed climate change data under SEC rules was scuttled. The SEC, charged to regulate financial markets for integrity to protect shareholders, was compromised as a "whole-of-government" vehicle to implement ultra vires "climate" requirements on farms.

The proposed rules would have bankrupted many small- and medium-sized businesses through uncompensated compliance costs. Tennessee tomato farmer Renea Jones, of Jones and Church Farms, testified that "From a record-keeping standpoint, my small family farm operation would have to hire extra staff just to keep up with the data the SEC is asking for."[33]

The EU sought to implement similar agricultural climate change reporting but backed off due to political backlash and burdensome compliance costs.[34] Other regulatory strictures directed toward wildlife or ecological goals have a dramatic and disproportionate impact on small farms and food processors. Broadening the list of protected endangered species and their habitats encroaches on existing farmlands.[35] Small farms are once again disproportionately impacted, and farms in general are economically impacted with no offsetting compensation for what is essentially a regulatory taking. Similar rules are slowly strangling UK farmers, although at least farmers there are compensated for caring for wildlife.

Meanwhile, New York Attorney General Letitia James sued JBS Foods for false advertising over its claims that it was striving to achieve net-zero in its beef rearing operations. The suit alleges:

> Even if it had developed a plan to be "Net Zero by 2040," the JBS Group could not feasibly meet its pledge because there are no proven

> agricultural practices to reduce its greenhouse gas emissions to net zero at the JBS Group's current scale, and offsetting those emissions would be a costly undertaking of an unprecedented degree. As of 2021, the JBS Group's estimated annual greenhouse gases were more than those of the entire country of Ireland, and the JBS Group plans to substantially increase its meat production over the coming years.[36]

JBS Foods and other large industrial agricultural enterprises may be the biggest polluters, but that is precisely why they should be encouraged to adopt regenerative practices where possible, as the nation seeks to recover from a century of farming consolidation. New York's suit threatens the unintended consequence of dissuading these large market actors from trying to improve their operations at all. If they cannot cater to consumer preferences by improving their farming methods, there is little reason for them to change. But more, New York's lawsuit alleges falsehoods about cows parroted by climate warriors who never shoveled a cow pie—the claims of the lawsuit are bogus, focused on greenhouse gases while ignoring manure solids, pressuring the world's largest beef producer to embrace the very industrial agricultural system from which it must uncouple.

This partial list of inefficient, counterproductive federal and state regulatory intrusions into American farming practices parallels the growing burden of similar (often conflicting) wildlife and environmental regulations thrust upon European farmers by the EU and their native countries. UK farmers have been particularly hard-pressed: wildlife and climate regulations, coupled with rising input costs and land prices, reduced protectionism, and shrinking available farmland, are making farming undesirable as well as unprofitable. These same pressures are growing in the United States, where the small farmers suffer most.

The ever-increasing regulation of farming operations assumes greater significance when compared to the environmental impacts of government spending and regulations in other sectors. Solar panel "farms" are often presented as farm-friendly.[37] Still, they largely depend on Chinese coal-fired power for their production, emit deadly ecotoxins during manufacture and disposal, and usurp fertile farmlands. Irish sheep farmer Michael NicAoibh warns, "Solar panels are the death of farming. Why don't they put them on the roofs of factories instead of in the fields that feed us? This is about food security! I'm afraid it will take a world war for people to understand what they are doing to agriculture."[38]

A study commissioned by the Indiana legislature in 2023 found that the state had lost 345,682 acres of farmland from 2010 to 2022. The detailed analysis states: "The results show that agricultural land was most likely to be lost in areas around the edges of cities and suburban areas." Ironically, the Indiana study included solar panel arrays as farmland in its calculations: "Agriculture officials relied on data from the state Department of Local Government Finance [DLGF] and the U.S. Department of Agriculture to create its findings. The report stated that the DLGF includes uses like renewable energy in its counting for farmland."[39]Addressing the 2022 US Census of Agriculture data showing the nation's farmland had shrunk by 2 percent since 2017, and the number of farmers had declined 7 percent (142,000 farms), USDA Secretary Tom Vilsack expressed this ominous query: "Are we okay with losing that much farmland or is there a better way?"[40]

European Farm Extinction Coming to America

The aggressive climate, wildlife, and animal rights policies that have slowly choked Europe's farmers and sparked riots there are already well entrenched in America to similar effect—US farmers are demoralized and struggling. In "Down on the Farm: Why America's Food Producers Are Hurting," *Washington Examiner* writer Jeremy Lott undertook a rare but crucial deep dive into the regulatory and market pressures pinching down on US farmers, noting "Across the Atlantic, farmers became exceedingly fed up with attempts by the European Commission and some European Union members to micromanage them via regulation."[41]

The parallels with Europe are clear to see, except the coming "farmageddon" for America promises to be *worse.* US farms are already more consolidated than in Europe, meaning there are fewer farmers to drive tractors to Washington, D.C., to defend the American food supply (and they are much farther away if they wanted to). Hedge funds and billionaires (and China) have bought up millions of acres of US farmland: oligarchs and millionaires have closed in on European farms as well—particularly in Ukraine. Small or start-up farms are cost-prohibited from the land market, while existing farmers struggle with tight margins and regulations. Why then are Bill Gates et al. so interested in buying farmland when farming is currently so unprofitable? Billionaires and globalists know full well that food is, in fact, extremely lucrative.

The current trajectory for American farming is not a reversal of decades of consolidation, soil degradation, and aquifer depletion—it instead propels industrial farming into hyperdrive, *increasing* technological dependency, including for GMO crops and synthetic fertilizers. "Efficiency" and climate change are intertwined as justification for either "get even bigger or get out" globally. The US is pushing full-bore to become even more synthetic fertilizer and chemical dependent, not change course and heal the land and humanity.

European farmers have understandably balked at this agenda. The political recoil propelled farmers in many European nations to descend on city centers in droves, while political parties and influence shifted dramatically. The EU's Green Deal plans were scrapped due to partisan blowback, a big win for Big Ag, which seeks to ensure complete dependency on its products.

In the United States, reducing the use of pesticides and synthetic fertilizers was not even part of the Green New Deal. There has been no push by the USDA to eliminate synthetic fertilizers or pesticides—the *opposite* has occurred under the moral auspices of climate change, with vegetarians and animal rights activists joining the push to eradicate cows and their manure in favor of industrial processes.

To the extent that it can influence European farming, the United States has promoted a similar massive industrial predominance there. Larger European farms employ industrial practices more commonly than small producers (as in the US), receive the lion's share of Common Agriculture Policy (CAP) subsidies, and thus have the most significant political influence.[42] While the USDA has mouthed approval of "multiple" approaches to farming, it faces economic hurdles in the EU selling US food products such as GMOs, gene-edited crops, and synthetic meats or meats containing growth hormones. Consequently, "Alarm bells are sounding in Europe over concerns it could open the bloc to imports that don't meet European production standards."[43]

In November 2021, the EU's commissioner of agriculture Janusz Wojciechowski and United States agriculture secretary Tom Vilsack announced the Cooperation Platform on Agriculture (CPA) to advance "a greater exchange of knowledge and information, and the promotion of mutual understanding between the US and the EU on agricultural issues." The stated goals of this (corporate-collaborative) effort are summarized as:

- approaches to improving the mitigation of greenhouse gas emissions
- carbon sequestration
- climate adaptation strategies
- improving the climate resilience of agricultural production systems
- research and innovation[44]

This is a list not of regenerative policies, but of a frenzied techno-manufacture that replaces food security, human health, and soil and water purity with a *climate* agenda that destroys all of these goals while churning out enormous amounts of harmful chemicals. "Envisaged activities" include "promote ties between the agricultural sectors of the US and the EU, . . . identify opportunities for collaboration to raise climate and environmental ambition in agriculture and land use through research and innovation . . . [and] The future of the livestock sector: pressures and opportunities."[45] The war on European farms is not just coming to America—it has been waged all along on both sides of the Atlantic by multinational corporate agricultural "stakeholders."

The focus of these proposals is not to revert extensive agricultural facilities to small-scale, sustainable production, but the reverse. The "EU-US Collaboration Platform" hosted a June 18, 2024, event titled "Empowering Rural Areas: The Role of Rural Investments in Accelerating Climate Resilience."[46]

Wojciechowski and Vilsack claim this effort represents a "new chapter" in EU-US collaboration toward "climate-smart agricultural production" to "bolster food security" and "digital connectivity." Tom Vilsack veiled this climate agenda as food saving, claiming, "We initiated this coalition because it is clear that increasing agricultural productivity is essential to meet the needs of a global population and ensure that food is affordable to hundreds of millions of people around the world."[47]

This bait and switch over climate change and food security, as well as industrial agriculture's role in both, obfuscates the conflicting missions involved, shielding practical analysis of ecotoxins, soil and water degradation, and other harms to sustainability inflicted by "climate-smart" technologies that are actually sustainability-dumb. Suppose soils and water are destroyed in the pursuit of "climate change remediation" and maximizing food production. In that case, the entire system will implode, the environment will be decimated, human health will continue to decline, and billions of people will face food insecurity. Is that the *plan*, or just the consequence of short-term profit-seeking shrouded as a global rescue plan? Either way, that plan is already underway in America—but US farmers are not rebelling.

Notably, Secretary Vilsack has consistently "taken issue" with the Farm to Fork goals of reducing pesticide and synthetic fertilizer use, claiming "this approach will result in additional costs to farmers and lower productivity." How will reducing synthetic fertilizer use (costs have skyrocketed in the EU and US, linked to fossil fuel prices) increase farming costs if farmers can eliminate those expensive inputs while securing higher prices for organic goods? And how will productivity look in two decades as soils weaken and erode, and ever more pesticides and synthetic applications are required to maintain productivity artificially? What of the soil microbiome, water supplies, and the human gut? USDA Secretary Vilsack, who earned the moniker "Mr. Monsanto" for his consistent servitude to that company during the Obama administration, does not address these crucial questions.[48]

Farming Demographics and Food Security

Complex, overlapping regulations that pit agricultural productivity against climate, wildlife, and animal rights ideologies have been a chief complaint of European farmers and are now increasing in the US. So, too, are upward pressures on farmland, fertilizer, equipment, and energy costs. However, there will likely not be farmer protests in the US, as seen in Europe. US farmers are divided between very small and very large operators. USDA defines anyone earning over $1,000 annually in agricultural sales as a US farmer, but this segment won't be storming Washington, D.C., with John Deere tractors. Larger operators, meanwhile, are heavily subsidized to grow the GMO monoculture crops endorsed by the globalist climate change agenda and are not rioting against their federal gravy train anytime soon. America's midsize farms are practically extinct. This bodes poorly for our coming food supply battles.

European farm production is diverse and evolving, but lessons can be drawn from the EU for farmers and consumers in the United States and beyond. As recounted earlier in this chapter, Europeans suffered profound privations during two world wars that only hit American shores in the Pearl Harbor attack—never its farmlands or food supplies. Ireland's identity is entwined with its potato famine, a poignant lesson in the dangers of relying on foreign nations (in this case, Britain) to provide food when self-reliance and food security are lost. Additionally, *all* European cultures remain deeply rooted in food traditions, savory dining experiences, and a passionate appreciation for local farmers. These differences make the EU a harder sell for globalist industrial agriculture than America, where people have been eating ultra-processed foods for seventy-five years. Many Americans don't even know what healthy food tastes or looks like, so long have they been enamored with Burger King, Fritos, Ring Dings, and Jiffy Pop.

Europe has long "protected" its farms and farmers in ways that America has not. This has been criticized as an intrusion on free markets, but the current plight of European farmers shows what happens when the market is a tad too "free." For decades, farmland has been protected throughout most of Europe by strict zoning requirements that restrict much land to "agriculture only" and prohibit residential or commercial development. In the United States, "free" markets have steadily devoured fertile farmland that attracts far more money for commercial or residential development than could ever be earned growing lambs or barley. US farmland is appraised for real estate tax calculations at its "fair market value," which is its residential or commercial development value, and so taxes also unfairly burden farming operations.

Absent farm-favoring programs at the state level, the productive value of most agricultural ventures is absorbed by the government in property taxes. The result has been what Wendell Berry called "the Unsettling of America": the more people were ushered into cities, the more land was needed for suburbia. Farms disappeared or were consolidated rapidly. Suburban lots chopped up and tainted with lawn chemicals will never be reclaimed for food production at scale. At the same time, crops and animals (industrially housed in misery) raised ever farther away have become less trustworthy, more processed, and less nutritious. They have also become exponentially more susceptible to disruption, disease, and desertification.

Similar economic forces are now crushing farms in the United Kingdom, as reported by farming writer Chris Smaje:

> Here in the UK, yes, there are ag land use restrictions via the planning system, but that's another uneasy compromise with market forces. The new government is committed to reforming the planning system, so it'll be interesting to see what comes out of that, but the noises are for more housebuilding and 'cutting red tape' around infrastructure projects. So I'm guessing that'll nibble into farmland and further cut national food self-reliance. In southern England, farmland sells typically for something like £15k per acre, whereas bare land with outline permission for residential building would be more like £750k, so it's not hard to see where the pressure lies—although this applies more to edge-of-town situations than deep countryside. The farm workforce is aging, and farmers are encouraged to diversify out of food production to make ends meet. Though more young, educated people are getting interested in farming out of environmental concerns—land access is a problem for them.[49]

Michael NicAoibh in Ireland similarly reports that farmland there has become so expensive that very few new market entrants can afford to farm, except for the ultrarich or corporate investors. The problem began during the "Celtic Tiger" (An Tíogar Ceilteach) economic boom there in the 1990s and early 2000s, which opened the country to foreign direct investment. Irish farmers couldn't afford to buy land, and current prices are not much better.[50] Michael describes himself and his neighbors as "lifestyle farmers" who cannot compete with wealthy investors and warns that UK farmers are "being destroyed by solar panel farms"—these, too, compete with farmers for open lands.

Chris Smaje confirms Michael's account:

> Here in the UK, now that we've left the EU, we're headed more towards a US-style free market with less support for farmers and trade deals that shred the remaining elements of protectionism, but with a lot of narrative about wildlife-friendly farming and "public money for public goods." Upland livestock farmers here are under pressure to sell up to corporations for dodgy plantation forestry carbon-offsetting schemes, but are trying to articulate their own carbon-offsetting credentials within the farm sector. Generally, morale among farmers is pretty low about how all this will play out.[51]

The farm-destroying forces in Europe seek to undo the traditional "agricultural exceptionalism" that has shielded local agriculture for a century, claiming that farmers are welfare recipients who must answer for their destruction of the planet (ignoring their "carbon-offsetting credentials," also known as rotationally grazed livestock). *Vox* declared that this regulatory ideological noose must be tightened yet further, in what is seen by farmers and farm-supporting Europeans as an unfair marginalization and denigration of farmers:

> But to the extent that [CAP] remains primarily a subsidy program, there is no reason why conditions on meeting strict climate and environmental targets should not be massively strengthened, rather than weakened, and enforcement ramped up. And there is no reason not to use policy to steer production away from highly polluting industries like meat and dairy toward less harmful ones.[52]

European farmers are quick to explain that there are very important reasons for price supports—farmers already suffer from relatively low incomes and cannot bear the burdens being thrust upon them by bureaucrats. Unrestricted land sales will drive agricultural properties out of production. Adding irony to injury, *Vox* described CAP as "an ever-open spigot gushing taxpayer money." The proposed solution to nitrate pollution and climate change is to make renewables manufacturing that spews forever ecotoxins "an ever-open spigot gushing taxpayer money"—to multinational corporations instead of local farms.

The disconnect between such policy prescriptions and their impact on small farmers is astounding. *Vox* acknowledges that "Between 2005 and 2020, the EU lost over 5 million farms, virtually all of them small operations sold by retiring farmers or those simply unable to compete with their larger neighbors." The callousness of the author's conclusion that "there is no reason" why "strict" environmental regulations should not be "massively strengthened" is borne out more clearly by the economic plight of Europe's farmers: "the EU acknowledges that farmers earn about 40% less than non-farm workers."[53]

Punishing small farm operators for the sins of large-scale facilities (who receive the lion's share of CAP subsidies) and then subsidizing multinational corporations to litter European countrysides with solar panels is more than merely unethical and inequitable—it creates exactly the dependencies that Europe historically strove to prevent via land use restrictions protecting its farms (and food culture) from profit-making development pressures. Like suburban sprawl, solar panel sprawl cannot be quickly reverted to food production in a time of economic or climate crisis—let alone war or hyperinflation. People cannot eat solar panels or grass. Cows convert grass (a renewable resource) into food. Calling these mass arrays of silicon and plastic "solar farms" is an oxymoronic travesty.

The grand plans of the European Green Deal are hurting small family farms:

> The overwhelming majority (about 93 % in 2020) of the EU's farms are classed as being family farms, defined as being farms on which 50% or more of the agricultural labour force is provided by family members. Family farms were the dominant farm type in all Member States . . . .
>
> Almost two-thirds of the EU's farms were less than 5 hectares (ha) in size in 2020. . . . These small farms can play an important role in reducing the risk of rural poverty, providing additional income and food.[54]

This data presents several other inequities for European policymakers to consider: Ireland and other farming cultures attract tourists to their green vistas, which will soon be ideologically compromised and marred by the proliferation of subsidized solar panels. Agritourism will fall in tandem with farm production. Meanwhile, Finland and Sweden need to give up little—their forests are viewed as carbon-sequestering, though rotationally grazed pastures sequester far more carbon dioxide than forests while yielding food. It is a further inequity to pin compliance costs on farming communities who feed northern denizens who can't grow many food crops because of their long, cold winters—Sweden and Finland get most of their food from the Netherlands.[55]

Meanwhile, proponents of renewable energy stress the importance of boosting solar panel and EV subsidies to secure Europe's *economic* stability. A 2024 article in *Foreign Policy* titled "Countering Europe's Backlash to the Green Transition" argued:

> Despite political stigma, key components of the Green Deal, such as policies that drive decarbonization in industry and support resource efficiency through circular economy business models, are essential for European competitiveness and economic security and must be upheld.[56]

Which is it?—Climate change, food supplies, or economic growth for renewables? All three are in conflict: the economies of Germany, France, and the UK are wobbling as high energy costs that began to spike well before the Ukraine War (compounded by the destruction of the Nordic Stream natural gas pipelines and the shutting down for the first time since 1991 of gas pipelines through Ukraine in late 2024) destroy competitiveness. Volkswagen has laid off tens of thousands of workers as European manufacturing jobs and farming shift to environmentally dubious nations such as India and China. Germany's elimination of coal plants and nuclear power has only aggravated these market pressures.

This brief overview of agricultural and policy developments in Europe demonstrates that the United States is (1) implementing similar farm-stifling regulations against American farmers and processors without compensation for increased compliance costs and lost production; (2) pushing for complete dependence on synthetic fertilizers and GMOs; and (3) increasing land pressures on already struggling American farmers and food supplies. This combination is a death knell for the nation's family farms.

American farmland has been acquired by billionaire investors, foreign nations including China,[57] and hedge funds, driving up farmland costs beyond the ability of new farmers to afford, let alone make them cost-effective when farming margins are plummeting. At the same time, US hay and other field crops are being shipped to China and Saudi Arabia, taking the nation's precious water aquifers with them in the bargain. Arid Arizona allows Saudi Arabian interests to lease lands for hay crops that it ships abroad.[58]

Such pressures have also strained America's water-dependent breadbasket, California, where many dairy and beef farmers have closed up due to high feed prices driven up by foreign buyers from China.[59] This "free market" economic result mirrors its environmental harms—both water aquifers and domestic food supplies are being undermined. America's farmland has been shrinking for decades, but much like in Europe, the nation has diverted massive resources to "farm" solar panels in lieu of food.

The EU includes small farms that generate €4,000 (Euros) in annual sales in its demographic studies. The USDA includes farms producing merely $1,000/ per year in revenue in its assessments, obscuring the loss of midsize farms, which serve a crucial function in providing food locally and at scale. As in Europe, small and family farms provide a small share of total US food supplies, while large operations have expanded. The National Sustainable Agriculture Coalition reported the 2017 census showed that agricultural consolidation is driving medium-sized family farms out of business and concentrating wealth among large operators.[60] Vital midsize farms have shrunk into obscurity.

American farms have long been in decline, steadily compressed into larger facilities overseen by fewer people. The number of US farms declined by 141,733 between 2017 and 2022, accompanied by a reduction of 20.1 million acres of farmed acres.[61] Another 14,950 farms closed in 2024, withdrawing 2.1 million acres of farmland from production.[62]

These numbers reflect an ongoing trend of consolidation. In 2022, more than three-quarters of US farm production was generated by fewer than 105,384 large operations comprising 6 percent of US farms.[63] Lacking the vital food and farming traditions and land protectionism that have long preserved European farming, US farms have grown fewer and larger even though America remains the world's largest agricultural exporter. Since the largest farms receive the bulk of federal crop subsidies (as under the EU's CAP system), these farms are not inclined to oppose but to embrace the industrial methods they are paid to employ.

About half of all US farmland is expected to change hands in the next fifteen years due to the aging-out of the current generation of farmers—will these lands become fallow? Will they be transferred to a younger generation of human farmers or absorbed by industrial farming operations?

America's Pantagruelian farms and their shrinking cadre of aging operators are not likely to storm the US capital and spray liquid manure on statues of Abe Lincoln and George Washington or rally in complaint at the Washington Monument. They are very few in number; most are thousands of miles away from Washington, D.C., and many receive hefty federal subsidies against which they do not rebel. Divisions over organic versus conventional farming methods are used to further splinter organized action and thwart restorative policies.

Understanding European farm revolts and the globalist pressures being exerted on small-scale family farms in the EU reveals a pattern already well established in the US. American farmers require every American who eats food to stand with and for them, including those receiving large subsidies, who can be incentivized to transition to sustainable production models rather than corporate subservience.

The future of food security—and thus liberty itself—depends upon it.

CHAPTER 7

Personal Liberty or Globalist Food Control?

> Hunger is not a problem. It is an obscenity. How wonderful it is that nobody need wait a single moment before starting to improve the world.
>
> —Anne Frank

The fabric of global domination of humanity is woven before us. An examination of the statements of globalist organizations such as the WHO, WEF, World Bank, and United Nations reveals their plans to "save" humanity by controlling all global food production. The threads of globalist supremacy and the erosion of national and individual sovereignty are plain to see, knit together by emotional pleas to feed the world, protect human health, mitigate climate change, and institute "social justice" and equity.

This kaleidoscope of rationalizations to surrender individual liberties and national cultures into an all-absorbing international blob has been peddled by these organizations for decades, rising to a chorus of urgency and totalitarian oppression in recent years. The proposed cure to solve hunger and climate change while instituting equity and justice is a prescription of universal industrial GMO agriculture.[1]

"Climate change" ideology was crafted and promulgated decades ago by the UN and has consistently stained fields of scientific inquiry and political action. This uncheerful picture of climate doom invites fear, confusion, and the inaction it is intended to seed. At the same time, the supranational globalist cabal appropriates power and wealth to consolidate its exploitation of human health and human wealth. A brief review of past efforts to impose order (tyranny) by controlling food supplies is instructive of the lurking catastrophes attendant not just on the Netherlands or Ireland, whose histories bear bitter witness to past famine and oppression, but to any people in the world who seek to retain and nurture their liberties. Any meaningful resistance to global corporate food control requires sufficient localized food supplies.

Control the Food, Control the People

Food has been used as a weapon of war, coercion, genocide, or control for at least as long as there has been recorded history. Sieges in Rome and ancient Britain were strategized to inflict famine: the siege of Jerusalem in 70 AD was a horrible bloodbath that included imposed famine, leading to riots and cannibalism within city walls. The primacy of food never left humankind, from hunter-gatherers who painted cows on their cave walls, to the first agrarians who cultivated grains and made urban centers possible.

Recounting the plethora of such food war horror stories is the foodstuff of another book. Yet, several catastrophic twentieth-century examples are worth noting because they were carefully and deliberately orchestrated by left-wing totalitarian regimes, including those of Joseph Stalin and Mao Zedong. Pol Pot's Khmer Rouge sought to create an "agrarian socialist republic," killing or starving an estimated two million people.

Stalin's and Mao's political ideologies and brutal totalitarianism sprang directly from Marxist ideas of statist domination justified on behalf of improved living conditions for the downtrodden masses, who were then the very people ruthlessly destroyed using famine as an instrument of ideological coercion. Tens of millions of Chinese, Russian, and Ukrainian citizens were systematically starved to death. In Stalin's "dekulakization"[2] program directed at small farm peasants ("kulaks"), there is no question this was deliberate.

The important lesson here is that the greatest human-created famines of history have resulted either from deliberate genocidal eradication using food or reckless top-down plans that went awry. The globalist cabal of international organizations that are overseen not by nation-states but a Star Chamber[3] of corporate actors is a *pretender* of human liberation. Already, farmers revolting against its stifling statist domination (the EU takes its food policies directly from the UN) are being labeled "far-right extremists," a page from the books of Mao and Stalin.

Above the EU farmer fracas, funding and controlling the unfolding melee are the usual suspects of ultrarich elites playing God to save humanity. The sinister collection of multinational corporations that have profited by sickening the world seeks to employ their greedily gained largesse to "rescue" humanity (and all life) in a grand, globalist gesture of feigned goodwill.

Food security requires *local* food, locally controlled and grown, not distant food, factory-farmed, processed, and distributed. An impersonal, techno-dependent, far-reaching food supply network is subject to numerous vulnerabilities that could unintentionally—let alone intentionally—inflict on America suffering and famine far exceeding what Hitler, Stalin, or Mao could have imagined.

The solutions to local problems, including food supplies and pollution generation, are *local* in scale. The risks associated with surrendering local control of food production and distribution to any large institution, let alone an inefficient, sprawling, unelected international body with a proven record of failure and corruption, should be obvious.

The infamous Kissinger Report of 1974, prepared by Henry Kissinger[4] (Rockefeller lackey and darling of the UN), is officially titled "National Security Study Memorandum NSSM 200: Implications of Worldwide Population Growth for U.S. Security and Overseas Interests." Kissinger's "National Security Study" secretly called for an international collaboration led by the United States and the United Nations to combat human overpopulation by various means, notably via widespread implementation of birth control or "fertility reduction" technologies and incentives. Given the current international treaties that are used to consolidate agricultural production under industrial methods, the importance of this voluminous document, dated December 10, 1974, but not declassified until 1989, cannot be overstated. The "National Security Study Memorandum 200" that authorized the Report demonstrating the direct involvement of the CIA, USDA, and USAID was not declassified for public consumption until February 8, 2007.[5]

There are sociopolitical aspects of the Kissinger Report that raise additional reasons to distrust both the motives behind this plan and the viability of its proposed solutions. The report connects the globalist industrialist dots by its terms over a long period, revealing a vast and ever-broadening network of international public and private entities. The potential for even a well-intentioned globalist plan to fail miserably in its self-appointed mission to rescue and feed humanity cannot be overstated.

Fear has a long history of manipulative deployment to control people, often in conjunction with food—consider climate change alarmism used to push people toward bug or synthetic burger diets, or to eliminate cows. Every human in the world should be fed, but empty declarations that "food is a human right" do not put a single crumb in a hungry mouth—reliable, healthy soils and food supplies will always remain the sole source of food security.

The Kissinger Report presented an industrial blueprint to feed the world using wasteful, soil-destroying synthetic fertilizers and technological "advances" that were clearly shown to inflict ecological and human health harms. Despite evolving revelations about industrial agriculture's deleterious effects on soil, water, and human microbiomes, the current international proposals to "save the planet" from climate change and famine remain firmly rooted in the proposals of Kissinger's 1974 manifesto. They are now advocated by the WEF, a bevy of NGOs, and the largest multinational corporations of the world.

Kissinger's report exploited ideals of future human happiness and "global peace" to veil efforts to manipulate and control human population growth. The proposed UN-WHO-US (and related agencies) network outlined in Kissinger's nefarious population control report has grown larger and has expanded its mission far beyond mere food control. The report called for surreptitiously persuading poor nations to implement "fertility reduction measures" as a condition for relief funds, linked famine in other countries to a US national security interest of securing natural resources[6] present in those nations for US industry (and protection of US agricultural and other exports), and contemplated human sterilization and mandatory control of food supplies both abroad and domestically. Kissinger arrogantly assessed the world's nations individually in his report, positing which ones were overbreeding and should be better controlled for their own benefit, what criteria should be employed (behind closed doors) to decide who should be awarded for compliance, and why some "experts" believed that voluntary compliance would be inadequate and more draconian mandatory methods would be required.

The interrelation of the agencies involved in Henry Kissinger's report, the evolution since that time of technologies including AI, surveillance, GMOs, and mRNA vaccines, and the exponential expansion of bureaucratic power and mission creep, are additional cautions meriting concern. The globalist toolbox has grown terrifyingly powerful.

The central premise of the Kissinger Report (and climate change today) is that human overpopulation threatens the world, and therefore governments and private entities must unite supranationally to rescue humanity from this growing scourge.[7] The Report includes recommendations for a techno-mystical toolbox of synthetic fertilizers, fossil fuels, and industrial agriculture. Even before GMOs had been developed, Henry Kissinger called for their creation. There is no mention of regenerative agriculture, organic food, or improving soil health. Instead, Henry employed the pollution, water loss, and soil erosion *caused* by industrial agriculture as justification for eliminating more humans and pitched the marvels of modern agriculture as a grand solution to famines and wars, thereby creating "world peace."

Kissinger was not above using complete speculation about unforecastable climate change to invoke climate change forecasts (and climate-caused famine fears) to justify yet more "equitable" salvation of the nations he sought to colonize industrially:

> Climatic changes are poorly understood, but a persistent atmospheric cooling trend since 1940 has been established. One respectable body of scientific opinion believes that this portends a period of much wider annual frosts, and possibly a long-term lowering of rainfall in the monsoon areas of Asia and Africa. Nitrogen fertilizer will be in world short supply into the late 1970s, at least; because of higher energy prices, it may also be more costly in real terms than in the 1960s.[8]

The lie of Kissinger's climate-rooted call to control food and human reproduction suffers from precisely the same defect as the Green Deal in Europe and the Green New Deal in America—industrial agriculture will inevitably *cause* global desertification and famine, whether the climate is warming or cooling. About that, the soil, water, and agricultural science is abundantly clear.

The 1974 prescription exploiting climate change fears is the same agricultural prescription that economically destroyed America's family farms and is slowly destroying the nation's water and soils:

> We do not know whether technological developments will make it possible to feed over 8 much less 12 billion people in the 21st century. We cannot be entirely certain that climatic changes in the coming decade will not create great difficulties in feeding a growing population, especially people in the LDCs who live under increasingly marginal and more vulnerable conditions. There exists at least the possibility that present developments point toward Malthusian conditions for many regions of the world.[9]

Kissinger did not really care at all about the poor people of the least developed nations and only about his own power and that of the elite industrialists he so eagerly served. Kissinger was no farmer of the soil, just a rapist of the Earth, serving the same global industrialists the UN, WEF, WHO and other fake rescuers serve today, invoking the same Orwellian fear-lie: "There is a major risk of severe damage to world economic, political, and ecological systems and, as these systems begin to fail, to our humanitarian values."[10] Henry Kissinger invoked threats of a "failure of humanitarian values" as his rubric for enslaving third-world nations so that their cheap natural resources would remain available to US interests.

The Kissinger Report was adolescent compared to the sophistication of today's globalist fear-spinners. However, the same old caveat applies—be cautious about who is influencing your thoughts. Alex de Waal, one of the world's foremost experts on humanitarian crises, warns that globalists themselves could cause famine:

> Famine is a very specific political product of the way in which societies are managed. The single overwhelming element in causation—in three-quarters of the famines and three-quarters of the famine deaths—is political agency. Yet we still tend to be gripped by this idea that famine is a natural calamity.[11]

The framework to expand Kissinger's Machiavellian scheme to control the world on behalf of corporate profiteers and billionaire elites (including the use of NGOs and other "private actors")[12] was seeded by Kissinger's 1974 worldwide road map for totalitarianism.[13] Since that time, globalist organizations and NGOs have proliferated in ways that would make Kissinger beam with elitist joy. The push toward industrial food production in Iraq, Mexico, the EU, and Ukraine has all but fulfilled his planned globalist vision.

As the previous chapter revealed, France has already proposed meat limitations for its population as part of a strange technocratic bovine calculus that determines how many cows the nation needs, and the mayor of Lyon banned meat with the wave of his bureaucratic wand. Humans can freely raise cattle on grass, with zero (not net-zero, simply *zero*) industrial chemical adjuncts. To manage humans like cattle, globalists must seize those cattle—to "save" the world from cow farts and switch humans to compulsory diets of impossible-to-make synthetic meats, bug burgers, or chemical-dependent, ultra-processed "plant-based" foods that destroy the soil and human health. People will fall in line at the (social credit) techno-trough and eat what they are told—like cattle.

Food, Food, Food

John Kenneth Galbraith observed, "There are two kinds of forecasters: those who don't know, and those who don't know they don't know." Henry Kissinger was likely a third kind—one who knew he didn't know but didn't care at all. He also represented a pernicious kind of especially dangerous forecaster—a technocrat who knows nothing about agriculture, telling all the world's farmers how to farm. Raising food at the local ("peasant") level is always the bulwark against totalitarianism, climate change, war, economic or currency collapse, and toxic agricultural production and food processing.

The Kissinger Report foreshadowed the exponentially larger network of entrenched globalist forces arrayed against humanity by the United Nations, the WHO, the WEF, the World Bank, the World Trade Organization, USAID, and a dizzying array of companion NGOs. It addressed food and agriculture almost as much as it called for fertility reduction, increased birth control, and the sterilization of humanity.

Today, science is clearer than ever that industrial agriculture is destroying the ecosystem, yet more clouded than ever by the same globalist elites who claim they are all-knowing and technologically equipped. The big plan to control humanity has expanded to include plant life, animal rights, biodiversity, and gender, race, and queer "theories." Still, its prescription for solving all of these problems remains unchanged: "control the food (with Big Ag only) to control the people (for the greater global good)."

The Report highlighted the problems of industrial agriculture, despite calling to implement industrial methods on a grand, leveraged scale that would crush peasant and organic farming:

> The estimates of production capacity do not rely on major new technical breakthroughs in food production methods, but they do require the availability and application of greatly increased quantities of fertilizers, pesticides, irrigation water, and other inputs to modernized agriculture, together with continued technological advances at past rates and the institutional and administrative reforms (including vastly expanded research and extension services) essential to the successful application of these inputs. . . . [14]

Kissinger calls for even more industrial research and to increase yields and farmed land areas in the developing nations he claims are clearing too much land: "A strengthened research effort, including long term, to develop new seed and * farming technologies, primarily to increase yields but also to permit more extensive cultivation techniques, particularly in LDCs." Stunningly, the asterisked footnote claims the USDA at that time "favours U.S. commercial interests holding any national stocks in an international network of stockpiles."

This is an intriguing inclusion. As it happens, just such an international "network of stockpiles" was created through the International Treaty on Plant Genetic Resources for Food and Agriculture in 2001, with 148 countries as signatories. The Svalbard Global Seed Vault functions much like a safe deposit box, where owners can reclaim or share seeds according to the Treaty. Unknown to most Westerners, Iraq boasted one of the world's most comprehensive seed banks, in a place called Abu Ghraib—destroyed by US bombing in 2003 in the US-led Iraq War (enthusiastically supported by Henry Kissinger, of course). Another seed bank in Aleppo, Syria, has barely escaped destruction in that war-torn nation.

Kissinger's report outlined a strategy of globalist domination.[15] As chronicled throughout this book, farming is not an easy task, and unpoliced "free" markets are not free—industrial agriculture is very heavily subsidized, while small farms are not. This is true in America (the subject of my previous book, *Small Farm Republic*) and increasingly throughout Europe (including Ukraine). Industrial chemical manufacturers and seed sellers have steadily increased their wealth and control at the expense of local agricultural production worldwide.

Food Liberty 101

> People who are hungry and out of a job are the stuff of which dictatorships are made.
>
> —Frankin D. Roosevelt[16]

Despite illusions of plenty, humanity (especially in highly industrialized America) is more vulnerable to widespread starvation than at any time in world history. This unprecedented threat is concealed behind a short-term transition to technological dependence and destructive industrial agriculture that has provided inexpensive, seemingly abundant food supplies. The farms and farmers that once fed America are largely extinct, replaced by and consolidated into massive industrial operations that depend on tractors, specialized equipment, inexpensive fossil fuels, and synthetic fertilizers.

One need not believe that globalists are conspiring to diminish human numbers or methodically inflict genocide to comprehend that there are risks in even a well-meaning undertaking of such global proportions. As Niccolo Machiavelli counseled, "Always assume incompetence before looking for conspiracy." Since the 1974 Kissinger Report, soils have been depleted, waters polluted, and glyphosate and GMO technologies have been implemented globally. Kissinger proposed globalizing his report's US national security population control plan, targeting even domestic US citizens for inclusion.

Throughout history, maintaining local food supplies—not third-world mineral supplies—has been a cornerstone of national security. During the War of 1812, Vermont enacted a law (the "Safe Syrup Act," still in effect) that required every household to keep on hand a supply of maple syrup to ensure the five thousand troops stationed there were always provided with "the elixir that turned the tide in the Revolutionary War." British troops were far from home: Americans defended theirs.

Vermont now imports most of its food, where a century ago it fed cities and suburbs around New England. The contraction of Vermont dairy farms has been accompanied by an expansion of food factories and mega-farms in out-of-state or even out-of-country facilities. Vermonters have largely relinquished their truest elixir—healthy local food supplies.

As a young child staying with my grandparents in Brookfield, Vermont, my grandmother Cesarine carefully taught me how to make maple syrup. We walked down to a maple tree at the bottom of the gravel driveway, bored a tap hole with a hand auger drill, inserted a sap spout, and hung a mason jar to await the sweet sap. It overflowed with sap more than once a day, so Grammie upgraded the jar to a plastic bucket. That tree still stands but is no longer tapped.

It requires approximately forty gallons of sap to produce one gallon of maple syrup. Grammie boiled our collected sap in a battered pot on her ancient wood-fired cookstove. Years later, I repeated the same lesson with my children—I used steel sap buckets, and we left the sap on the woodstove similarly. Two trees provided enough syrup for our family of five for more than a year.

Vermont still produces maple syrup, but it is predicted that Americans in other states may soon have to give it up in favor of artificial substitutes that will never come close to matching the potent maple flavor of the tree. (I still love to drink the faintly sweet sap right from the bucket when gathering, which our family has done here for generations.)

An article explaining the anticipated inflationary prices for future maple syrup production echoes many of the cautions about inflation for other food sources documented herein:

> Small-scale producers are struggling to keep up, while larger operations are using advanced technology to maintain production. However, this isn't enough to meet growing demand. The result? Higher prices for smaller bottles of syrup, turning this breakfast favorite into an occasional treat. Additionally, the *rising cost of land and labor is making it harder for new producers to enter the market.* The impact on local economies in maple syrup-producing regions is significant, as many rely on this industry for income. . . .[17] [emphasis added].

America's food production faces threats similar to those faced by Vermont's maple syrup industry. Food insecurity is already on the rise in the United States. Post-COVID, data reveal that an increasing number of Americans are unable to afford a comprehensive dietary regimen. An October 2023 Census Bureau Household Pulse Survey[18] concluded that 12.5 percent of the adult US population, or 28 million adults nationwide, were "living in homes where there was either sometimes or often not enough to eat in the last week." The USDA considers a household to be food secure "if it can eat an adequately nutritious diet without resorting to using emergency food supplies, scavenging, stealing, or other measures."

The 1996 World Food Summit defined food security as "when all people, at all times, have physical and economic access to sufficient safe and nutritious food that meets their dietary needs and food preferences for an active and healthy life." This is a remarkably high standard, rarely achieved in any society. To achieve this goal requires at least three factors: "Physical availability of food, economic and physical access to food, [and] food utilization. . . ."[19]

All three pillars of US food security have become entirely dependent on: affordable energy sources; GMO monocrops susceptible to disease; sophisticated planting, harvesting, processing, and distribution technologies; wage and social program stability; and fiscal/monetary integrity. Steady increases in foreign food sources, the vanishing of rural farmland converted to suburban or other development, or left fallow, nutrient-depleted and eroded soils, dwindling aquifers and rivers, and long-distance transport within US borders have all exacerbated these vulnerabilities.

Considering the multiple other glaring Achilles' heels of Americans' modern food supplies, as discussed in Chapter 3, a "national security" priority that supports rather than shuts down local farms seems more than sensible; however, there is currently no such priority. Zoning laws that prohibit chickens or milk-cows impinge on the most fundamental right of all—the right to grow one's own food. Relinquishing that right is a dereliction of duty.

The unforeseen disaster looming above Americans' larders will be readily recognized when it is widespread. The next chapter discusses the globalist plan to implement *total control* over the world and its human inhabitants, encompassing food, currencies, land, waterways, oceans, and essentially every molecule of creation.

One need not believe that the globalist corporate cabal is conspiring to control all food market share to perceive the many benefits of a local food supply, or the risks associated with the interruption of a long-distance, fossil-fuel-dependent technological supply chain. However, there is indeed a plan afoot, built upon the shockingly insensitive machinations of Henry Kissinger's grand 1974 scheme. As will be discussed in Chapter 8, the noose being twisted around EU family farms' necks is rooted in globalist corporate hegemony that denigrates farmers resisting its domination as "far-right populist extremists," "climate change deniers," or "welfare recipients."

It is terrifying that so many people in the world have been conditioned to believe that cows and agriculture are their enemy, and that their rescue from a warming climate should be entrusted to the world's largest corporations and a globalist power structure committed to GMO crops and chemical dependency for food. Kissinger found an elitist audience willing to believe his prescriptions for globalist control were world-saving. The eugenicists whose pseudoscientific racism flourished in Germany believed that sterilizing and aborting humans was a good cause.

The US Supreme Court was tainted with similar hubris. In 1927, Oliver Wendell Holmes Jr. penned what may be the most infamous decision on the US law books, *Buck v. Bell*, in which he justified forced sterilizations of fellow citizens:

> We have seen more than once that the public welfare may call upon the best citizens for their lives. It would be strange if it could not call upon those who already sap the strength of the State for these lesser sacrifices, often not felt to be such by those concerned, in order to prevent our being swamped with incompetence. It is better for all the world if, instead of waiting to execute degenerate offspring for crime or to let them starve for their imbecility, society can prevent those who are manifestly unfit from continuing their kind. The principle that sustains compulsory vaccination is broad enough to cover cutting the Fallopian tubes. *Jacobson v. Massachusetts,* 197 U. S. 11. Three generations of imbeciles are enough.

> . . . Of course, so far as the operations enable those who otherwise must be kept confined to be returned to the world, and thus open the asylum to others, the equality aimed at will be more nearly reached.[20]

Reasonable minds will likely agree that it was Holmes, and later Kissinger, who belonged in asylums. The current "world leaders" and billionaires who machinate plans to dominate all food production in the name of saving the human race are no different. They are deranged elitists who play God, as Holmes did.

CHAPTER 8

Reclaiming Food Sovereignty for All

> Under capitalism, man exploits man. Under communism, it's just the opposite.
>
> —John Kenneth Galbraith

America enjoys the most diverse and affordable food choices that any society has ever had (though not all are healthy). The idea that the United States might one day, perhaps soon, suffer a sudden interruption of its food supply system, or battle hyperinflation, seems an unfounded paranoia. Yet as history shows, such shocks are rarely foreseen.

Largely lost on the modern American conscience is that something similar has happened here before, during the Great Depression. Revisiting that chapter of US history offers imperative lessons for our present times.

The trauma of the Great Depression was severe, though its causes are often disputed. What is not in controversy is that the trouble began with a stock market collapse, bank failures, and a precipitous drop in national economic productivity. The famous stock market crash of October 1929 marked the beginning of a long descent in stock prices that revealed highly leveraged stock portfolios fueled by lax "margin" rules that permitted investors to essentially buy stocks on credit at ratios as high as ten times their actual holdings. Many investors lost their entire portfolios virtually overnight, leading some to commit suicide in despair. The stress of losing their job in a one-income family caused suicide rates for men in the 1930s to skyrocket, leaving their wives and children destitute.[1]

Many employees were compelled to take pay cuts of 25 percent or more. Unemployment rates increased. Many schools closed, especially in hard-hit rural areas. It is estimated that half of American children struggled against starvation, mostly without health care. Tens of thousands of adolescents became homeless hoboes.[2]

Small banks, too, were caught in the financial melee, prompting bank runs by millions of Americans who learned their savings had evaporated due to bank stock market speculation. Both margin rules and banking activities have since been improved—the Federal Deposit Insurance Corporation, or FDIC, was created in response and insures individual investors' deposits up to $100,000. During the Great Depression, no such protections existed, and it was the "little guys" who were typically burned.

My grandmother, Cesarine Stoddard, then a nineteen-year-old Cesarine Alexander, had scrimped and saved for her future, but trusted the banks that went bankrupt—she never got a dime back. Many Vermont families lost all their savings and were unable to pay their mortgages, taxes, or bills at the local general store. When the Dust Bowl of the 1930s followed the market implosion, Southwestern farms suffered far worse than those in Green Mountain, which still had access to water, healthy crops, and lush green grass.

The soils of the semiarid grasslands of the American Southwest had been built by the hooves and manure of millions of bison, slaughtered recklessly for sport and genocide.[3] The rapid western expansion of settlers growing wheat and other crops by tilling up these healthy soils eliminated the grasses that held the soil in place during storms and prevented erosion. Overgrazing for livestock ranching similarly degraded essential soils until an environmental crisis lurked.[4] Then came the winds.

Massive storms ravaged the now-vulnerable prairie lands, lifting weakened topsoil into the air in a legendary natural disaster. Houses, vehicles, and barns were buried under the enormous storms, which carried millions of tons of topsoil as dust across the nation and deposited it in East Coast cities. John Steinbeck's classic novel *The Grapes of Wrath* chronicled the resulting devastation to farmers uprooted from their homes, much as the grasses had been uprooted from the prairies. Photographers like Dorothea Lange captured iconic images in black and white to convey, through pictures, the suffering of farmers and their families. A massive migration ensued, leaving "Okies" from Oklahoma treated horribly in other states where locals felt their jobs and livelihoods were threatened by the exodus from the dust storms that joined the stock market crash in economic destruction.

"Tink" Camp

Vermonters were not immune. I interviewed Lawrence "Tink" Camp to share his experiences living through a struggling but still surviving Vermont farming economy. He milked fifty Holstein cows for fifty years, enabling him to put his five children through college. He has twelve grandchildren and thirteen grandchildren, but laments that not a single one is farming. This is the story of the death of American family farms and local agricultural economies, told through the eyes of a man born on January 24, 1932, who graduated from high school in 1950. A boy at the time, Tink describes how egg and pork prices plummeted in the 1930s, and how urban people struggled to survive more than country folk: "We had people walkin' the road and come up askin', 'Could I get you to give me a slice of bread, you know, and maybe a drink a water.' And we were poorer 'an hell, but we did it. But the problem with that, they keep comin'."

Tink relates that Vermont agriculture has changed radically over his lifetime:

> I have lived through four major changes in farming. My grandfather had sheep. They disappeared when the imitation fiber come about. Sheep left. Then it was, course everybody had some pigs for themselves and some folks raised pigs to sell, and then it turned from that to poultry and now the poultry's gone except for those who have a dozen hens for their own use and their neighbors. And now we got down to dairy cows that all just moved into a big operation, a thousand milkers and up in a lot of cases. . . . So, it's entirely changed but I've seen those four major things happen in my lifetime.

For a ninety-three-year-old, Mr. Camp also offered insightful perspectives about the healthiness of our current food supply:

> [Health and Human Services Secretary] Kennedy is on track. Pesticides, the sprays that we've got here that have got condemned here, sent down to South America and they use it. So we don't get away from that so I'm gettin' it whether I want it or not 'cause I have to be on fruits, vegetables, and meat twice a day [for my diabetes]. Kennedy's trying to cut some of that stuff out, and he's right about all these synthetic materials that we're gettin' in our food line, he's workin' on that.
>
> Poisons and imitation food is the worst thing for us. No question about it. He's tryin' to do somethin', but it's gonna take a long time 'cause these big corporations that are makin' this imitation crap as well as the pesticides, you know, they don't go away easy. It's a long haul to get it done.

Tink's decades' long perspective also applied to my question, "How do we help young people who want to farm succeed?":

> Make farming profitable for young people. That's the key. It has to be profitable and we can't do it. And now I don't see how a young fella can start, when dads can't turn the places over to them. That's gone.
>
> Here's the problem with all this. It starts when the government was lettin' out so much money to the farmers to get bigger. They knew what they were doin'. They priced the milk. And so they've got 'em, once they've got 'em in debt, they got 'em.
>
> And it's just about like it is in a communist country in a sense. I had a [tenant] in my yellow house over there before it burned down. He come from Russia. He went to law school down here [at Vermont Law School in South Royalton] and he was tellin' me 'bout the farmers over there. The government loaned, and more and more of it gets sucked up by the government. And that's what's happenin' here.

Tink was extremely aware of current farming markets when I met with him in his East Randolph, Vermont farmhouse on September 21, 2025. He knew the current price of milk, the current price of both dairy and beef cows, prices for newborn calves, the proportion of Holsteins used in production, and other agricultural statistics. Farmers are far more intelligent and informed than societal stereotypes envision them. It is common for retired farmers to stay abreast of the farming markets and developments until the day they die.

Despite contracting polio as a child that left one leg partially paralyzed and a severely curved spine, Tink had just returned from a tractor pull. His living room is adorned with hundreds of trophies accumulated over decades of tractor-pulling competitions. He told me he only did five tractor pulls in 2025, "but I used to do twenty-five every year."

I've been blessed to have known many old farmers like Tink Camp. They never complain, they always work, and they waste nothing. Tink knew many of my family members, including my grandparents and my grandmother Cesarine Stoddard. Toward the end of my meeting with him, I related how I once asked Grammie Cesarine what would happen if the Great Depression reoccurred today. Tank let out a hearty but eerie chuckle:

> Ha-ha-ha-a-a-a. Wouldn't it be somethin' for our country for them city people to try to get a livin' for themselves, don't know anything

> about it. But you see, we here, we have a garden long as we can, and we had our own meat and stuff.
>
> That's really what happened before. The Great Depression of '29, people commenced to come out of the cities to the country 'cause they had no work and it was hard 'cause they couldn't borrow money much and even though things [cost] a lot less than they are now.
>
> I believe we're building for a depression again. I hope it don't happen but you see stuff keeps goin' up, taxes, and insurances, health insurance—ah, they're beatin' me to death, but I gotta have it. . . . It's pretty near impossible, and the taxes on this old dump! This is the farmhouse I was born in, bedroom in there [points to neighboring room].[5]

Roland Greene

Roland Greene, born in 1927, tells the story of his father securing a town job at twenty-five cents an hour, a relatively good income at the time that shielded him and his seven siblings from the extreme suffering of many in the community. Roland and his family milked cows by hand at the time on their modest dairy farm:

> Well, I think we had eight [cows] on the first farm. My dad did the milkin' by hand until we were nine years old, really, and then we moved to the village. He went to work on the road for the town, I think we were probably maybe a dozen years that we didn't farm and then he rented another farm and we went on the farm and we had fourteen cows there and my brother and my dad and I each had our cows that we milked, all by hand then even. We had a big trough that run in front of 'em and we had a hand pump on the end. We kept it filled with water for 'em and they stayed in the barn but there was an upstairs stable. It was the best stable they ever made, open the trap and throw everything down, but you know I always loved the horses and that's what we did our work with. And I would work myself to death throwin' manure so I could drive those horses. But when my dad wasn't around I still threw manure. We had to load it by hand and spread it by hand.
>
> Oh it was a good life, I loved farmin'. . . . Back then people got a dollar a day, you were lucky if you could get a job for a dollar a day. You couldn't sell a day-old calf, they were worthless, and so my dad

> would take 'em from [the farmer] in the winter and hang 'em in the shed and freeze 'em up, and then he would shave that meat off for the hens. But you know, they would lay, you'd get an egg every day. They had to raise what they had, you know, that you could in a garden. One thing we had that you don't find much now, most anywhere you went along the roadside you could find berries and raspberries, blackberries, blueberries. When we finally moved to the village and my dad went to work for the town of Wolcott, when he would draw gravel on the hill, all one side of it was filled with blueberries. We'd ride up there with him in the mornin', my brother and I when we didn't have to go to school, and pick berries all day. And even when I was a small kid, we had currant bushes along the roadside, but you know women could pick those berries and kids would too. When I stayed with my grandmother, if I stayed there I had to go berryin'. She knew where they all were. In the evenin', she knew where the berries were and we had to go berryin' in the evenin'.
>
> I was nine years old when I first went into the hayfields to work. My dad had an old four-tine pitchfork and he cut the handle off to fit me so I could tumble hay. Everybody worked. If you were big enough to do somethin', you worked. I always loved the horses. I never cared a thing about an automobile, but I just couldn't wait til he let me drive the horses.[6]

My grandparents and other elderly people at whose knees I grew up hearing such tales all relate that the privations were profound, and that "today's generation" lacks gratitude for what it enjoys. Henry Labrecque, a dear personal friend who was my neighbor in Barton, Vermont, taught me how to make square bales and winch cedar trees with my tractor in deep winter. Henry often told stories about rumrunners from Canada storing moonshine in caves along Vermont's Lake Willoughby, and firsthand tales of truckloads of booze concealed in local dairy barns.

Henry also related his family's experiences as dairy farmers in Barton: picking through potatoes in the cellar to sort out the rotten ones when he was a young boy during the Great Depression, and scrounging for work at a pittance through the 1940s. Barton sits in Vermont's famed "Northeast Kingdom," close to the Canadian border and its harsh Arctic blasts. Temperatures can easily plummet to forty below zero there, and most of the roads remain unpaved gravel even today. During the Great Depression, Henry explained, barefoot families walked along these dirt roads, wandering through Vermont in search of food. He said it was very depressing to watch, and that when his family heard some of these travelers raiding the family vegetable garden, they didn't stop them because they knew how desperate they were.

Stories like this have faded into distant fog for most Americans alive today, but such scenes can easily recur—and much worse. Americans across the country have flocked into cities since 1929, leaving once-fertile farmland to be "developed" into suburban enclaves, "rewilded" to sequester greenhouse gases, or consolidated into vast industrial operations that employ synthetic fertilizers and pesticides, destroying soils and accelerating erosion. These practices are not "sustainable," either economically or environmentally.

Vermont's 27,000 dairy farms in 1929 were scattered across the landscape like my many relatives, and families such as the Labrecques, Camps, and Greenes. These farms were self-reliant, mostly off-grid, and generally biologically diverse—sheep, chickens, and pigs were communally available. But no more. Vermont has fewer than six hundred operating dairies remaining, and that farm animal diversity has been abandoned.

America fed 122 million people in 1929; now it feeds 330 million, with very few farmers remaining and agricultural production highly concentrated in industrial operations dependent on cheap energy, factory processing, and long-distance distribution systems. The national debt when the Great Depression and Dust Bowl struck in 1929 was a modest $16 billion, roughly 16 percent of gross domestic product (GDP).[7]

The United States enters 2026 with a daunting $38 trillion national debt, a dangerous 121 percent of GDP.[8] This number was increasing by approximately $1 trillion every 100 days in 2025.[9] The nation's modern goliath of entitlement obligations did not burden the economy and government in 1929. One 2025 Penn Wharton study estimates the actual calculus of federal debt obligations (when considering total federal obligations) to approximate $162.7 trillion.[10]

This number conceals an additional $1 trillion in state debts,[11] uncommon or nonexistent in 1929. Consumer debt hovers at an additional $18.4 trillion.[12] Credit cards weren't much in use in 1929, and that generation would not have embraced 30 percent interest rates very warmly.

If America's stock market and currency crashed in 2026, the country would witness a far different event than in 1929. America now imports far more food, and necessary DEF, microchip, and other gadgetry upon which its miracle-appearing food system relies. Such massive debt burdens mean the federal government would lack the capacity to maintain payments on debt service and entitlement payments if the economy began to decline, let alone borrow for a twenty-first-century New Deal. Americans already strapped with high-interest debt would similarly lack any more room to borrow. Default rates would quickly increase; bankruptcies of small businesses and international lenders would soon join those of individuals, clogging up the nation's bankruptcy courts.

In such a crisis, urban Americans in 2026 would quickly learn where their food comes from (and where their garbage goes) when New York City, Chicago, and Los Angeles watched their grocery shelves empty and their streets pile up with rat-infested heaps of rubbish. Flocking desperately to the countryside in far greater numbers and frantic panic than during the COVID-19 pandemic, they would find the farms long gone. Vermont hosts many tourist stops, art galleries, and pottery shops in today's rural hillsides, but not much more than trees to eat. Civil order and police protection would evaporate overnight, threatening physical as well as food security. (During Hurricane Katrina, hundreds of law enforcement personnel simply abandoned their posts—imagine what a currency collapse or national emergency would entail.[13])

If this type of unthinkable calamity befell modern America, food, water, and electricity would quickly disappear in urban centers. Highways would be indefinitely blocked as panicked civilians walked on foot seeking precious necessities once taken for granted. The great "unsettling of America" described by Wendell Berry would rapidly reverse. But there is no place for this populace to settle, and they lack the oxen and axes that my great-great-great-great-grandfather Solomon Stoddard likely owned when he ventured from New London, Connecticut into the Vermont wilderness in 1798.

No government agencies to call. No neighbors to shelter with. The LA wildfires are a minor inconvenience compared to the widespread death and destruction such an event would inflict.

All of this could descend in an instant from a nuclear war, an electromagnetic pulse, or an asteroid, earthquake, or volcano in the American homeland. Such threats are obvious to Vermont homesteaders who endured the Great Depression of 1929; they are largely invisible to the modern dependency on trucks and plastic-packaged, ultra-processed foods that have replaced the balanced agrarian way of life that once dominated the nation's landscapes.

This is the generation of cellphone addicts and computer junkies, munching Skittles, Oreos, and Pop-Tarts in ill-health. Some 7 percent of Americans think chocolate milk comes from brown cows,[14] and only 44 percent know how to boil an egg.[15] How will they find food, if they don't even know where it comes from or how to prepare it? The mega-farms and CAFOs that churn out tens of millions of eggs[16] and chickens[17] daily will quickly collapse without power and fuel, as will the swine farms in which the pigs[18] will die in mere hours when the fans that evacuate toxic fumes from their factories fall idle. There are not enough fish in the nation's chemically tainted rivers, or deer in the suburbs, to feed such a massive population for very long. The roadside berries have vanished in Vermont, as has the knowledge where to find them in the forested hills.[19]

Vermont's roads will again see sunken-eyed, barefooted travelers on its dirt roads, but these will be the fortunate few who managed to escape the concrete metropolises, and they will pass rotting barns and collapsing stone foundations where the wanderers of Henry Labrecque's time found farm after farm after farm. This is a people that has mostly abandoned backyard gardening for swimming pools and manicured, chemical-soaked lawns. Cows, sheep, and goats eat grass, converting it to human food—the attack on them as climate villains will be seen as the great folly it is when Americans can't feed their cats or dogs and begin eyeing them for protein.

Modern Threats of a Greater Depression

This doomsday scenario may never occur. The purpose of this book is to warn people, especially non-farmers who indeed don't know where their food comes from or how tentative their connection to that primary need has become, so that government policies and individual actions will combine to reduce this threat. Humans mostly don't change behavior until necessity mandates it: that luxury is not available in America if chaos and suffering are to be avoided. A deeper consideration of these risks is warranted to fully comprehend just how monumental our modern peril has become.

The comparison above was premised on a juxtaposition of the Great Depression's financial tragedy and the agriculturally created Dust Bowl with what could unfold today. A tripled population, urbanized, heavily indebted and government-dependent, means twenty-first-century Americans would suffer exponentially more substantial trauma if such events recurred. But there are other even greater threats, unimagined in 1929, that are very real a century later.

The ideological push toward reversing "climate change" is a technologically driven plan that profoundly increases human dependency on technology for heat, travel, and food supplies. Even assuming humans are contributing to global warming, such dependency creates unprecedented threats of a horrific famine never witnessed in human history. Additionally, renewable energy manufacturing generates significant amounts of ecotoxins that adversely impact human and environmental health. This is consistent with a century-old pattern of using technology to conquer the soil and earth, which should serve as a testament to the perils of human folly. The corporate domination of the world advocates for amplifying and universalizing this techno-servitude.

These pressures have been augmented by a climate change ideology that seeks not just to consolidate farms under the GMO model and convert humans to diets based on plants and insects, but also efforts to "set aside" vast areas of land that will no longer be available for farming of plants or livestock. The Biden administration pushed its 30x30 agenda, designed to "conserve" 30 percent of all American lands by 2030.[20] This was repealed by Donald Trump, but this policy remains in force in many states, with more aggressive efforts calling to conserve 50 percent of all lands by 2050.[21] This reduces available croplands and drives up land prices for farmers. Regenerative agriculture enhances ecological and soil biodiversity and sequesters carbon dioxide more effectively than forests. However well-intentioned, reductionist land conservation that blindly removes land from food production is a threat to farmers and future food production.

For over a century, industrial agricultural and food-producing corporations have sold small farmers and consumers a toxic bill of goods, funding research and development at universities (also supported with taxpayer dollars) that has eliminated or consolidated farms, depleted or eroded soils, increased water pollution and water loss, and consolidated animals into "efficient" CAFOs. This was perpetrated in conjunction with growing monopolization of food and agriculture markets.

The story begins with the slaveholder states of the Deep South and Abraham Lincoln's efforts to defeat their plutocratic domination of the nation's nineteenth-century economy. The Homestead Act of 1862 fulfilled a Republican campaign promise by providing 160-acre lots to Americans willing to work and develop the land for five years. Hundreds of thousands of families, including African Americans, migrated to new farms and settled over 270 million acres of US lands. Lincoln also created the USDA to support farmers and local production.

Resistance to this egalitarian effort led to a deterioration of these initiatives through the 1890s, as railroad and telegraph companies that had grown into prominence during the Civil War created unprecedented financial behemoths intent on amassing market control. Commodity prices plummeted as monopolies took control of food crops, prompting a populist alliance of farmers, workers, small producers, and local merchants to galvanize in support of "antitrust" legislation to curtail market abuses by large business trusts. The result was the Sherman Act of 1890, which forbade contracts or agreements designed to restrain free trade or commerce, declaring "[e]very person who shall monopolize, or attempt to monopolize, or conspire with any other person or persons to monopolize any part of trade or commerce . . . [shall be] guilty of a felony."

Succeeding years witnessed the watering down of the Sherman Act and the ascendancy of the usual abusive suspects (led by J. P. Morgan) to consolidate many businesses in the "Great Merger Movement." Industries that sold agricultural supplies to farmers were particularly targeted. American Tobacco acquired over 250 rivals, which ultimately led to the destruction of tobacco farmers. The International Harvester Company controlled approximately 80–90 percent of the agricultural equipment market. Meatpackers (the "Meat Trust") consolidated small slaughter and processing plants, enabling them to control 70 percent of the nation's livestock slaughter and half of its poultry, eggs, and cheese production.

Later administrations began to reestablish restraints on monopolization, including through the 1914 Clayton Act, which restricted the use of business practices that were "common and favorite method[s] of promoting monopoly." Woodrow Wilson empowered the USDA to investigate misconduct and set standards to prevent deceptive business practices. The advent of World War I paused these relief measures, as the US feared that its industry would be disrupted. This also spurred a dramatic increase in US crop production to feed the struggling populations in Britain and France. When the war ended, US crop prices plummeted as Europe resumed agricultural independence.

Crop prices fell, but the costs of equipment, fertilizers, and other manufactured goods remained high. This oft-repeated pattern consistently leaves small family farms at a disadvantage, while larger farms and capital interests gain position to capitalize at their expense. Heavy-handed industrial interests reduced production and kept prices high, while indebted farmers were unable to either increase production or reduce costs. Federal policies that favored a laissez-faire approach to freedom for powerful postwar industrialists sparked another wave of corporate mergers through the mid-1920s, which pummeled vulnerable farmers and consumers alike.

The consequence of unregulated monopolization was the Great Depression of 1929, "the ultimate consequence of a monopoly-friendly public policy that endorsed agricultural overproduction and evermore intensive exploitation of the land by the wealthy few at the expense of economic and environmental degradation for the many."[22] One in four family farms was sold off in the aftermath.

The Roosevelt administration steered America back to a free market for farmers, stabilizing prices by reducing production and saving many family farms by assisting them in securing prices for crops that covered their production costs. The nation did not permit monopolies to run rampant during World War II. On the contrary, the Antitrust Division scrutinized cartel arrangements between American, German, and Japanese companies that used unlawful practices to dominate markets for phosphate fertilizers, nitrogen ammonia, and the chemical industry.

The federal government vigilantly sought to protect small businesses from domination by big business from the late 1930s through the early 1950s. Competition increased for pesticides, fertilizers, electricity generation, meat and grain processing facilities, and farm equipment. This effort functioned effectively to prevent widespread farm failures into the 1980s.

Lax USDA oversight in the 1960s, combined with shifts in administration by the 1970s, led to a new wave of anticompetitive attacks against small family farms. The Nixon, Ford, and Carter administrations pursued deregulatory policies that undermined fairness and competition in agriculture, reverting to the pro-monopoly farm and antitrust policies of the 1920s. This accelerated under the Carter and Reagan administrations, which both approved rapid consolidation in the nation's food system and abandoned the supply management programs that had shielded crop prices from rapid decline. Agriculture Secretary Earl Butz infamously declared to farmers, "Get big or get out!" Small farms were decimated: by the end of the 1980s, nearly 300,000 mostly small farms (less than five hundred acres) had vanished, a sixth of the country's farms.

This food and farming takeover has endured in the United States for the last century without interruption and has been leaping to the globalist stage. The WEF and its corporate stakeholders claim that the world's remaining small farmers must be force-converted to this same mythologized techno-industrial methodology (owned by the WEF stakeholders) to stave off climate change.

The United Nations claims those poor peasant farmers around the world, like America's rural farmers, must be rescued from farming and "resettled" into well-managed cities:

> It is estimated that the livelihoods of about 4.5 billion people globally are tied to food systems. With food system workers often affected by

> poverty and hunger, economic transformation must allow for expanded off-farm job opportunities while improving employment conditions in the agricultural sector. The introduction of new agricultural technologies can raise the productivity and incomes of family farmers and help to ensure the sustainability of the agricultural sector.[23]

This is a global prescription to destroy small and widely distributed small farm holdings, just as they have been decimated in America. The various reports advocating for this "final solution" to climate change and famine recite that enormous amounts of public money are needed to transform the world's food production, and that people's diverse cultural dining traditions must be controlled and changed rapidly to eat what will be produced:

> Government policies can create market incentives to encourage shifts in production, while also using consumer education and school curricula to affect consumption habits. Policy approaches including incentives, regulations and dietary guidelines can encourage people to adopt healthy diets based on foods that have lower environmental burdens.
>
> Targeted social protection programmes, protections for vulnerable food system workers, including migrant workers, protections for import-dependent countries, and increased diversity and resilience of production and distribution systems—including temporary measures implemented during the COVID-19 crisis—can also contribute to a long-term transformation of food systems.[24]

The same end result awaits—dependency, enabled by the big lie about "which foods carry the highest environmental burdens."

Other "partners" at the WEF farming makeover table include TikTok, Walmart, BlackRock, Vanguard, Ralph Lauren, Toyota, and Pfizer. The world's peasant farmers were not consulted, but Bayer has ample corporate partners to refashion agriculture with chemical dependency, aiming to save the world from carbon dioxide. The EU announced mealworm flour may be used in pasta and other foods beginning in February 2025,[25] and is pushing frantically to implement an electronic currency which it says is vitally important but would allow complete statist control of all food supplies.[26]

One potential use of modern technologies is to control food dining choices, which these unelected organizations claim is "necessary" to save humanity from its warming climate. A hint of what this will look like is gushingly endorsed by German chemical manufacturer BASF:

> Ever look at your cotton-made attire and wonder, where did that come from? How was it grown and does it deliver improvements from a sustainability standpoint?
>
> Now, all those questions can be answered thanks to a new technology developed by BASF. The global company's agricultural solutions business created a one-of-a-kind e3 sustainable cotton program. Why is it called e3, you might ask? Because customers know their clothes meet all three E's—they're socially **e**quitable, **e**conomically viable and use **e**nvironmentally responsible sustainable practices. (The three pillars of sustainability are society, environment and economy, and this program covers all three.)
>
> The unique program delivers the comprehensive level of e3 cotton farm-to-retail traceability, along with third-party verification and BASF certification.[27]

The e3 system tracks cotton products from seed to fabric through an "entirely traceable" supply chain back to each cotton field. Especially with the growth in AI technologies, companies will soon be able to "item-level" track every morsel of food from the field it is planted in to the shelf it is sold on. This is a template for total food domination. The government and its corporate partners will regulate foods using societal, environmental, and economic metrics (whatever those are). These are the same entities that claim cows are harmful and that the world's millions of peasant farms must be replaced with industrial methodologies, including satellite tracking of RFIDs (radio frequency identification) ear tags on livestock, GMOs, and now the BASF tracking system. The Wars in Iraq and Ukraine offer ominous warnings about what this agricultural transition portends for the world.

The Refashioning of Iraqi Agriculture to Serve US Corporations

As the cradle of modern human civilization, Iraq and its people have made enormous contributions to the food supplies Americans consume today. Its ancient farmers developed many strains of nourishing wheat and barley, as well as date palms, beans, peas, lentils, cucumbers, leeks, lettuce, and garlic, along with fruits such as grapes, apples, melons, and figs. Also called the "Fertile Crescent," the region originated many domesticated animal species[28] including sheep and cows used for milk and butter, giving rise to the next big step in human progress: the "urban revolution."[29]

Mesopotamian farmers of the Neolithic Revolution (also known as the First Agricultural Revolution) transitioned societies from hunter-gatherers to farmers. This period is estimated to have commenced some ten thousand to twenty thousand years ago, led by the ancient Sumerians.

The modern nation-state of Iraq under President Saddam Hussein experienced declining farm productivity during the 1990s due to international (US-led) sanctions implemented following the 1991 Gulf War, increased soil salinity (from overuse of urea), deteriorating irrigation supplies as Turkey diverted water from Iraqi irrigation, and other influences. On the eve of the Iraq War, the USDA's Agricultural Research Service (ARS) conducted a comprehensive analysis of Iraqi agriculture in 2002, detailing its rich biodiversity, ancient contributions to farming, and long history of peasant seed-saving.

The ARS noted the nation hosted "[m]ore than 400 species of medicinal plants," "97 medicinal plant species belonging to 43 plant families," and "a tremendous wealth of vegetables adapted to the various bioclimatic regions of the country."[30] The report recounted the nation's domestic farming focus on local genetics, and the creation of its seed bank at Abu Ghraib to protect this heirloom heritage.[31]

Before the Iraq War, 97 percent of each year's seed stocks were sourced by Iraqi farmers using small-scale seed-saving.[32] America's 2003 Iraq War disrupted or destroyed the country's agriculture, including the seed bank at Abu Ghraib. Monsanto, Cargill, Dow, and other US companies maneuvered to "help" the nation by providing (proprietary) GMO seed varieties. Of the 100 orders imposed by US Director of Reconstruction and Humanitarian Assistance Paul Bremer, Order #81 controversially protected the patent rights of US GMO corporations

Journalist F. William Engdahl chronicled the law's impact:

> As soon as Order 81 had been issued, USAID began delivering thousands of tons of US-origin "high-quality, certified wheat seed" for subsidized, initially near cost-free distribution through the Agriculture Ministry, to desperate Iraqi farmers. The USAID refused to allow independent scientists to determine whether the seed was GMO seed or not. . . .
>
> Under the USAID program, the State Department, working with the US Department of Agriculture (USDA) set up 56 "wheat

> extension demonstration sites" in northern Iraq, "introducing and demonstrating the value of improved wheat seeds." The project was run for the US Government by Texas A&M University's International Agriculture Office.
>
> This $107 million USAID agriculture reconstruction project had as goal the doubling the production of 30,000 Iraqi farms within the first year. The idea was to convince skeptical Iraqi farmers that only with new US "wonder seeds" could they get large harvest yields. Desperation and a promise of huge gains would be used to trap Iraqi farmers into dependence on foreign seed multinationals.[33]

One commentary alleged "Order 81 allowed Monsanto to promote the benefits of its seeds to a suffering population without warning farmers of the potential financial risks." Order 81 was justified as assistance for Iraq's farmers to improve efficiency and modernization and engage more fully in international markets, yet some claimed "A closer examination of these '100 Orders' and U.S. policy in Iraq shows that the war on Iraq had nothing to do with WMD, terrorism, 'democracy' and 'liberation,' but to colonise Iraq and enrich U.S. corporations at the expense of the Iraqi people."[34] Another commentator alleged "Iraq is one more arena in a global drive for the adoption of seed patent laws protecting the monopoly rights of multinational corporations at the expense of local farmers."[35]

Order 81 was never fully implemented,[36] likely due to farmer opposition, international outcry,[37] and the dubious legal authority to usurp Iraq's constitution, which had long prohibited the patenting of biological life. Yet the effort displayed an industrial agricultural playbook that manipulates crises and farmers to wean them *away* from traditional, localized, biodiverse farming systems into the consolidating mono-cultures of industrial/chemical dependency. Iraq was unusual because most of these changes were instituted unilaterally by occupying US forces and "allies," yet similar US agreements have been instituted through bilateral treaties with Sri Lanka, Cambodia, and Afghanistan.[38] In 2025, Iraq's agriculture sector, which traditionally accounted for one-fourth to one-third of Iraq's GDP, had dropped to a paltry 10 percent.[39]

The Agri-Industrialization of Ukraine, the "Breadbasket of Europe"

A similar GMO conquering of Ukraine was undertaken in exchange for military armaments, in which vast tracts of domestically owned farmland were sold off to oligarchs and foreign investors while GMO cropping technologies—previously banned there, as in Russia—were irreversibly implemented.

Before the Ukraine War, estimates that Ukraine alone could feed 400 million people (nearly the entire population of the European Union) were not far-fetched. The nation's 42.5 million hectares of highly fertile organic farmland is equivalent to more than a quarter of the EU's total farmland.[40] Russia and Ukraine together account for about half of grain exports to Africa.[41]

Ukraine gained independence from the former Soviet Union in 1991. The country distributed agricultural land to small-scale farmers who were restricted to using it privately or leasing it to agribusinesses. Beginning on July 1, 2021, these restrictions were relaxed to permit private citizens to purchase larger parcels and allow agribusinesses to buy up to 10,000 hectares at auctions beginning in 2024. This shift still prohibited foreigners or foreign corporations from purchasing farmland without a national referendum.[42]

The Russian invasion of Ukraine on February 24, 2022, resulted in escalating foreign debt conditioned on drastic structural adjustment, including cuts to social programs and privatization of key areas of the economy.[43] International financial institutions demanded the creation of a land market and deregulation of the agricultural sector "to improve the sector's productivity and access to finance." Foreign actors, including oligarchs and agribusinesses, quickly bought up large tracts of arable land. This further increased consolidation of the global grain trade, "with four companies exercising an oligopoly over the market by controlling about 70–90 percent of the worldwide grain trade. . . .[44]

The Oakland Institute reported in April 2023, that "the majority of Ukrainian agricultural holdings are actually owned by 'American NCH Capital, French AgroGeneration, German ADM Germany, KWS, Bayer and BASF, Saudi PIF and SALIC.'"[45] This controversial takeover resulted in false media claims that international corporations and investment firms were not in fact buying up land or sowing GMO crops. One "Fact Check" outlet declared in October of 2023:

> It is not true that GMO crops are being grown legally in Ukraine; Ukraine's parliament has never allowed foreigners to buy agricultural land. That right is reserved solely for Ukrainian citizens and companies owned fully by Ukrainians; The investment company BlackRock was invited by the Ukrainian government to participate in the creation of a fund for the future rebuilding of the country after the war. The company has no right to purchase agricultural land in Ukraine. . . .[46]

The potent negative blowback following public awareness of the corporate GMO takeover of postwar Iraq likely caused global corporations to more quietly insinuate their dominance into Ukraine's immense agricultural lands, including the promulgation of patently false propaganda. In truth, at the time the foregoing article was issued, Ukrainian president Volodymyr Zelenskyy had already signed a law authorizing the use of GMO crops, and large agribusinesses had indeed been amassing agricultural lands. Zelenskyy signed a 2023 law to establish "the legal and organizational framework for state regulation of genetic engineering activities, ensuring the ecological, genetic, food, and biological security of the state, and state control over the placement of GMOs and their products on the market."[47]

Only a year into the war, Western financial institutions were maneuvering to exploit the conflict for profit in the name of rescue. Much like the pseudo-beneficence following the US invasion of Iraq, the most prominent new landowners included Ukrainian oligarchs, European and North American interests, and the sovereign fund of Saudi Arabia. Prominent US pension funds, foundations, and university endowments invested through US-based private equity fund NCH Capital: "Most of the large landholders are substantially indebted to Western funds and institutions, notably the European Bank for Reconstruction and Development (EBRD) and the World Bank."[48]

This was made possible after Zelenskyy implemented land reform laws in 2020, "against the will of the vast majority of the population who feared it would exacerbate corruption and reinforce control by powerful interests in the agricultural sector." Ukrainian farmers were afforded virtually no financial support, while Western financial institutions offered massive funding for larger landholders and corporations.[49]

Farmland acquisitions accelerated rapidly: agricultural entities accounted for 83.5 percent of all legal entities purchasing land lots during the first five months of 2024, acquiring 14,500 hectares (358,000 acres), according to a report by the Agrocentre of Kyiv School of Economics.[50] By mid-2024, three companies had acquired more than half of all Ukrainian agricultural land at discounted prices, totaling 17 million hectares. Some described this as "a purely colonial scheme typical of the Western world."[51]

Much of this rapid development paralleled the transition of Iraq's traditional agrarian culture to GMO technologies in the name of increased efficiency, productivity, economic growth, domestic food security, and international competitiveness and standards compliance. Ukraine reformed domestic laws to allow GMO patent protections, land sales to foreigners, and favorable business opportunities for large agricultural corporations and investment "partners," saddling the nation with debt. The administrative handmaiden of this corporate field day was, once again, the CIA-linked United States Agency of International Development that assisted the corporate piracy of Iraq. Shortly after the war began, USAID was on the ground with seeds and fertilizers provided by the agency to over 14,000 "agricultural producers" in 2022 and 2023. The agency launched a $100 million program dubbed the Agriculture Resilience Initiative—Ukraine (AGRI-Ukraine) in July 2022, providing seeds, pesticides, and fertilizers to 20 percent of the nation's registered agriculture businesses, as well as "drone technology that allows Ukrainian farmers to apply fertilizer and pesticides by air rather than on the ground."[52]

USAID expanded grain storage facilities in Ukraine in 2023 with alliances with Grain Alliance, Kernel, and Nibulon,[53] and "expanded" its partnership with Bayer Corporation, which agreed "to provide an additional $15.5 million investment in Ukraine for innovative technology, new donations of high-quality seeds, and a farmer safety campaign."[54] In October 2024, USAID announced it had expanded its AGRI-Ukraine program with $1.75 billion in investments with "Astarta, Best Leasing, Crédit Agricole Bank, the U.S. International Development Finance Corporation (DFC), the International Finance Corporation (IFC), IMC, OTP Bank, and Universalna Insurance Company. . . ."[55]

In just two years, Europe's GMO-free "breadbasket" was transformed from an organic, Ukrainian-owned agricultural powerhouse to an indebted, GMO-dependent industrialized system in which more than half of its farmland was owned by foreign interests, including international financial firms.

The Global Agricultural Landscape and the United States

The takeover and consolidation of small peasant farms in Iraq, Ukraine, and Europe is a tragic exploitation by powerful government and corporate actors. Americans are naive to look abroad at such piracy and not see their own countryside in the rearview mirror: the United States is *already* immersed in these chemical-dependent technologies, with attendant soil and water loss and declining human health as witnesses to the result. The diverse, family-owned and operated US farms that a century ago resembled Ukraine's and Iraq's peasant holdings were long ago consolidated into sprawling industrial systems or cookie-cuttered into residential lots and commercial "zones." As in Ukraine and Iraq, once small farms disappear, it is a mammoth task to re-create them.

This is a chief cause of America's current food supply peril. A Russia-China (and possibly Iran and other nations) alliance is emerging in the areas of food, trade, currency, and military technology. Animal rights, climate change, and social justice ideologies are conspiring to eliminate animal husbandry, dictate food choices, and control all agricultural production, processing, and distribution. Americans are becoming utterly dependent on an ever more fragile electric grid to heat and cool their homes, obtain water, communicate, and travel. All of these pressures are converging in a perfect storm of famine and collapse (or at least, sicker humans and soils), whether unintentionally or by design.

But it is by design. Large corporations have a long history of employing financial power to consolidate and monopolize farming inputs, food supplies, and farms themselves. A monopoly is defined as "a company or group having exclusive control over a commodity or service." Groups of companies now control the majority of farming inputs, including seeds, fertilizers, pesticides, and equipment. Even most of the animals in swine and chicken operations are owned by corporations, not the farmers who care for them. A handful of huge companies, in turn, control food processing, distribution, and retailing.

Tensions between free-market competition by small farms versus the Goliath of large business and financial interests seeking to consolidate markets for greater control and profit have existed for nearly two centuries in the US. This battle ultimately pits our nation's rural, individualist impulses against a totalitarian, government-subsidized collectivist cabal of monopolistic enterprises. Unregulated capitalism destroys the small family farm, much like statist communist forces historically ruined peasant farming in favor of state-run domination of entire economies.

The current plight of American diners and the farmers who grow their food is a shared servitude to enormous commercial ventures. This is the culmination of a long-standing battle between those who unethically manipulate markets to amass wealth and the antitrust movements that seek to restrain them.

High crop prices in the late seventies incentivized farmers to incur high debt loads to buy farmland; the ensuing high interest rates of the early eighties combined with plummeting commodity prices to propel many into bankruptcy as land prices dipped.[56] The first Farm Aid benefit concert, held on September 22, 1985, was led by Willie Nelson, John Mellencamp, Neil Young, and others to support American family farms. The effort has continued annually ever since but has not halted the steady decline of small farms.

The year 1985 coincided with the Reagan era's Food Security Act, which expanded federal price supports favoring large farmers while cutting target commodity prices for international markets. This was amplified exponentially under the Clinton administration's "Agricultural Improvement and Reform Act of 1996," which reduced conservation subsidies and pushed farmers to grow even more crops, often on marginal lands. Crop prices plummeted yet further. This regulatory climate prevails today: two major farm subsidy programs (the Price Loss Coverage program and the Agricultural Risk Coverage program) "channel their payments overwhelmingly to large grain and oilseed agribusinesses."[57]

This scheme provides massive subsidies per acre to the largest farms, effectively excluding small-scale farmers and those who grow multiple crops. It ensures chronic overproduction of corn, soybeans, and other grain and oilseed crops. Many large farms operate at a net loss, selling commodities at a price below their cost of production. Federal subsidies are their incentive to grow, as well as their ultimate source of profit. Meanwhile, monopolies in farm input industries (including seeds, pesticides, fertilizers, equipment, and processing) and finance and insurance ensure corporate control of every aspect of farm production.

Whether at the grocery store or for family dining, Americans are buying foods controlled "from soup to nuts" by an ever-smaller club of ever-larger corporations. The monopolization of food markets has returned with a vengeance, eliminating farms and backyard gardens alike from the American landscape and creating a dangerous dependency. These corporations control the health and trustworthiness of our food supplies, and can increase prices to consumers while reducing what they pay to farmers.[58]

This is a very deliberate monopolization that has reached a crisis point. As reported by the European Conservative, this is a calculated undertaking unseen by most "consumers":

> Food security, once a cornerstone of national policy and identity, is now being eroded by globalist ideologies and bureaucratic overreach, threatening not just agriculture but the very fabric of Western civilization.
>
> Under the guise of environmental sustainability and climate policy, the EU has declared war on its farmers, implementing measures that force them off the land. These policies, varying by country but united in their destructive outcomes, are choking the life out of European agriculture.
>
> At the heart of this assault lies a globalist agenda spearheaded by the United Nations (UN). Cloaked in the rhetoric of sustainability

> and equality, the UN's policies often serve the interests of unelected elites rather than the citizens they claim to represent. Through initiatives like Agenda 2030 and the woke climate agenda, the UN advances a vision of top-down control that sidelines national sovereignty and democratic accountability. The role of powerful NGOs, funded by wealthy philanthropists with vested financial interests, further illustrates how unelected actors dictate policy. These oligarchs, shielded by their philanthropic facades, wield immense influence over supranational organizations, bypassing the will of the people.[59]

The apparatus to effect this totalitarian control of the world's food supplies was outlined by Henry Kissinger's 1974 report and has grown to its dystopian fruition in the modern octopus of the UN, WEF, and WHO, all of which are dominated by multinational corporations and NGOs. Always those who would enslave humanity claim benevolent motives to conceal their expansion of power.

The *Epoch Times* has documented this attack on the world's farmers:

> The escalating regulatory attack on agricultural producers from Holland and the United States to Sri Lanka and beyond is closely tied to the United Nations' "Agenda 2030" Sustainable Development Goals and the U.N.'s partners at the World Economic Forum (WEF), numerous experts told *The Epoch Times*. . . . Indeed, several of the U.N.'s 17 Sustainable Development Goals (SDGs) are directly implicated in policies that are squeezing farmers, ranchers, and food supplies around the world.
>
> The WEF, a network of major multinational businesses that collaborates closely with the CCP, is a "strategic partner" of the U.N. on Agenda 2030. According to critics of the policies, though, the goal isn't to preserve the environment or fight climate change at all. Instead, the experts warn that the "sustainability" narrative and the other justifications are a tool to gain control over food, agriculture, and people. The U.N. Sustainable Development Goals, often referred to as Agenda 2030, were adopted in 2015 by the organization and its member states as a guide to "transforming our world."
>
> Using government to transform all economic activity is a critical part of the SDGs, with Goal 12 demanding "sustainable consumption and production patterns." . . . Among the specific targets outlined in

> Goal 12 are several directly linked to agricultural policies that undermine food production. These include "sustainable management and efficient use of natural resources."[60]

Currency failure, hyperinflation, international instability or war, economic or social turmoil, and dubious ideologies threaten to profoundly disrupt global or regional food supplies. An electronic currency will permit governments unprecedented power to control the citizenry politically and economically. A new disease justifying vaccine mandates and global lockdowns may appear. All of these unforeseeable risks threaten humanity's food supplies—even before considering the deliberate globalist plot to control all food production for nefarious goals.

The solution to totalitarian food control is to oppose such plans in favor of local agriculture.

CHAPTER 9

Restoring Healthy, Local Food Supplies

The hard-working farmer must be first to partake of the crops.

—1 Timothy 2:6

To be successful, a resistance to globalist food control, industrial food, hyperinflation, and food supply interruptions must be scaled to a size that best achieves the desired outcome, and it must offer specific, viable policies to do so. Ultimately, all pollution and food consumption is connected to individual choices. All environmental decisions—large and small—impact human individuals: We the People. And so, We the People must connect and restore community and individual awareness to buttress our local food supplies.

Not everybody can (or should) be a farmer. However, the current disconnect between city mice and country mice is mutually destructive and needs to be healed. The farmer-consumer connection is key, and represents a spectrum. Some people just consume fresh, local foods; some may dive in deep, and start breeding pigs, sheep, or cows; others may dabble in backyard gardening, raising chickens for meat or eggs, or canning foods they grow or buy. All must share in the effort to educate themselves in order to spread good health outcomes, cultural and economic benefits, and improvements to the nation's food supplies by fostering and nourishing regenerative agricultural methods and localized agriculture.

Most American consumers are largely unaware of the world of agriculture and do not realize the significant impact their buying decisions have on the farming economy, particularly on food quality and local availability. They also mostly don't appreciate just how much their own health (and perhaps their very lives) depend on those fast-disappearing, misunderstood farmers. The fact is, *every* American *can* impact local food supplies, and *all* are threatened if corrective action is not taken immediately.

Wendell Berry has described food-informed consumers as "consumer-conservationists." He explains that the connection between consumption and the environment is built on food, but that something much more than mere victuals is gained. Consumers must raise awareness of a *relationship*:

> Now consumer-conservationists must begin to feel these strains and stresses also. They will have to acquaint themselves with the requirements of good agriculture. They will have to see that a good food economy does not enrich the agribusiness and grocery corporations at the expense of everything and everybody else, but pays to the real producers the real costs of good food production in capital, labor, skill, and care. They will have to become active and knowledgeable participants in their local food economy. . . .[1]

To follow this counsel, consumers must become aware of the origin of their food—how it was produced, processed, and transported. Dr. Sina McCullough counsels that "The most effective way to change the system is to change our behavior and let the market respond. That requires us to read our food labels and act on that information."[2] This also means people either need to pay more for healthier food, or government programs must be reformed to subsidize healthy, whole foods rather than GMO crops that destroy soils and are used to create unhealthy, ultra-processed foods.

The threats to the interruption or adulteration of global food supplies are numerous, but the remedy of local food immediately incorporates healthier food, healthier soils and water, and healthier humans. As people become more aware of where their food is grown, processed, and packaged, and seek to improve food security, they will inevitably enhance food freshness, quality, and trustworthiness. Farmers' markets, CSAs, food cooperatives, farmstands, and gardens in backyards or on rooftops offer an immediate path to preventing food inflation or supply disruption.[3] As consumers source foods from local producers, those food avenues will be economically nurtured. More aspiring farmers will find economically viable paths back to the land, allowing them to join existing local farming operations.

Buying organic is not just about avoiding GMOs and chemicals in one's food—it is about avoiding their use on soils and water in the production of food, regardless of whether food safety is directly impacted. As is increasingly apparent from multiple scientific disciplines, GMO foods, and their means of production, are mostly *not* safe. Even if food is not certified organic, if it is local it has required less fossil fuel in its transportation, is likely fresher for the same reason, and supports a small or midsize business rather than a multinational corporation or an industrial farm in Wuhan.

Americans must support laws and policies that revitalize local farms and reverse the decades-old regulatory and subsidy imbalances that favor large industrial producers and processors over local rural enterprises. This requires becoming aware of how farming works in particular regions of the country. Water, farming inspections and certifications, local meat processing, crop subsidies, distribution systems, and other factors all vary across the country. Understanding local nuances as well as federal laws and regulations is imperative to fashion a meaningful response to existing industrial favoritism and to restore rural farms and supportive communities. This education begins by farming, connecting with farmers and learning from them, and investing in understanding the laws, regulations, and subsidies that impact them and you. This also begins with piercing the veil of mystery surrounding how specific foods are produced and processed, allowing us to make informed buying decisions at grocery stores.

A brief list of helpful books and other resources to learn more about food choices is supplied in the Resources at the end of this book. Central to all these works is an effort to expand consumer information to discern between what is healthy and what is dangerous. Simply put, organic and local = good; foreign and industrially processed = bad. The closer one is to the source, the more it can be trusted not to have been adulterated for profit. As Joel Salatin puts it: "Consumers who care about their food need to understand that security does not come from bureaucrats or labels; the best way to know the quality and safety of your food is to see the source and visit the farmer."[4] As Joel hints here, this includes food *security*—having access to any food at all as well as being "secure" in the knowledge that it is trustworthy.

Finding good foods entails abandoning old dining choices. And while modern efforts to organize effective targeted boycotts of large retailers may serve to impact their food policies, personal shopping choices *do* impact markets. The key is to avoid toxic food like the plague that it is. Many of the "products" on modern food shelves are essentially that. They are also often shipped extremely long distances from foreign factories. Buy local.

Would-be Farmers

More small- and medium-scale farmers are desperately needed to reverse the industrialization that has steadily eliminated most family farms from rural

American landscapes, along with the crucial knowledge and genetics they have stewarded. Considering the food security provided by local agriculture, this need is urgent, regardless of CO_2 emissions and the abundant environmental benefits of regenerative practices. As food safety expert Mark Bittman presents it, "Providing the food we need to sustain ourselves and flourish is the single most fundamental and important human occupation. How we do it defines our present and determines our future."[5]

Bittman presents a comprehensive array of specific policy areas that will bolster regenerative agricultural practices broadly, and for local farms specifically: "positive government action to change agricultural and nutrition policies ultimately is the most effective way to change the way we grow and eat food."[6] Such policies at either the state or federal level will make entry into farming easier for new producers, reverse decades of unfair discrimination against small farms, and accelerate the return of people to the land. This will make farming more profitable on a small scale than it has been in many decades, and the profitability of local farms will increase quickly as current inflationary pressures push food prices ever higher. Creating lending or grant support for young wannabe farmers to purchase land and equipment will also help counteract the high land prices that bar new entrants.

Mr. Bittman advocates an "agroecological" system, which in many ways summarizes the path outlined in this book to reverse industrial dependency and rebuild national (food) security:

> [D]eveloping an agroecological system would ultimately transform the global food system by first cutting back on the toxic techniques innate to industrial agriculture, starting with chemical fertilizers and pesticides.
>
> Next comes replacing those materials and their associated techniques with alternative practices, such as the use of compost, cover crops, crop rotation, and multicropping; the encouragement of beneficial animal and plant interactions; and the complete elimination of chemicals. To this point, what we're really talking about is organic farming, but this is where farmers will begin to rebuild the system, using from-the-farm fertilizer, intercropping—planting a number of crops together—to reduce pests and unwanted plants, encourage pollinators, [etc.]. The next step involves shortening the food supply chain, reducing the distance between growers and eaters, and establishing new ways of getting food to people.[7]

A word here about "organics." The term often evokes sneering derision from conventional farmers, who are convinced of the productivity and efficiency benefits of conventional industrial farming systems. There is no doubt that industrial agriculture creates long-term problems for soil health, including erosion, water loss, and other issues. Yet, the core message here regarding food security and thus national security, is not about the ecological and nutritional differences in production methods: either conventional or organic food is better than famine.

However, this is where organic foods unequivocally surpass the industrial food system—local food systems have historically been organic and are inherently disengaged from industrial dependency. There is no arguing with that conclusion. Food liberty *is* liberty, and self-reliance is the opposite of chemical-industrial dependency.

It is essential, however, that conventional farmers are not demonized as enemies of food security who destroy the Earth. For decades, federal regulatory and subsidy policies have been directed at encouraging the nation's farmers to invest in chemicals and equipment rather than in healthy soils and nutrient-rich foods. Conventional farmers have been paid to embrace industrial farming practices. Rewarding organic alternatives is common sense, but it is folly to abandon the large farms we have invested in, which have become dependent on industrial inputs; they can be incentivized and supported to transition. They also continue to be the primary producers of our nation's food supplies. America needs *all* its farmers.

From a policy perspective, existing federal programs that encourage conventional farms to transition to regenerative practices must be expanded and funded to increase scale. Paying corn farmers to convert their acreage to grass, upon which beef and sheep can be raised, is a win-win for farmers, consumers, and local economies. Increasing funding and support resources to assist farmers in shifting from conventional to regenerative agriculture will liberate them from the high input costs of fertilizers, pesticides, and patented seeds while nourishing soils, preserving groundwater, and building higher profit margins by meeting the demand for healthier, nutrient-rich food options.

Profitability has long been the most significant problem for small farms, not a lack of people willing to toil for a decent wage. Many people would love to work and live on a farm even today; many try and fail. People who undertake the hard work of tending the land and the humble task of caretaking beasts *should* be decently paid.[8]

Sadly, farmer and writer Wendell Berry's decades of warnings about the dangers of industrial aggregation of agriculture have gone largely unheeded.

His encouragement to restore farmers to the land and soil has become more and more fantastical as fertile lands have been "developed" or rewilded, and agrarian knowledge has faded. In an ongoing conversation with Wendell about the positive benefits of Robert F. Kennedy's MAHA mission to reclaim agriculture, he wrote to me on January 11, 2025, with sobering remarks:

> Making America Healthy Again is desirable, but neither party can do it. Where would they find the necessary people?
>
> Politically, I remain a New Dealer. The tobacco program of this region, begun in 1940 under Franklin Roosevelt, *worked* democratically and economically. I *saw* this. I saw it for many years, as a field hand in this region's tobacco patches. Such a thing is now impossible, not for want of tobacco, but for want of people.

My first book, *Small Farm Republic*, advocated supporting local farms primarily by reducing burdensome regulations on small and midsize operators, and phasing out federal crop subsidies for industrial production of GMO monocultures (mainly corn, soybeans, and wheat).[9] With the implementation of policies supporting local farms and regenerative practices, one of the oldest human motivators—economic profit—will attract many people to invest time and treasure into local agricultural ventures.

Existing USDA programs supporting small farms, organics, soil conservation, etc., can be bolstered and expanded.[10] There are already good profits to be made, especially for value-added goods like meat and fruit pies, canned goods, jerkies, salsas, breads, and other baked goods, as well as cheeses and yogurt. These markets must be supported and improved. Farms that are going concerns must be strongly supported economically to maintain or increase local production with improved regulations while phasing out subsidies that undermine local, small-scale farming.

There are many different types of farming—Joel Salatin's terrific book *You Can Farm: The Entrepreneur's Guide to Start and Succeed in a Farming Enterprise* is an excellent resource for the interested beginner. As with any business, it is essential to gauge the economic viability of agricultural enterprises. There is a broad range of profitable agricultural business models from which to draw inspiration and income for the would-be back-to-the-lander. These vary in required acreage, start-up capital, skill level, and time commitment: those "daily chores" can range from five minutes each morning feeding laying hens, to all-day-long, 365-day-a-year toil. The farmer's adage is "Work Is Life." To weld oneself to the land in productive stewardship provides priceless benefits: a factory-lensed world has reduced human productivity through labor as an illness to be avoided.

America *needs* farmers to succeed. The nation's industrialized society has been acculturated to strange ideas completely inconsistent with agriculture, such as "weekends," "overtime," "days off," "parental leave," "sick time," and other modern factory-clock accoutrements. Many people who set out to farm will find these lifestyle changes too challenging. But to farmers, such strange fictions are much like T. S. Eliot's lament that modern man "measures out his life in coffee spoons"[11]—socially anxious because leading a dull, meaningless, materialistic life. Agrarian life can be the cure.

This presents a host of reasons, in addition to profitability, as to why more Americans are considering a fruitful career in agriculture. A survey of possible motivations includes:

- There are numerous threats to human health from food additives, hormones, pesticide residues, and antibiotics in retail grocery food. This short list barely scratches the surface of the various potential threats of chemical contamination and foodborne pathogens, especially to more sensitive, vulnerable children and sick or immunocompromised adults. Allergies, asthma, and other illnesses diminish when humans live among livestock—that can't be bottled for pharmaceutical ingestion. The human microbiome flourishes when healthy bacteria abound, which they are inclined to do in manure-fed soils, rather than in petroleum-tainted sidewalks.
- Choosing a farming lifestyle offers numerous priceless benefits, if enough conventional money can be earned to sustain it economically. Exercise is part of this life; stress levels are lower, gratitude higher; relationships with neighbors, customers, family members, and animals perpetually nurture mental health; food is fresh, wholesome, nutrient-dense, and absolutely delicious. It is an unjust assessment to exclude these numerous benefits from consideration by weighing merely the monetary income of a farming enterprise; these factors also merit contemplation when evaluating the trade-offs of those weekends, vacations, etc. Unless it is seasonal, farming must become both work *and* vacation—it is a way of life.
- It is a healthy way of life. The Amish are perhaps a model community in their enviable communion with the land, and their physical health

> is generally superior to that of the industrially fed population that surrounds them. So, too, is the health of the average person who returns to the land to farm or eats exclusively from trustworthy, whole-food sources—disease wanes; prescriptions are discarded; inflammation subsides. Switching type 2 diabetics to a low-carbohydrate diet liberates many of them completely from illness and prescription medications, including insulin: imagine what switching to a farming way of life does for physical health. There is toil, but that's partly the point.

The specters of politically encouraged looting of cities following the death of George Floyd, and sardine-packed hospital wards in New York City and Los Angeles under COVID, have motivated millions of people to confront the numerous vulnerabilities and health threats created by urban dependency. Americans are migrating in droves from urban chaos to rural food security and physical safety.

Over the decades, there have always been defectors from suburban consumerism who dig holes in mountainsides for bunkers or stockpile bullets and preserved foods. Sometimes called "survivalists," but now more often referred to by the pejorative label "preppers," this instinct to escape is understandable when the skyscraper-and-traffic-jam claustrophobia strikes. The negativity toward so-called preppers arises from anxiety among the unprepared that they are vulnerable, exactly like vaccinated people project their fear of having made a misjudgment by taking experimental vaccines onto unvaccinated scapegoats. Those entirely dependent on industrial food and government are made uneasy by those whose self-reliance holds a mirror up to their folly. Thus, the social pressures against prepping are the *opposite* of rational and should themselves encourage people to . . . prep.

To most farmers, this is silly. They *are* prepped. And this is really how preparing for disaster (which is always a possibility) should be viewed: as a win-win, commonsense approach. If there is an interruption in the food supply, prepared citizens will eat better than the unprepared—as they would in the absence of a collapse or disruption. How could people sneer at the good old Boy Scout idea of preparedness? The explanation is in their underlying anxiety and suppressed awareness of the monstrous vulnerability lurking always in human dependency on the earth, severed today like never before in human history by techno-industrial dependency.

This currently denigrated idea of individual household preparedness (prepping) has a long history of being considered entirely rational. This was the preindustrial state of human societal structure throughout *all* human history, in *all* cultures, since humanity transitioned from a hunter-gatherer to a crop-growing society. Now, there is a Brave New Human Food World, as urbanites have gathered themselves apart from any connection to the source of all life and eschew hunting, gathering, digging, and even eating or "enslaving" animals. That Brave New Industrialization is favorable solely in their deluded minds, as what they attack (much like those who attack US history, culture, or the Constitution, which guarantee liberty and prosperity) is that which has afforded the foundation for their slippery soapboxes.

Americans need not hark back to precolonial or prehistoric imaginings of self-reliant food production and storage to appreciate the current importance of those skills. After all, the twentieth century gave them the Great Depression. Had the nation not still been predominantly agrarian at that time, the suffering would have been exponentially worse. Livestock, farms, and fertile lands blanketed the American landscape; yet, people still starved. Imagine if a similar calamity were to befall us now.

Especially following the Great Depression, a generation of Americans were quasi-religious in their dutiful storage of food in canning jars, freezers, and root cellars—they weren't going to be fooled again. Victory Gardens further supported this creed during World War II. Those generations have faded, and how quickly this modern, soft, privileged society has displaced that collective wisdom with an unprecedented degree of collectivist industrial folly.

Marie Antoinette was not nearly as surprised when she faced the guillotine as today's pampered generation will be when they face an abrupt interruption of their food supplies. The hundreds of millions of unsuspecting industrial-food dependents in today's America resemble a swarming mass of nonswimmers on the *Titanic*, pushing away lifeboats because they laugh that Big Ag can never sink. But Big Ag will unquestionably sink: it is already sinking, along with the subsiding San Joaquin Valley and the nation's dwindling underground water aquifers and vanishing topsoil.

It is that kind of rational survey of the present landscape that leads many people to feel uneasy, not by preppers, but by *not being prepared*. This gradual awakening from the Industrial Food Matrix is accompanied by an increased awareness of what has been introduced into the food supply as acceptable for humans to consume. As more Americans see the common sense of raising food locally and healthily, they will become "preppers" and reap all those benefits without any real sacrifice. Their anxiety will diminish while their health improves.

Many Americans will then begin to think past self-reliance and toward the broader journey of agrarian life. An intriguing 1930 collection of ideas endorsing distributism called *I'll Take My Stand: The South and the Agrarian Tradition* describes a diverse group of thinkers who

> . . . endeavored to stimulate reconstruction of an agrarian society in the Southern states, where agriculture would again be the "leading vocation, whether for wealth, for pleasure, or for prestige." Happiness, they said, is the primary goal of an agrarian economy: "the culture of the soil" is" the best and most sensitive" form of work. The self-sufficient farm assured the family of "perfect economic security." An agrarian order provided "a right attitude toward nature" and the preconditions for art, music and marriage to flourish. Hostile to this humanistic framework for life was industrial society, "the capitalization of the applied sciences," which produced satiety, aimlessness, debilitating surpluses, and "the illusion of having power over nature."[12]

Economist and visionary E. F. Schumacher was thinking outside the industrial prison-box almost fifty years ago:

> The whole point is to define what constitutes progress. And the homecomers believe that the direction which modern technology has taken and is continuing to pursue—towards ever-greater size, ever-higher speeds, and ever-increasing violence, in defiance of all laws of natural harmony—is the opposite of progress. Hence the call for taking stock and finding a new orientation. The stocktaking indicates that we are destroying our very basis of existence, and the reorientation is based on remembering what human life is really about.[13]

Here then are the two poles of the modern human condition: one "sustainable," more frugal and respectful; the other rapacious, shortsighted, a lustful "progress" toward more, and ever more immediate, gratification of ever more useless, wasteful wants. More obvious now than ever are the human consequences of that ignorance: alienation, obesity, addictions, overdoses, suicides, and sickness from a lifestyle that "progress" promised would be easier. Man has fallen yet again.

The man (or woman) who wants to get up again must get to the land as the source and foundation. The proper relation to nature is a requisite for a "right attitude" toward life and even an appropriate appreciation of one's place in the world: without it, of *course,* humans are alienated, anxious, and vulnerable. Much as some theologians would say a proper relation to God is necessary before that restless unease can be quelled and a man come to be whole, so most humans are unaware of their separation from the Creation until they rejoin it in unity. Gratitude and wonder are unavoidable consequences, unmeasurable in monetary profit. Humanity must get "back to the Garden."

Raising a Family

The small-farm reputation for being the ideal home in which to raise functional children is well-founded, for apparent reasons. Dietary and exercise benefits are yoked to discipline, work ethic, initiative, community, self-confidence, humility, an agrarian education, and perhaps most valuable: gratitude. Industrial society is opposed to this "humanistic framework for life": its educational institutions lack classes for these subjects.

Crime rates are lower in rural areas. Schools are smaller and safer. Bullying can still occur, and young boys and girls can be killed in farming accidents. However, the benefits outweigh these risks, as popular sentiment reflects: everyone knows that farm kids are more likely to possess that strong, uncomplaining ethic that was widespread after the Great Depression.

The hypnotized silliness of Homo sapiens' modern alienation from agriculture is perhaps most revealed in this contrast: popular culture denigrates farmers, simultaneously extolling the benefits of farm life for children. Common sense would suggest it can't be both. In fact, the first premise is false (created by government subsidies and regulatory forces that destroyed small farms economically); the second is true. Restoring small farm economics through a genuine reformation of the industrial food system will allow more young families to make the leap to raising their children separated from the chaos, dependency, violence, and alienation that is seeding anxiety and depression in a generation of public-school-educated children. The more families return to the land, the more food they will produce to sell to urban and suburban customers who desire and can afford healthier foods. All of society will benefit from increased food security, which is currently threatened by the reliance on foreign imports and distant food factories.

It may be that younger people today, most of whom reject parenting as imprisoning, are not willing to sacrifice their own perceived comforts (and weekends and vacations) to become farmers to shape their children's lives the best they can. However, many very much are, and must be fully encouraged and supported. The truth is that almost no parent who leaps into farming with their children ever reports regret, even if things don't go well—that's the point.

Distributist writer Edwin O'Hara believed the health of the family was central to the social cohesion of rural communities and agrarianism:

> As O'Hara explained, "the primary product of the farm is not wheat or potatoes or cattle, it is people." Indeed, the farm is "the natural habitat of the family," because country life embraces home ideals, avoids excessive consumption, favors early marriage, cements the functional partnership of husband and wife, and receives children as economic assets. In short, "on the farm alone . . . the economic forces work for the unity of the home."[14]

Notwithstanding today's ill-advised contempt for strong marital foundations, many young people, including those of faith, seek precisely the stability, security, nurturing, and happiness that only such functional arrangements can provide. Farming is generally nonsexist, in that husband and wife are united in labor along whatever lines are appropriate to their circumstances, abilities, and relationship. Women can drive tractors or horses, and men can wash milk pails or watch kids—it is a perpetual familial rhythm, unifying and nurturing. It is also alien to the modern, loud, busy, techno-dependent life of the majority of unhappy, unhealthy, anxious Americans, in which husband and wife depart daily to separate jobs and lives. Instead of climbing into a spaceship to escape modern nihilism, expectant mothers are wise to flee to a remote farm to protect their babies from that unnatural industrial churn.

Spiritual/Psychological Health

Rather than a boring, artery-clogging, sedentary fade near a golf course in Florida, a modest agricultural retirement might be one of the healthiest transitions for Americans to dream about. Increasingly more Americans are burning out and switching careers midlife—farming is often seen as the great escape. It will strengthen the tired heart and amplify that "still, small voice." Many retirees mow their lawns and watch TV for a short time before realizing that their "dream" of relaxing golden years more resembles a padded prison or asylum, a tragic epiphany too late to reverse.

Agriculture offers proven salutary therapeutic benefits: working the soil and feeding animals psychologically heals many sufferers of mental trauma, such as sexual abuse, PTSD in veterans and others, or substance use disorder.

The daily routine, healthier diet, ritualistic exercise, connection to the earth, responsibility, and resultant bonds with animals, plants, and soil all speak silently to the soul, whether wounded or soaring high. Wendell Berry writes that "agrarianism had, and where it survives it still has, a sort of summary existence as a *feeling*—an instinct, an excitement, a passion, a tenderness—for the living earth and its creatures."[15]

Whatever one's spiritual tradition or pursuit, an agrarian life challenges mind, body, and soul in unique ways, which is why nature and agrarian imagery saturate all mythological, spiritual, and religious traditions. A book could be written surveying Christian theology/spirituality relating to animals, nature, and agriculture in particular—let alone the ancient cultures (or Muslim, Judaic, Buddhist, etc. traditions). The question raised here ponders the potential spiritual as well as food-security implications of a trusting dependency on food staples from compromised, regulatorily captured state and federal governments that serve industrial profiteers selling toxic, polluting food at the expense of environmental health and humane animal treatment. Is it all worth the price?

The questions asked of Christians might "spiritually" be asked of all:

- Is it sinful to eat meat from animals treated horribly during life and inhumanely at slaughter?
- Is it sinful to contribute to the pollution of soil, water, and air by commuting, drive-thru dining, consuming, disposing, and mindlessly speeding through life?
- Will switching to a more self-reliant lifestyle or conscientious food choices reduce humanity's pollution of Creation?
- If the human body is a temple, is it sinful to knowingly sicken oneself with poor food choices? The chronic conditions of diabetes, obesity, congestive heart failure, and cancer are now established to often stem from a toxic, industrial diet.
- Is it wise to become knowingly dependent on government and distant corporate entities for both the provision of all food and for its safety and healthfulness?

Increasing numbers of Americans are disenchanted with the dystopian "progress" of the American Dream and the environmental deterioration it is wreaking. For those waking up morally and spiritually to the growing threat this poses to *all* dreams, there is a pull not to just protest or finger-jab others but to "walk the walk" and change personal behaviors to become part of the solution. Admittedly, this is difficult, so people must not be judged for doing otherwise.

It is further moral slavery to have no choice what to eat; physical slavery to have no food at all. The options available to store-going families have narrowed for decades to ever-more addictive, toxic, or nutritionless offerings. The universal problem with moral assessments of which environmental or health path to choose is that it cannot be selected for another; each individual must assess the externalized pollution costs of their own consumption and existence. Just as it is wrong to condemn others for their drug addiction, it is wrong to judge people for their food addictions.

But now, increasingly, people *do* know better. A flight back to the land is an escape from a terrifying, Orwellian food addiction:

> Wrestling free of an addiction requires us to give up something that came to define our lives, and then fend off forever the myriad temptations that try to reel us back in. This only gets harder with eating, where enticement is the calculated business of those who make and sell processed food. They have nearly boundless resources in knowing our vulnerabilities.[16]

Personal awareness in food choices begins with information and necessitates action at the same individual level. Urban shoppers will suffer the consequences of personal responsibility for starvation or ill-health if they do not adopt informed personal responsibility for their eating habits and dining choices—so will those in the suburbs and rural areas, where they too can easily find cheap junk food. However, all of this depends on small-scale, trustworthy (primarily rural) farmers to provide reliable food supplies as alternatives to toxic foods and to survive in the event of a sudden calamity.

These food choices are much more beneficial to the environment than "conserving" land through rewilding. Libertarian Christian Joel Salatin is a blunt activist when it comes to this issue:

> If all the grand matriarchs and patriarchs who fund environmental organizations would withdraw their daily patronage of industrial food, it would do more to preserve farmland than all the preservation regulations and easements put together. I'm a believer in personal responsibility. If you don't like something, clean up your own act first. But how many feel-good Sierra Club grandparents take their kiddos to

> McDonald's and fund Tyson chicken? Telling someone else what to do is always easier than cleaning up your own act.[17]

Aldo Leopold also saw personal responsibility as an ecological imperative and viewed responsibility-shifting to government as a dangerous way to *avoid* dealing with environmental problems:

> Conservation is our attempt to put human ecology on a permanent footing. Milk-and-water education has convinced people that such an attempt should be made, and they have told their government to act for them. Some other force must now persuade them to act for themselves.[18]

Americans have largely abandoned their personal responsibility to oversee the environmental health of waterways, skies, and soil to an irresponsible, industry-biased government. That milk-and-water industrialized education has yielded plastic-plugged oceans, smog-choked cities, asthma-sickened infants, and a long list of destruction that need not include CO_2 or climatic warming to be chilling. It has also enabled total dependency for the fundamental need of nutritious food for healthy and physical survival to be exclusively controlled by an Orwellian superstate.

As Wes Jackson ominously muses, "I fear that the industrial model for agriculture may be regarded as even more necessary in the last years before the collapse."[19] Those who claim destructive agricultural practices are vital to "feed the world" are the industrial voices who ply yet more poisons as the cure for the industrial toxification of the planet.

It is imperative that the federal government champion the antitrust legislation of a century ago to enhance competition, promote fairness, and preserve family farms and rural landscapes. The Federal Trade Commission (FTC) and the Department of Justice (DOJ) have played a leading role in alternately relaxing or enforcing these laws over the last century. These agencies must now lead an antitrust revival to scrutinize the handful of companies that now dominate the nation's entire food supply. *Both* political parties have been complicit in permitting this consumer-farmer strangulation: bipartisan action is required to liberate Americans from this food tyranny![20]

The assistant attorney general for the Antitrust Division at the DOJ, Gail Slater, is reportedly "deeply committed and believes aggressive antitrust enforcement can benefit consumers in countless ways."[21] Existing antitrust laws and regulatory powers will permit her office and the FTC to pursue relief. Additional funding for these agencies would expand free market protections by empowering regulators to police more mergers and anticompetitive practices in agriculture, food processing, and retail grocery establishments. Several draft bills would support the DOJ and FTC's powers to restrain food monopolies from engaging in anticompetitive practices or further consolidation.

What this book has primarily emphasized is the importance of regenerative, localized agriculture for achieving long-term national food security, as well as environmental and human health. However, the impact of humans on soil, water, and air is not confined to agriculture: the externalized costs to the environment from toxic pollution extend to almost every single human activity, and many of those harmful chemicals in the air, soil, and water circulate back into food supplies. This is why individual responsibility is necessary for effective environmental remediation, why the government alone should not be entrusted with stewardship, and why government coercion of individuals is counterproductive.

For there to be any serious effort to reduce pollution and improve food security, public awareness and responsibility must be increased, and the delegation of authority to corporate and government entities must be reduced. This is a movement of values, as Kirkpatrick Sale explains in *Dwellers in the Land: The Bioregional Vision*:

> We will have to measure our lives in terms of clean air rather than large cars, of healthy chemical-free food rather than supermarket frozen convenience, of autonomous workplaces rather than fat paychecks, of days without rush hours and TV commercials and junk mail. Such things are not measurable by the traditional GNP (aptly called gross) but they are not without value—indeed for many they are of primary value—and in any sensible reckoning ought to be considered part of one's living standard.[22]

In a culture that incessantly barrages people with messages to consume, spend, eat, play, travel, and accumulate worthless crap, it would be stunning if more Americans were *not* waking up to this tragic condition. Hoarding is the subject of a TV series; purging homes of accumulated junk has become a trendy form of conspicuous-consumption bulimia. Humans are drowning in the "blessings" of materialistic existence and yearning for something more genuine. Instinctively, people sense that this industrial life is not desirable, let alone every day. Somewhere within that growing awareness, Americans must awaken to the peril of their food dependency. The rest of the useless clutter of possessions distract from that core threat.

This is the focus of this book: toxic food dependency and a loss of self-reliance. In the quest for profits, aided by advancing technologies, the confabulations packaged and presented as "food" are increasingly sickening Americans physically, but perhaps also spiritually. There must be sympathy for the human diner, who at some point must look at his or her plate and simply want to barf:

> [T]he closer we look at our food, the more disgusting it will turn out to be. And this always seems to be the case! Every time the best food minds and investigative journalists dig into a particular part of the supply chain they find some new horror.
>
> The real object of our scorn might not be in our food safety standards, in the revolving-door regulators, in the rise of industry, or even in the abuse and commodification of men, but in ourselves as agents in this world: for knowing what we want and what we are willing to give up to get it, for understanding that this is a moral outrage we've been digging for all along because it verifies what we know but also don't quite want to acknowledge about ourselves.[23]

When the OPEC crisis struck America, President Jimmy Carter implemented speed limit restrictions and gas rationing, and counseled Americans on how to conserve energy. Now Americans are told the world will end in ten years, and the answer is not to consume less, but to drink an entire line of new products peddled as a solution that requires the burning of coal and other fossil fuels to manufacture them. They are not instructed to make personal changes or consume less, but that global totalitarianism must be embraced to protect them from their neighbors.

Anthropogenic ecotoxin pollution extends far beyond food consumption. Americans should begin to apply the analysis that none of the environmental activists seem to embrace: there is a tremendous difference between pollution generated for food production (food being a necessity) versus pollution generated for recreation or almost any other cause, except for heat or shelter (which are also necessities). How can any sane environmental policy not distinguish between the two?

The Transportation Climate Initiative (TCI) aims to encourage rural residents to relocate to cities in an effort to combat high commuting costs.

However, those are costs associated with making a living, such as commuting. The TCI does not mention the long commute to ski slopes or why vacation-consumed gasoline should be (equitably) taxed at higher rates than that for workers trying to make a living. It also ignores the environmental costs of trucking food into cities and hauling garbage out, rather than promoting a sustainable rural culture where both are close to home.

A study posted by NASA in 2005 estimated that Americans mowed an area of lawns three times the size of the land area dedicated to corn crops. NASA's website[24] has not updated this data since 2005 and says that these lawns are beneficial to the planet because they are a "net carbon sink." Only, this conclusion is reached by ignoring the gasoline used in the lawn mowers and the energy and materials used in their manufacture. It also overlooks water usage—in pursuit of carbon dioxide as the primary climate culprit.

This lawn mowing frenzy consumes some 800 million gallons of refined gasoline annually,[25] much of which is spilled on the ground. Many lawn owners mount massive, $15,000 zero-turn commercial ride mowers for solely residential use, and mow their lawns before the new growth can be discerned. These lawn mowers lack any pollution control protection and get worse mileage than most cars. Before considering leaf blowers, lawn thatchers, lawn fertilizers, and pesticides (which kill dandelion-loving bees), consider how unworkable and undesirable it would be for government agents to "police" lawn mowing. But what if all this energy was instead put into food production?

A 2020 *Psychology Today* article assessed the cognitive dissonance inherent in this American fascination with manicured lawns:

> Using lawns to create an illusion of order or to inflate a sense of personal success suggests they can act as psychological buffers. Like moats around castles, our neatly tended yards become barriers between the worlds we create inside our home and the hardness of reality outside. And while the downside risk of these types of mental stories may not seem significant by itself, the damage associated with lawn maintenance is more than just psychological.
>
> The USDA estimates that lawns account for about half of homeowner water use, much of which is wasted. Additionally, Americans are reported to use 80 million pounds of fertilizers and pesticides on their lawns each year. Perhaps of even more import, the particles generated by lawn mowers are a major source of toxic, carcinogenic air pollution.[26]

Climate change ideology has shifted attention to carbon dioxide rather than personal consumption of chemicals, such as drain cleaners, laundry and dish detergents, soaps, fragrances, shampoos, body lotions, floor waxes and cleaners, bug sprays, and tire cleaners: an ever-growing menu of specialized chemicals for specialized consumer projects and products. Plastic residues and microplastics now coat Creation. In oceans, there are islands of plastic. Reducing plastic use would help reduce CO_2 emissions and decrease reliance on fossil fuels. Where is the plan to reduce plastic consumption that doesn't involve consumers and personal decisions? Which is to say, there *is no plan* to significantly reduce plastics manufacturing, as it is a multibillion-dollar industry. The problem is not one of economics but of moral breakdown and a collapse of personal responsibility. The greater lurking threat is that this same folly has essentially severed local food security in the bargain.

Instead of amplifying that growing awareness (guilt) in modern humans for the obvious harms being inflicted by their consumption, corporations are pacifying Americans with bold lies—that they can keep right on consuming with no environmental impact. EV cars and solar panels accelerate ecological destruction, and the argument that they "save electricity" is used to conceal the fact that they exponentially compound all of the problems faced by the Earth while distracting consumers away from reducing their consumption. This ideology safeguards and amplifies corporate profits and ongoing pollution. Similar arguments about the need to shift all agricultural production to GMO crops and industrial systems achieve the same illusion regarding food supplies.

If Americans do not return to self-reliance by rebuilding local food resources, some will find themselves horrifically dependent on untrustworthy sources for their very survival. Agricultural knowledge is hard-won but easily abandoned.

Wes Jackson explains the importance of this heritage:

> High energy (such as fossil fuel or nuclear energy) contributes to the arrogance of university professors who, though righteously appalled when species disappear, pay little attention to farmers driven from their lands or to the loss of cultural information this represents. This cultural information, which was hard won through sweat, tears, injuries, and death, will have to be won back in the same manner, and not just for the land, but for the urban culture too. Though cultural information can evolve faster than biological information, once lost it

> will be difficult to regain. Reestablishment will be gut-wrenching and the land will experience further abuse.[27]

The concern that America and the world may be on the precipice of a tectonic shift or economic collapse is increasingly common and not just a Chicken Little fringe. British farmer and writer Chris Smaje devoted an entire book to the subject called *Finding Lights in a Dark Age*,[28] in which he suggests small farms are the only path forward for humanity's survival and so agrarianism has something important to offer in the face of seemingly numerous existential threats:

> The collapse of the business-as-usual world—which has been the chief opponent and great inhibitor of agrarianism—creates an environment where agrarianism can position itself the best means to feed, clothe, and house people, and as the optimum pathway for conviviality and flourishing in the chaotic new world. In fact, Chris is adamant that it may only be through chaos and collapse that widespread agrarian localist communities are enabled to emerge and thrive.[29]

Here then, dear reader, is "what you do": get informed about where your food comes from and examine where your own externalized chemical-generation footprint leads. How far will you get when the stores all close because social chaos or a national calamity descends, the POTUS says you can't eat without a vaccine or social credit card, or the lights go out from a neglected grid? The list of potential disruptors of the food and consumer goodies train, deliberate or unforeseen, is indeed long.

If the goal is to leave children—of Democrats and Republicans alike—a "better" life than their parents, that cannot be achieved by leaving them money instead of clean air and reliable food sources. If the World War II generation was America's greatest, this one will one day be remembered as its *worst*: selfish, cowardly, and shallow in character and pursuit. If there is any hope whatsoever for the children and grandchildren of today's America, it is that individuals exhibit the character and personal responsibility to reclaim personal and community food sovereignty.

Food inflation looms. The long-standing illusion of cheap, trustworthy food is over—it was always a lie. This truth will become increasingly evident in a very short time. Economics and fiscal integrity cannot be compromised, especially when it comes to food. It is the great tragedy of the modern age that, instead of growing humility, humans, flying wickedly toward the sun, become only giddier as they plunge into its furnace.

John Greer believes this inevitable descent back to the realities of earth can be accomplished gradually, while rescuing some of that vital lost knowledge of which Wes Jackson speaks, like casks of gunpowder or molasses from a ship wrecked at sea:

> One of the most hopeful features of this side of our predicament is that the revitalization of old technologies can be done successfully by individuals working on their own. . . . These same technologies—if they're recovered while time and resources still permit—can make use of the abundant salvage of industrial civilization, help cushion the descent into the deindustrial future, and lay foundations for the sustainable cultures that will rise out of the ruins of our age.[30]

Few observers are as sanguine about future prospects as Greer. It is much more likely that the transition to self-reliance will be very sudden. Americans will ultimately be individually responsible for their position in the world when that interruption inevitably occurs. To think that things will simply continue as they have been requires an unprecedented level of cognitive dissonance.

Political bickering and fake crises are conjured to keep people in a constant Orwellian fight-or-flight distraction from their greatest peril: famine. One day, humanity will awaken to the true crisis facing the planet—complete global domination by an evil cabal of corporate fascists pretending to be social justice rescuers, a complete breakdown of the food supply leading to anarchy, possibly "rescued" by martial law and government currency (and food) control.

Learning to reconnect with the soil and source of all life and food is a reward in its own right—a win-win. It is also the sole path toward healthy food and liberation from globalist corporate domination. In this scenario of supporting small farmers and homesteaders and incentivizing conventional farmers to employ sustainable practices, everybody wins except corporate and bureaucrat fascists. Consumers and farmers need each other; urban and rural Americans need each other.

Just as Americans have always needed and helped one another. If we cannot come together for food quality and food security, we will never come together over immigration, transgenderism, climate change, or social justice. If we don't come together to reclaim food security, a horrifying future awaits us all.

CHAPTER 10

Preventing Famine and Finding Unity

> It is easy for me to imagine that the next great division of the world will be between people who wish to live as creatures and people who wish to live as machines.
>
> —Wendell Berry, 1999[1]

The inhabitants of the world's developed nations are embroiled in an existential tug-of-war against an industrialized food production and distribution system that feeds them much like industrial livestock. Modern "consumers" are voluntarily confined to their homes, relying on computer and TV panaceas, much like cows or sheep masticating cud in comfortable, mechanized barns, often gaining weight like tender calves kept sedentary for fat gain. Humans reach into bags of processed feedstuffs specially formulated to encourage them to eat more, frequently employing ingredients derived from the CAFO livestock industry.

Americans are currently fractured along numerous belief-system lines: systemic racism, transgenderism, politics, faith, etc. Yet the most crucial division is between those who eagerly embrace an industrialized food system to feed humanity—imposed tyrannically to "save the planet" from climate change, or to stop people from eating meat diets to rescue animals, or for perceived health benefits, and those who challenge the sustainability or wisdom of yet greater reliance on technology and industrialism for future food supplies. (Notably, the second group does not seek to compel the first to stop eating Cheerios for breakfast, Cheetos for lunch, and Cheese Nips for supper.)

The United States is engaged in a decisive battle at home and abroad, which will determine whether its citizens decide to sever themselves en masse from this industrial codependency or double down on what will essentially be a globalist, government-compelled weaning from any last individual strings of connection to earth and soil. Which way will America lean?

The collapse of trade and food supplies considered in these pages will inevitably occur, at which time those weaned from the soil may quickly perish, and those weaned from chemical soup will be more likely to live and thrive. The sooner America chooses the better path, and the more people at every level and station individually inform themselves and bend their wills to a self-reliant approach, the less disastrous will be the impacts when the system unravels, and the fewer forever chemicals will be released in the interim. People can heal themselves, just as soil and life can heal. Society must heal and reclaim what it means to be human—community, shared hardship, honest labor, history, culture . . . connection with one another and the Earth.

A Grammie's-Eye View

My grandmother, Cesarine Alexander (later Stoddard), was born on a modest cow-dairy homestead in Williamstown, Vermont, in 1910. Grammie was eight years old when her mother succumbed to Spanish flu, leaving a single father of five children—the youngest merely five months old—to hand milk the family cows.

The milking maid became my grandmother's (strict) stepmother, and several siblings (my great-aunts) joined the family. At age nineteen, Grammie lost all her savings in 1929's October Crash, which marked the onset of the Great Depression. She grew up riding and working with Percheron draft horses and, naturally enough, because he lived just over the ridge in Brookfield, married my grandfather, Milburn Stoddard.

Milk prices plummeted by half during the Great Depression, as did the prices paid for most farming commodities. Milburn's herd dwindled as his drinking increased; Grammie became a schoolteacher, and most of her career was spent in a one-room schoolhouse. "Mrs. Stoddard" remains a local legend for her infamous milk hose—a length of rubber milking hose she kept handy for dissenters and ne'er-do-wells (the word is, she used it sparingly and softly), Grammie was also known for taking the chains off (or putting them back on) her car tires herself after (or before, as the commute might be) navigating the muddy Vermont mountain roads in spring and winter.

Grammie was an amazingly resourceful, humble woman. She never complained and was habitually frugal. She saved the leftover vinegar from pickle jars and drank a teaspoon daily. She went trout fishing, grew vegetables, and picked berries and hazelnuts independently, into her nineties. Every spring, she ate piles of cowslips and dandelion greens, her favorite. She would never buy expensive cuts of meat, and nothing went to waste uneaten.

Reviewing the themes of this book through Cesarine Stoddard's eyes means stepping out of time and examining contemporary American society from a distance. Cesarine witnessed the replacement of the horse with the tractor, the human hand with the milk machine, the milk can with the bulk tank, and cow manure with government-subsidized synthetic fertilizers. She watched roads paved, farmlands disappear, markets collapse, banks close, and wealthy suburbanites buy up farms and build "modern" homes dependent on the electric grid. She watched as independent Vermont farmers failed, and farm families dissolved and moved to cities.

My Grammie Cesarine and the other Great Depression generation quieted down over the decades, so long dismissed by their own children. Yet they still stored food, never wasted it, and were grateful for every morsel. My father's mother, Marjory Hemenway (Klar), was born in 1911 on a dairy farm in Sheldon, Vermont, and similarly witnessed the transition of a rural culture to a technologically dependent tourist destination. Both women maintained well-stocked root cellars and copious rows of canned veggies until they were incapacitated by age, unpersuaded by the collective trust in this cowardly New World expressed by their grandchildren and great-grandchildren. Gramma Klar passed away in 2008, at the age of ninety-six. Grammie passed in 2010, just after her hundredth birthday.

Neither of my grandmothers walked about proselytizing about how the economy would implode one day and people would again have to fend for themselves. Many old Vermonters claim they suffered far less during the Great Depression than Americans trapped in big cities, begging on sidewalks, selling apples for a nickel, or standing in soup kitchen lines. Relinquishing their self-safety net was folly to the grammies from that time; my grandmothers had simply given up trying to persuade this soft generation of its peril and folly.

After farming livestock in Vermont for a decade, I gained a deeper understanding of my grandmothers' culture and life experiences. This created a bond that was unique while they were alive: both grandmothers loved to hear about our cows and horses, our sheep and goats, and the making of cheese and bacon, as well as brined pork shoulders. Both admired my wife Jackie's ability to cobble together a meal out of scraps and odd bits, creating a special bond of mutual understanding and nostalgia with my grandmothers.

Visiting Grammie Cesarine when she was ninety-seven, talking as farmers do about farming, milk prices, and the importance of food, I asked her a simple enough question: "Gram, how do you think America would look if the Great Depression happened today?" Sitting in her favorite recliner with a view toward the Green Mountains and Camel's Hump, a thin smile flashed wryly across her lips. "Oh, I don't think it would be too good."

This understatement masked a deep understanding—deeper than most of the current American generation can comprehend—of just how disastrous such a calamity would be for a population completely disconnected from the traditional tools, knowledge, land, plants, and animals necessary even to begin to surmount such a dramatic shock. Tremors of such an event have periodically signaled the potential for a recurrence of an even more dramatic interruption of markets, distribution, and food availability than occurred during the Great Depression. Recent and ongoing food inflation reveals another facet of this American Achilles' heel.

The 1973 OPEC oil embargo crushed the US economy, doubling the price of oil virtually overnight, tripling it within one year. Oil prices doubled quickly also in the "second oil crisis" of 1979, sparked by the Iranian Revolution. These shocks to the US economy were related to disruptions of oil supplies.

A second threat to energy prices is posed by monetary policy. Federal spending under the Reagan administration artificially boosted a war economy funded with borrowed money. The S&L "crisis" (the bailout of which is still quietly costing ever-higher interest on the federal tab: the entire debacle was simply added to the national debt) displayed threats of banking corruption seen again in Bernie Madoff and the mortgage derivatives failures of the 2007–2008 market crash. Money mischief has permitted the US government to defer the normal economic impacts of such market shocks by rolling them into a giant equivalent of a national reverse mortgage. The United States has repeatedly staved off economic hardship by simply printing more money.

Through Grammie's experienced eyes, there is nothing new under the sun here. These near-disasters have swayed the public to place even greater trust and responsibility in the bureaucratic agencies which are so obviously captured by the financial interests that recklessly inflict these massive economic harms. That thin, wise smile would cross Grammie's lips when such tremors shook the nation. She saw the bullet narrowly dodged each time. Each time, she had a full cellar of canned veggies and a freezer full of berry pies and meats that would feed a small family for months.

A Vermont farmer who survived the Great Depression is unlikely to engage in the cognitive dissonance required to trust the government to this degree. As bankers issued hundreds of billions of dollars in mortgage loans to borrowers with no jobs, assets, or incomes during the unrealistic investment banking euphoria that led to the 2007–2008 financial crisis, the societal cognitive dissonance involved was almost mystical. Groupthink reaffirmed the mania—if everyone at Morgan Stanley and Goldman Sachs was comfortable with these derivative securities, they *must* be okay. After all, "they don't make any more real estate."

A similar disconnect pervades today's America with regard to food supplies and prices. For most people alive today, food has always been plentiful and affordable. Humans value what is rare, and waste what is abundant. Ultra-processed food is abundant and obviously unhealthy; nutritious food is rare. The entire food supply is susceptible to utter collapse, much like the mortgage derivatives market in the early 2000s, and most Americans are oblivious. It would be best to have some canned foods and a chicken coop in such a time.

Through Grammie's eyes, bug burgers are preposterous, and lab-grown meats are a scam—she doesn't have to read a book about them. Making an illegal deer hanging in the woodshed stretch through meals for a family of ten in brutal Vermont winters did not condition Grammie to veganism. If there was one Grammie lesson, it was never to trust the government—or banks, or TV announcers, or corporations—to take care of you. This seems wise, but so few people today see through Grammie's eyes.

Many things recounted in this book have occurred since Grammie's passing. European farmer revolts, and globalist plans to eradicate cows in favor of bug foods or patented plant-based meat substitutes, were not discussions heard at Grammie's chatty table. She knew better than to trust bureaucrats, egghead experts at universities, agri-corporations, or other sweet-sounding voices that tempted humanity to slip into techno-captivity. She would have suppressed that same ironic smile if she had witnessed these final chapters in society's collective self-extinction.

That lifetime of Great Depression and Vermont farming knowledge, which Grammie's children dismissed, would still serve today—and a century from now—to counter or survive the various unique threats to the modern food supply chronicled in this book. A well-developed homestead is the enemy of globalist plans to implement totalitarian domination, the alternative to dependency on dubious processed foodstuffs, and the source of health and security during market disruptions or social chaos.

From this "Grammie's-eye view," the folly of twenty-first-century techno-dependency for heat, transportation, medicine, security, and most of all, food is visibly short-term folly. In this view, an interesting companion to Grammie was author and historian John Lukacs, whose perspective was not that of a Vermont agrarian but that of a world-renowned historian and philosopher.

Many of Lukacs's observations merit consideration in this discussion. He opined that roughly half of what humanity has believed at any one point in history was false. This is an interesting optic to consider in the current era—society is split over "scientific" issues such as vaccine efficacy, COVID-19 origins, the merits/harms of transgender treatments, whether the climate is changing, whether renewables do more ecological harm than good, and whether cows are good or bad. In each case, both sides can't be right. In each case, the stakes are very high. The stakes may be highest for food supplies—is cheap, industrial food the "only way to feed the world," or the "surest way to reduce the global population by destroying the soil"?

Lukacs offers an additional consideration to ponder that may have lurked in Grammie's distrust: the energy sources that have enabled the modern miracle of farming, transportation, and technology are finite and will eventually be depleted. Regardless of availability, reckless monetary supply can rapidly increase the price of these vital resources exponentially. In Lukacs's long view, the plenty and ease humanity is currently enjoying will prove to be a brief blip in the arc of human existence.

Moreover, Lukacs observed that modern society is rapidly deteriorating as a result of that same technological culture:

> We are at the end of an age: but how few people know this! The sense of this has begun to appear in the hearts of many; but it has not yet swum up to the surface of their consciousness.
>
> This will happen, even though there exist many obstacles to it—among them, enormous but corroding institutions. As these lines are being written, something is happening in the United States that has had no precedent. A great division among the American people has begun—gradually, slowly—to take shape: not between Republicans and Democrats, and not between "conservatives" and "liberals," but between people who are still unthinking believers in technology and in economic determinism and people who are not. The nonbelievers may or may not be conscious or convinced traditionalists: but they are men and women who have begun not only to question but, here and there,

> to oppose publicly the increasing pouring of cement over the land, the increasing inflation of automobile traffic of every kind, the increasing acceptance of noisome machinery ruling their lives. Compared with this division the present "debates" about taxes and rates and political campaigns are nothing but ephemeral froth blowing here and there on little waves, atop the great oceanic tides of history.[2]

This historian's 2002 prophecy has more fully taken shape in 2026, and at first blush, it might appear he is mistaken—Republicans and Democrats, "conservatives and liberals," have become bitterly alienated to the point of talk of civil war.[3] Yet Lukacs is correct about this slow-simmering division for two reasons: it has indeed increased over the previous two decades, and it will accelerate in the years to come.

Over the past two decades, public awareness of food toxins, microplastics, and "forever" chemicals has increased. More and more research links human health to the gut; more and more evidence links that gut to the soil. There is a war on cows, and the nation's children are fatter and sicker than ever before. The COVID-19 pandemic rightly caused many citizens to realize that their federal government may suffer from a deficiency of competence, if not integrity. Record inflation reminded hazy-memoried consumers of its existence and struck food fiercely.

These issues all indicate an increasing bifurcation between Lukacs's techno-believers and non-believing skeptics. When a major shock strikes or food inflation accelerates even faster, that rift will be complete, with very few believers left in the fast-food pews, and those starving fast.

Cultish Faith in Technology and Science

John Lukacs is also insightful in his characterization of people's trust in technology as something perhaps irrational and even mystical, against which more and more people are rebelling in search of mental, physical, and spiritual health. Lukacs contrasts "unthinking believers in technology" with "nonbelievers" who seek an escape path as if from a cult, questioning and opposing the industrial world man has fashioned into his own prison. Add to this the specter of artificial intelligence, which is increasing daily. Interestingly, this transects traditional religious and party lines—Grammie, for instance, was secular in her worldview but was never beguiled by the techno-cult described by Lukacs.

If faith is defined as "belief in what is unseen,"[4] then the constant secular refrain that "the scientists/technology will figure it out" is a fantastical religion.

Wendell Berry, a longtime friend of Mr. Lukacs, shared this view that science and technology take on "irrational" (unscientific) attributes of religiosity when modern human advances lead people to believe that science will eventually know everything, and will ultimately solve all human problems.

Scientists have long acknowledged that it is not within their discipline to devise a moral code to address nonscientific philosophical or ethical questions about how best to apply the advances of technology. Money, and thus human moral frailty, drives investment in technologies that pollute streams and poison trout, toxify oceans and wipe out salmon fisheries, saturate urban groundwater with forever chemicals, and kill the continent's soil microbiome and drain its precious underground aquifers. Technologies have inflicted these wounds, yet people place ever-greater faith in technology as a cure.

Science cannot know everything—it has only recently discovered that the PFAS it has been producing since the 1940s are toxic and persistent, and that the human gut microbiome is intricately connected to health. Science and technology cannot solve all human problems if the majority of those problems are *caused* by technological advances coupled with human moral frailties, such as greed, jealousy, gluttony, and sloth, which, by definition, do not claim the authority or ability to be solved. To the extent modern science, and modern industrial agriculture in particular, serve Americans as a religion, it is a particularly pernicious cult that has soaked the world in ecotoxins, dotted it with mountainous landfills, paved vast expanses, and even cluttered space with useless flotsam propelled skyward after being "manufactured" from the Earth's finite resources.

Grammie's six children were evenly divided between Republican and Democrat. Still, they aligned mainly on the same side regarding their faith in the techno-cult. Unlike Grammie, their lives have been marked by what is historically the most productive and profligate period of any culture in human history, enabled by that technology that is now culminating in the death throes of industrial agriculture and the rapid sickening of humanity and almost all life. They have little experience from which to expect the future to deprive them of what they have never not known.

Yet many people—again, regardless of party, race, or other tribal/identity caste placement—are intuitively aware, even spiritually sickened, by the cancerous expansion of asphalt, traffic congestion, and noise recounted by Lukacs. EVs and solar panels do nothing to curb toxifying consumption, merely repackaging the path to the landfill while the roadways clog and dead rivers congeal. A society religiously told it can consume without moral accountability because "science will fix it" results in today's disintegrated American culture, utterly dependent on factories and machines for unhealthy, uber-processed "food."

This modern plight, as Lukacs observed, has arisen "gradually, slowly." Rachel Carson's book *Silent Spring* warned in 1962 that migratory birds were wiped out by insecticides that were potent endocrine disrupters in humans. Jack Kerouac's *On The Road* in 1957, and Aldous Huxley's *The Doors of Perception* in 1954, respectively explored societal rebellion and human consciousness under the influence of psychedelic drugs.

Modern American consumers have closed themselves up behind flat-screen TVs, exotic phones, and social media on an electromagnetic internet, with groceries delivered by Uber Eats or DoorDash, or easily selected at low cost from a "box" or "convenient" grocery store. The narrow chinks remaining are focused on entertainment, politics, sports, or maybe porn, through which are seen nothing at all of the perils recounted in this book, or the inexorable waste, destruction, and contamination of the environment this narrow-minded and selfish blip in human history has inflicted. Ironically, Jim Morrison named his famous hedonistic band the Doors after Huxley's tome, influencing a generation of Timothy Leary tune-outs to gyrate in the park and have sex in the woods to escape something undefined and unnamed.

America's sixties generation railed against war and corporatism, but they loved Pepsi-Cola, free love, and freeing weed. If humans must choose between consumption and conservation, the world dies. The snake-oil industries manufacturing renewables and fake meats rake in trillions of dollars peddling technological "indulgences" that promise consumers a chance to atone for their eco-guilty consumption—while still consuming. The consumption continues conspicuously, even as Joni Mitchell's lyrics about the shame and tragedy of paving over paradise jingle in most every head.

In 2026, America's food supply and farmlands have been profoundly compromised by GMO monoculture cropping technologies that Lukacs could not have fully contemplated in 2002. This dramatic shift in production technologies is becoming harder and harder for Americans to ignore, swelling the ranks of the nonbelievers disenchanted with the perpetual lies of industrialism.

Readers of this book hopefully see what Wendell Berry saw: "People are fed by the food industry, which pays no attention to health, and are treated by the health industry, which pays no attention to food."[5] Healthy food is central to health and essential to liberty and the pursuit of happiness.

The slow, gradual division between those who do and do not see this peril is inevitable. The hippies lamented war and industrialism while dropping synthetic psychedelics like LSD, and though Dr. Suess's Lorax warned of the loss of trees, while the world united symbolically behind the beloved honeybee, little in personal responsibility for food choices or to improve the plight of small farmers (or honeybees) has been accomplished. Richard Nixon created the EPA to tackle a few high-profile chemical offenders. Still, the chemical "industry" and its proliferation of new toxins offered its stream of novel concoctions not just to Big Ag but every industry manufacturing new gadgets for recreation, convenience, or pleasure for their evolving "consumers." The shift to a carbon dioxide obsession distracted humanity just a tad longer.

But something *has* changed. The hypocrisy of condemning pollution and waste while engaging in it has grown more visible, not just with carbon dioxide. The climate cult has managed to strike sufficient fear of "greenhouse" warming into consumers to persuade many to purchase technologies (with hefty public subsidies) they believe will reduce their impact. That this is another marketing scam, and that these technologies will spew yet *more* nasty chemicals into the ecosystem, is still dawning on consumers. Perhaps the perversion of the very phrase "solar farms" and their contrast with fields of alfalfa that absorb the sun will dawn on the human consciousness before it is too late.

That dawn is darkened, striving to inflict that persistent cognitive dissonance that has trapped the techno-believers in servitude to corporate domination. The "Drill, baby, drill!" crowd on the American Right is increasingly realizing that their corpulence, cancers, diabetes, and heart disease are infecting their children and grandchildren more negatively than the fentanyl scourge. Meanwhile, the "sky is falling" histrionics of the carbon cult are yielding to the scientific fact that cows are better for soil and air than synthetic lab options; EVs cannot replace cars without destroying the planet in search of lithium, cobalt, and other toxins, and exponentially amplifying the release of toxic rubber tire particulates into the air and ocean; wind turbines eruct more plastic than decades' worth of plastic straws; solar panels require an astronomical scale of mining, fossil fuels, plastics, and coal, all environmentally destructive. All of these supposedly salvific products end up in landfills, joining the vast majority of plastics Americans have been collecting and sorting under the misconception that they were being recycled.

Just in case it went unnoticed, this realization about the actual toxicity of renewables manufacturing exposes that the far-left seizure of every available facet of federal, state, and local government and every conceivable international NGO (often created for the very purpose) to advance these supposedly earth-saving technologies have constituted the most vicious, relentless, unconscionable rape of the planet and its resources in human history. Perhaps this will be leveled at capitalism—those nasty companies selling people defective products that don't perform as advertised. Or maybe it is socialists—those nasty partisans allocating unwilling taxpayers' money to this bevy of corporate profiteers. As Wendell Berry has documented, neither socialism nor capitalism (nor science) can lay any special claim to environmental protectionism.

The crisis upon humanity is one of self-destruction by faith in the technologies that are torturing and killing us. John Lukacs did not shirk at criticizing this anthropogenic toxification of the earth and the atrocities lurking in human hubris:

> Recall Gibbon's sentence of more than two hundred years ago: barbarism and its catastrophes are now inconceivable "unless the face of nature is changed." . . . So at the end of the Modern Age the control and the limitation and even the prohibition of some of the applications of science—including genetic engineering—becomes a, sometimes global, necessity. At the same time there exists no international or supra-national (and in most cases not even a natural) authority that would enforce such measures.[6]

Artificial intelligence is an additional unregulated, unregulatable menace to the global human order. It, too, could create catastrophic natural disasters that propel humanity into a *Mad Max* (or *Terminator*?) barbarism. Humans are indeed a natural disaster: while the global order is identifying cows and farming as the greatest threats to humanity, the toxins spewed into the environment by the corporate masters seated at prestigious panels of experts are destroying and mutating life.

The threats of industrial food production (or its potential disruption) are not being remediated but exacerbated. Powerful technocrats and pseudo-environmental groups openly strive to regulate and eliminate local agriculture in favor of even greater centralization, technologization, processing, and tracking, shipping food over ever-greater distances in a politically and economically volatile world.

The zeitgeist that is "slowly, gradually" shifting in this milieu is the growing realization that denial is a deadly option and that there is no neutral ground. The toxins generated by recreational consumption are no longer in someone else's backyard—they are in the air, the soil, children's toys, fireproof sofas, dry-cleaned clothes, water (bottled or well), medical equipment, and pharmaceuticals. They are ubiquitous, swirling like an invisible potion, sickening and killing a generation. Robert F. Kennedy Jr. called this a "war on our children" when he announced his withdrawal from the 2024 presidential election—the media and public response displayed the two lines drawn: denial versus recognition.

Lukacs's 2002 hypothesized division was evident in this response to Kennedy's speech endorsing Donald Trump—will Americans choose tribal loyalties over healthy food and a clean ecosystem? Will they choose to "Make America Healthy Again?" Will that very issue be politically weaponized, as it has since Al Gore so conveniently hijacked the environmental movement and made it a greenhouse-gas-only monolith?

Gore's carbon dioxide crusade is fraying as (1) the nation has become divided to the point of paralysis on environmental issues, and (2) the government has leveraged trillions of borrowed US dollars to plow into a short-term renewables production frenzy that may be the last anthropogenic gasp of toxins life on earth can take, from bugs to birds to autistic human babies. Was that the plan all along—paralysis and debt?

"Build Back Better" was a government takeover by these industries during the Biden administration, as was the laughably monikered "Inflation Reduction Act." Long after the nation once called America has defaulted on its nosebleed financial commitments to accomplish this overnight planetary rape, the forever chemicals created will continue to course their way through soils, water, plants, livestock, human breast milk, and developing human fetuses. Perhaps there will be a political push for reparations in three hundred years, seeking ancestors to scapegoat for this gray dystopia bequeathed to the world.

Cognitive dissonance will not prevent these chemicals from compromising the human gut microbiome, regardless of political views, skin color, gender, sexual proclivities, or which national border they crossed (legally or illegally). The gut microbiome impacts virtually every aspect of human health and will determine how many people of *any* political or other identity persuasion will walk the earth over time. Just as foreign nations chuckle at an America politically paralyzed by partisan infighting over social issues while its economy, military, public safety, and health deteriorate, so too the chemical companies will keep peddling toxins as Americans argue over carbon dioxide. As Rome fell, this great nation will fall—if not into economic collapse, then into a self-induced communal chronic illness.

This division between people enamored with the glorious comforts of technological "progress" and the "nonbelievers" is shifting like an hourglass as more and more sand grains of human awareness filter into the reality of our plight. Perhaps 100,000 chemicals not found in nature have been created since Rachel Carson wrote about songbirds dropping dead from DDT. More and more of America's children are fat, stupid, autistic, anxious, addicted, or helpless. People increasingly understand that the best prevention for cancer and disease is to stop infecting themselves with ingested toxins.

If human and environmental health were not enough to amplify awareness of the risks of industrial food, then grocery inflation and food insecurity will accelerate those sand-grains passing through Lukacs's nation-dividing hourglass: how many people are already waking up as they must choose between paying their mortgage or feeding their family? The food inflation numbers provided by the federal government are obviously padded: any modest-income shopper can point to individual products and categories that have increased in price far more than official pronouncements gaslight. When there is limited or no food to be had on shelves, the complacent consuming crowd will bang on pots and pans, and perhaps be compelled to eat their own dogs and cats. The current poverty of Haiti might one day look preferable to what the Great Babylon America will exhibit if it continues on its present course.

The longer the delay, the greater the fall. Americans waking from a slumber of trust in their government and food supplies may choose to return to the artificial reality of fake meats depicted in *The Matrix* and a drug-like illusion of comfort through denial. However, more people are choosing to face the harsh reality of the world that has grown darkly around them, because they have no choice. They are getting sicker. They are starving, overdosing, and being pushed onto the streets due to poverty. Most of all, they are waking up to the fact that the technologies, industries, and mediocre governments that have been pretending to serve them have been preying upon them and their children all along.

Starvation, sickness, food inflation, and disruption of supplies will pop this bubble, either "slowly, gradually," through desertification or the exhaustion of North American aquifers, or overnight by an EMP, nuclear war, global pestilence, financial implosion, or asteroid. Perhaps the most baked-in threats are those in between: hyperinflation, growing resource scarcity, sociopolitical disruption, or a combination thereof. Current food inflation in the United States, China, and Europe is inconsequential compared to the unstoppable impacts of an always-accelerating hyperinflation.

Intelligence, individual responsibility, and taking initiative are required to exit what is essentially mind manipulation by a cabal of industries that have grown like swollen ticks feeding off human health and complacency. The government may be spending taxpayer dollars on resurrecting the woolly mammoth, splicing soybean DNA with pig DNA, or studying how to feed the population with snakes or roaches to replace cows, but it is *not* serving humanity to reverse the environmental destruction it has enabled—especially regarding food.

The intransigence of government regulatory agencies and policymakers in acknowledging the profound and rapidly growing human peril of unhealthy, vulnerable food supplies reveals to awakening consumers that these agencies are either complicit or incompetent. Exacting accountability is fruitless—fleeing the sinking ship of pollution and famine is the only escape, requiring individual thought, character, and action.

My first book, *Small Farm Republic: Why Conservatives Must Embrace Local Agriculture, Reject Climate Alarmism, and Lead an Environmental Revival*, sought to galvanize conservatives into action on toxic chemicals in general, and agricultural pollution in particular, as a higher ecological priority and more resonant environmental message than the idiotic, impossible war on life-sustaining carbon. This book similarly seeks to unite Americans of diverse political, social, and cultural backgrounds in a shared appreciation of the unprecedented peril that looms over all of us. Starvation, like fentanyl and cancer, does not care what race or political persuasion we are, and we must similarly elevate our common cause for health and survival above those less-important attributes that divide us.

This book has chronicled a myriad of very real and growing threats to the United States' food production, processing, and distribution system. Local action and responsibility are the only antidotes to globalist centralization and the threats it poses. Americans are indeed divided. Will they unite in a shared famine crisis and nurture the shared humanity of those they differ with, regardless of ideological divisions, or will they devolve under stress into barbaric tribal groups, drawing out their death and suffering, perhaps cannibalizing their neighbors?

That is a question that can be dragged out in the light and asked forthrightly, or people can stick their heads back in the sand and await the rumbling of their children's bellies to rouse them. Unless corrective action on a large scale is initiated to protect and rebuild our traditional, local food systems, it is only a matter of *when* this Great American Famine unfolds. The belief that technology will solve this crisis it created, or that the government that aided and abetted this modern condition will suddenly shift gears and serve We the People, is blind faith and trust in the very oppressors who delivered us here.

Grammie Cesarine Stoddard was self-reliant and knew how to be free from the government and shady technologies. Many moderns eschew the life of our Grammie forebears because it seems so harsh (in view of our relative comforts) and unrewarding. After losing his young wife to Spanish flu in 1918, Grammie's father, Jules, lost his right arm in a hunting accident and shifted from milking cows to planting a fruit tree nursery—I still eat apples from his one-armed efforts. Grammie's brother-in-law, Lester, a World War II veteran helping milk cows at the Stoddard farm, drowned himself in the cows' water tub. My mother, aged five, found his body, his wallet and watch set neatly beside him. Grammie's son Ronald (my uncle, beloved by all) was killed in a horrific tractor accident at age forty-seven when his legs were caught in a brush hog. His death devastated all of our family, and especially crushed Grammie.

These are just a few tragic experiences of poor Vermont farmers who were dependent on themselves rather than the government. It is a far less tragic life than the one endured by the vast majority of modern urbanites and suburbanites, their food spiked with toxins, their children dependent on that food, and their escape looking impossible. When the existing toxic, fragile, corrupt food supply system comes to a sudden halt or hyperinflation sets the price of a loaf of bread above a week's blue-collar wage, the life of Vermont subsistence farmers in 1900 will appear as an oasis of ease in contrast.

It is a haven still within our grasp. Supporting small rural farms nurtures soil, water, the ecosystem, and the residents of our cities. Agriculture enabled urban living, and still does today. Farmers and consumers desperately need one another; powerful business interests have severed that connection for profit. It must be rekindled for survival, and for our nation's food security. Supporting regenerative farming is the only path forward to accomplish this reversal of the damage done by modern industrial farming methods.

Resources

Here is a sampling of valuable resources to become educated about what to look for on those labels, as well as some foods for which labels need not even be consulted:

Beyond Labels: A Doctor and a Farmer Conquer Food Confusion One Bite at a Time is Dr. Sina McCullough and Joel Salatin's fantastic survey of various food safety traps and how to avoid them. Chapters are designed to progressively guide the unlearned diner through the labyrinthine variety of health risks presented in the conventional food supply. From Thai-farmed fish to grass-fed beef, imported greens to arsenic in rice, this encyclopedic resource is user-friendly and packed with information to equip American consumers to make more informed food choices.

Dr. McCullough's previous work, *Hands Off My Food!: How Government and Industry Have Corrupted Our Food and Easy Ways to Fight Back*, is an excellent companion volume that documents the history of how the federal government and industrial food producers repeatedly conspired to co-opt human and environmental health in favor of short-term profits. Included are valuable insights into how to "fight back," not legally but by becoming informed and changing buying patterns accordingly. An excellent summary on page 207 is titled "Easy Ways to Fight Back."

Sally Fallon Morell and the Weston A. Price Institute offer a wealth of materials at westonaprice.org explaining the importance to human health of whole foods, foods that can be best used for specific health needs, and the myriad homeopathic supplements that bolster immune systems and ensure a complete supply of nutrients, minerals, vitamins, and *fats*—especially for children. Mrs. Fallon debunks numerous industrial food myths, including the misconception that all animal fats are bad and that GMO vegetable fats are good (the opposite is actually true).

Sally Fallon Morell is recognized as a leading advocate for a return to nutrient-dense diets, which include raw milk, animal fats, organ meats, bone broths, and lacto-fermented foods. Her widely known book, *Nourishing Traditions: The Cookbook that Challenges Politically Correct Nutrition and Diet Dictocrats*, was followed by helpful specialized resources, such as *Nourishing Broth: An Old-Fashioned Remedy for the Modern World*, and *The Nourishing Traditions Book of Baby & Child Care.* Detailed resources concerning raw milk and raw milk products, including purchasing resources, can be found at Sally Fallon's invaluable website, realmilk.com.

Controversial Doctor Joseph Mercola offers numerous resources relating to the importance of food health in preventing disease. He remains up-to-date on current research and primarily offers health advice. For instance, one area of focus that attaches to industrial food production and human and environmental health is the impact of phthalates and other plasticizers—toxic chemical compounds exuded by plastic containers. Dr. Mercola offers valuable resources to minimize exposure to these invisible pollutants that accumulate in the body.[1]

Dr. Mercola is best known (notoriously so by some) for his whistleblowing book *The Truth About COVID-19: Exposing the Great Reset, Lockdowns, Vaccine Passports, and the New Normal.* Often overlooked in the disputes over the book's more provocative claims is that Dr. Mercola levels very pointed criticisms against industrial foods. Dr. Mercola argues that unhealthy, highly processed modern foods weaken the immune system and are deficient in nutritional content, as well as vital minerals and vitamins. They also cause obesity and diabetes. Habitual diets of unhealthy "manufactured goods" predisposed many Americans to death by COVID and other diseases by weakening their immune systems and the human body's natural ability to heal itself.

This problem of poor dietary health contributing to vulnerability to COVID should not be controversial—it is common sense and medically established. The reason many people have died not just from COVID but also from many other diseases (including diabetes, heart disease, and cancer) is that a toxic, unnourishing diet is making them ill. If people are to be helped, improving their diet should be of the highest priority. For those willing to consider Dr. Mercola's sensible advice regarding immune system support and preventive homeopathic modalities to prevent COVID-19 in particular, his book and abundant online resources are very insightful. Instead of scorning and unfairly discrediting his book, American media and political leadership should be exalting its valuable insights about the link between poor diet, weakened health, and COVID deaths.

Another more specialized food focus for urban and rural consumers is *Countdown: How Our Modern World Is Threatening Sperm Counts, Altering Male and Female Reproductive Development, and Imperiling the Future of the Human Race* by Shanna H. Swan and Stacey Colino,[2] which offers a horrifying assessment of the likely chemical causes of escalating infertility in young people. Recalling Rachel Carson's specific concerns about the impact of endocrine disruptors in her 1962 book *Silent Spring*, this book confirms Carson's assertion that the greatest threat of chemical exposures is both cumulative and collective—small exposures over a long period to a wide variety of chemicals which may interact more harmfully when combined. This book offers specific dietary precautions and suggestions for supplements for women during pregnancy,[3] and explains the importance of sourcing meats organically and locally.

Catherine Austin Fitts and her *Solari Report* (solari.com) provide a fascinating resource for understanding not only food supplies but also monetary policy, artificial intelligence, and the risks associated with fiat and electronic currencies. Catherine brings her extensive experience in finance to address a myriad of related issues. She understands the globalist effort to control humanity through money and food supplies, and has devoted her career to warning humanity of this growing threat.

Three other informative resources for the consumer food journey (all published in 2021) are Mark Bittman's *Animal, Vegetable, Junk: A History of Food, from Sustainable to Suicidal*; Dr. Stephanie Seneff's *Toxic Legacy: How the Weedkiller Glyphosate is Destroying Our Health and the Environment*; and Michael Moss's *Hooked: Food, Free Will, and How the Food Giants Exploit Our Addictions.* British writer Chris van Tulleken offers a thorough assessment of the evils of toxicity and addiction lurking on grocery store shelves in *Ultra-Processed People: Why Do We All Eat Stuff That Isn't Food . . . and Why Can't We Stop?* All of these books identify specific danger areas within the modern food chain and offer guidance on how to avoid them.

Acknowledgments

To my darling wife Jacqui, who suffered many months without me as a result of this effort, yet still fed me delicious, organic meals.

My gratitude extends also to Joel Salatin, Dr. Meryl Nass, Chris Smaje, Elze Van Hamelen, Michael Nic Aoibh, Catherine Austin Fitts, Pete Kennedy, Matthew Sheffer, Judith McGeary, and Greg Gunthorp for their insights into farming, government policy, and economic ramifications in the US, EU, and globally.

I am indebted to the outstanding mind power of Skyhorse editor Daniela Rapp and the meticulous copyediting of Jeannine Chartier Hanscom, to Margo and Ian Baldwin for believing in my work, to Leigh Merinoff for her unflagging support, and to Tony Lyons for his tireless devotion to the MAHA vision of a healthier food supply for America and the world.

My father, James Klar, supported me through college and law school, but did not live to see this book. I love you, Pop.

Notes

Preface

1 Walter Hooper, ed., *They Stand Together: The Letters of C. S. Lewis to Arthur Greeves (1914–1963)*, (Macmillan Publishing Co., Inc., 1979), 363–364.

2 Michael Crichton, *The Andromeda Strain* (Alfred A. Knopf, Inc., 1969), 18–19.

Chapter 1

1 Susan L. Flader and, J. Baird Callicott, eds., "Land-Use and Democracy," in *The River of the Mother of God and Other Essays by Aldo Leopold* (University of Wisconsin Press, 1991), 300.

2 "The Association Between Intestinal Bacteria and Allergic Diseases—Cause or Consequence?" PubMed Central, accessed November 9, 2025, https://pmc.ncbi.nlm.nih.gov/articles/PMC8083053/.

3 "The Impact of Diet and Lifestyle on Gut Microbiota and Human Health," PubMed Central, accessed November 9, 2025, https://pmc.ncbi.nlm.nih.gov/articles/PMC4303825/.

4 "The Dynamic Interplay between the Gut Microbiota and Autoimmune Diseases," PubMed Central, accessed November 9, 2025, https://pmc.ncbi.nlm.nih.gov/articles/PMC6854958/.

5 E.g., "Protecting Bees and Other Pollinators from Pesticides," United States Evironmenta Protection Agency, accessed November 1, 2025, https://www.epa.gov/pollinator-protection.

6 "Effects of Soil Compaction," Penn State Extension, accessed November 1, 2025, https://extension.psu.edu/effects-of-soil-compaction.

7 "Nitrogen cycle and world food production," World Agriculture, accessed November 1, 2025, https://www.world-agriculture.net/article/nitrogen-cycle-and-world-food-production; "Fertilizer feast and famine: Solving the global nitrogen problem," *Science Daily*, accessed November 1, 2025, https://www.sciencedaily.com/releases/2019/08/190805153709.htm.

8 Wendell Berry, *What Are People For?* (Counterpoint, 1990, 2010), 146.

9 Wendell Berry, *Standing by Words* (Counterpoint Press 2011), 58.

10 "In 80 years, thousands of fruits and vegetables went extinct," New Hope Network, accessed November 1, 2025, https://www.newhope.com/food-and-beverage/in-80-years-thousands-of-fruits-and-vegetables-went-extinct-infographic.

11 "Food for Thought: Celebrating the Vegetables of the 1890s," Chicago Botanic Garden, accessed November 1, 2025, https://www.chicagobotanic.org/blog/plants_and_gardening/food_thought_celebrating_vegetables_1890s.

12 "Per- and Polyfluoroalkyl Substances (PFAS)," United States Environmental Protection Agency, accessed November 1, 2025, https://www.epa.gov/pfas#:~:text=Basic%20information%20about%20PFOA%2C%20PFOS%20and%20other%20PFAS%2FPFCs%3B,EPA%20and%20states%20are%20doing%20to%20reduce%20exposures.

13 "Stay Ahead of the DEF Shortages in 2025: What Fleet Managers & Diesel Mechanics Need to Know," Keller-Heartt, accessed November 1, 2025, https://info.kellerheartt.com/blogs/def-shortages-2025.

14 "Sheep, Lamb & Mutton—Sector at a Glance," United States Department of Agriculture Economic Research Service, accessed November 1, 2025, https://www.ers.usda.gov/topics/animal-products/sheep-lamb-mutton/sector-at-a-glance.

15 "Food Waste in America in 2025, Statistics + Facts," RTS, accessed November 1, 2025, https://www.rts.com/resources/guides/food-waste-america/.

16 "Their land is also full of idols; They worship the work of their own hands, That which their own fingers have made." Isaiah 2:8, NKJ Bible.

17 Conservationist Aldo Leopold warned Americans of this modern plight seventy-five years ago: "We abuse land because we regard it as a commodity belonging to us. When we see land as a community to which we belong, we may begin to use it with love and respect." Aldo Leopold, *A Sand County Almanac: And Sketches Here and There* (Oxford University Press, 1949), viii.

Chapter 2

1 Albert Howard, *An Agricultural Testament* (Albatross Publishers, 2018), 158–159.

2 Susan L. Flader and, J. Baird Callicott, eds., "Land-Use and Democracy," in, *The River of the Mother of God and Other Essays by Aldo Leopold* (University of Wisconsin Press, 1991), 287.

3 Albert Howard, *An Agricultural Testament* (Albatross Publishers, 2018), 186.

4 Ibid., 223.

5 Wendell Berry has carried Howard's baton in this regard, for decades criticizing American universities for sacrificing integrity and critical analysis to become captured rubes of industrialists and corporations.

6 Albert Howard, *An Agricultural Testament* (Albatross Publishers, 2018), 20.

7 "Ultraprocessed Food: Addictive, Toxic, and Ready for Regulation," National Institutes for Health National Center for Biotechnology Information, PubMed Central, November 5, 2020, accessed October 26, 2025, https://pmc.ncbi.nlm.nih.gov/articles/PMC7694501/.

8 "Foods and Drinks Linked to Anxiety: What to Avoid and What to Eat," *U.S. News & World Report,* accessed October 26, 2025, https://health.usnews.com/wellness/food/articles/foods-and-drinks-linked-to-anxiety.

9 "Ultraprocessed foods may raise depression risks," Harvard Health Publishing, accessed October 26, 2025, https://www.health.harvard.edu/mind-and-mood/ultraprocessed-foods-may-raise-depression-risks.

10 "From the Fields to Inner City, Pesticides Affect Children's IQ," Yale Environment 360, accessed October 26, 2025, https://e360.yale.edu/features/from_the_fields_to_inner_city_pesticides_affect_childrens_iq.

11 See, e.g., Nicolette Hahn Niman, *Defending Beef: The Ecological and Nutritional Case for Meat* (Chelsea Green Publishing, 2024); Diana Rodgers and Robb Wolf, *Sacred Cow: The Case for (Better) Meat* (BenBella Books, Inc., 2020).

12 Internal Revenue Bulletin: 2021-16, April 19, 2021, states that "Qualified carbon oxide for which a section 45Q credit has been previously claimed ceases to be disposed of in secure geological storage (as described in §1.45Q-3(b)), or used as a tertiary injectant, if the leaked amount of qualified carbon oxide in the taxable year exceeds the amount of qualified carbon oxide securely stored in that same taxable year." The Internal Revenue Code includes a specific recapture provision to claw back tax credits when this happens, but the "lookback" period (§1.45Q-5(f)) is *only three years*. This means that if companies lose the carbon dioxide they were paid to sequester because it leaks back into the sky, they never have to repay more than the previous three years' 45Q credits. §1.45Q-5 (c) details how the release is to be measured: ". . . the quantity determined pursuant to CSA/ANSI ISO 27916:2019 must be certified by a qualified independent engineer or geologist" in accordance with "sound engineering principles."

13 "Greener pastures: Better ammonia production for a more sustainable future," Phys.Org, accessed November 1, 2025, https://phys.org/news/2024-09-greener-pastures-ammonia-production-sustainable.html.

14 "Glyphosate Herbicide Found in Breast Milk of American Mothers," *Mother Earth News*, accessed on November 1, 1015, https://www.motherearthnews.com/natural-health/glyphosate-herbicide-found-in-breast-milk-of-american-mothers-zwfz1404zswa/.

15 Glyphosate is used to increase yield and uniformity by killing the plants all at once, permitting natural desiccation to commence. In sugarcane, glyphosate increases sucrose concentration. In grains such as wheat, barley, and oats, yields are increased, and reduced drying time can serve to eliminate windrowing to assist faster harvests that especially benefit farmers in cold climes.

16 An excellent resource to more deeply study the saga and toxicity of glyphosate is Dr. Stephanie Seneff's *Toxic Legacy: How the Weedkiller Glyphosate Is Destroying Our Health and the Environment* (Chelsea Green Publishing, 2021). Bayer Corporation is leading efforts to insulate itself from legal liability by statutory immunity: see, e.g., "Bayer backs broadened effort to shield popular weedkiller from claims it failed to warn of cancer," Associated Press, February 10, 2025, accessed November 1, 2025, https://apnews.com/article/bayer-roundup-glyphosate-pesticide-liability-cancer-7d7885e55e228fae8ed8ec7b207a65b8.

17 "Bayer ordered to pay $2.25 billion after jury concludes Roundup weed killer caused a man's cancer, attorneys say," CNN.com, accessed November 1, 2025, https://www.cnn.com/2024/01/29/us/roundup-cancer-verdict-philadelphia-bayer-monsanto/index.html.

18 Krishna C. Thandra et al., "Epidemiology of Non-Hodgkin's Lymphoma," PubMed Central, accessed November 1, 2025, https://pmc.ncbi.nlm.nih.gov/articles/PMC7930980/#:~:text=NHL%20accounts%20for%204%25%20of%20US%20cancer%20diagnoses%2C,disease%20or%20a%20family%20history%20of%20hematological%20malignancies.

19 "In February 2020, after receiving and considering public comments on the glyphosate proposed interim decision, EPA published the interim decision registration review decision (ID) for glyphosate. As part of this action, EPA found that there are no risks of concern to human health when glyphosate is used in accordance with its current label. On June 17, 2022, the U.S. Court of Appeals for the Ninth Circuit vacated the human health portion of the glyphosate ID and held that EPA's registration review decision under FIFRA was an 'action' that triggered ESA obligations . . ." https://www.epa.gov/ingredients-used-pesticide-products/glyphosate.

20 "NAFTA Changed the Face of Mexico's Food System, Leading to Devastating Public Health Implications for its People," T. Colin Campbell Center for Nutrition Studies, accessed November 1, 2025, https://nutritionstudies.org/nafta-changed-the-face-of-mexicos-food-system-leading-to-devastating-public-health-implications-for-its-people/.

21 "Mexico is treating corn from the U.S. as a threat. Here's why," *National Geographic*, accessed November 1, 2025, https://www.nationalgeographic.com/environment/article/mexico-ban-genetically-modified-corn#:~:text=To%20protect%20this%20legacy%2C%20Mexico%20is%20fighting%20to,citizens%E2%80%99%20health%20and%20the%20country%E2%80%99s%20native%20corn%20varieties.

22 "Explainer: What is the US-Mexico GM corn dispute about?," Reuters, accessed November 1, 2025, https://www.reuters.com/markets/commodities/what-is-us-mexico-gm-corn-dispute-about-2023-03-08/.

23 "The U.S.-Mexico Genetically Engineered Corn Dispute," Congressional Research Service, accessed November 1, 2025, https://crsreports.congress.gov/product/pdf/R/R48083.

24 "Takeaways from Mexico's final rebuttal on the USMCA GM corn case," Institute for Agriculture & Trade Policy, accessed November 1, 2025, https://www.iatp.org/takeaways-mexicos-final-rebuttal-usmca-gm-corn-case.

25 "Does Glyphosate Affect the Human Microbiota?," PubMed Central, accessed November 1, 2025, https://pmc.ncbi.nlm.nih.gov/articles/PMC9145961/.

26 *Bowman v. Monsanto Co.,* 569 U.S. 278 (2013).

27 *Bowman v. Monsanto Co.,* 569 U.S. 278 (2013).

28 In 2011, a group of organic farmers sued Monsanto Corporation over the threat that the company would sue them for unintentionally appropriating Monsanto's patented seeds by cross-pollination. In dismissing their complaint, the United States Court of Appeals for the Federal Circuit ruled that they had no cause of action because Monsanto had promised it would not sue them. *Organic Seed Growers & Trade Assoc. V, Monsanto,* No. 12-1298 (Fed. Cir. 2013), 2013.

29 "Organic Farmer Dealt Final Blow in Landmark Lawsuit Over Monsanto's GMO Contamination," Ecowatch, accessed November 1, 2025, https://www.ecowatch.com/organic-farmer-dealt-final-blow-in-landmark-lawsuit-over-monsantos-gmo-1882173163.html.

30 "GMOs Plant Seeds For Corporate Control," Food & Water Watch, accessed November 1, 2025, https://www.foodandwaterwatch.org/2021/03/02/gmos-plant-seeds-corporate-control/.

31 Technically, Terminator gene technology is called "Genetic Use Restriction Technology," or GURT, and it consists of two categories: varietal GURTS (V-GURT) and trait GURTs (T-GURT). V-GURTs are genetic alterations that develop plants that grow and form seeds, but the second generation of seeds is sterile. T-GURTs incorporate the desired GMO trait (usually herbicide tolerance, i.e. "Roundup Ready"), but the trait is essentially "switched off" until a proprietary chemical "switch" is applied during growth to "activate" the valued traits. Terminator seeds are not presently in commercial use, but steady GURT patent filings indicate that many companies are waiting in the wings to unleash them.

32 "China White, Mexico's New Heroin Threatening the United States," InsightCrime.org, accessed November 1, 2025, https://insightcrime.org/news/analysis/china-white-mexico-new-heroin-threatening-united-states/.

33 "Tassel Emergence & Pollen Shed," Purdue University, accessed November 1, 2025, https://extension.entm.purdue.edu/newsletters/pestandcrop/article/tassel-emergence-pollen-shed/.

34 "Death by Crosspollination: The Uncontrollable Natural Occurrence That Could Kill Organic Farming and the Legal Solutions to Save an Industry," *Belmont Law*

Review: Vol. 7, Article 8, 2020, accessed November 1, 2025, https://repository.belmont.edu/lawreview/vol7/iss2/8/.

35 John Klar, "The Myth of GMOs Saving the Planet," Centre for Research on Globalization, accessed on November 1, 2025, https://www.globalresearch.ca/myth-gmos-saving-planet/5804013.

36 "Genetically modified crops support climate change mitigation," *Science Direct*, accessed October 26, 2025, https://www.globalresearch.ca/myth-gmos-saving-planet/5804013.

37 Susan L. Flader and, J. Baird Callicott, eds., Aldo Leopold "A Biotic View of Land," *The River of the Mother of God and Other Essays by Aldo Leopold* (University of Wisconsin Press, 1991), 269–270.

38 Wendell Berry, *It All Turns on Affection: The Jefferson Lecture & Other Essays* (Counterpoint Press, 2012), 22.

Chapter 3

1 Cormac McCarthy, *The Road* (Vintage International, 2006), 28.

2 "Iowa farmland consolidation expected to grow as state faces 'tidal wave' of transition," Des Moines Register, accessed November 1, 2025, https://www.desmoinesregister.com/story/money/agriculture/2025/08/05/iowa-farmland-consolidation-will-grow-experts-say/84429504007/?link_source=ta_first_comment&taid=6891dd33acc6ed00019b4610&utm_campaign=trueanthem&utm_medium=social&utm_source=facebook&fbclid=IwY2xjawMAVsRleHRuA2-FlbQIxMABicmlkETEzRHRIcm1WWWZpRzQ2bnBIAR6tPBF5E-xMOrx6h4qjSbp7p3_Dz4PCwmzBcw6rlrjGlYxM1TpRPOhXH-xoZQ_aem_qyZz0TjTeBsm6grLB8F_vA

3 "How Many Semi Trucks are on the Road?," truscksauthority.com, accessed November 1, 2025, https://trucksauthority.com/how-many-semi-trucks-are-on-the-road/; "Economics and Industry Data," American Trucking Associations, accessed November 1, 2025, https://www.trucking.org/economics-and-industry-data; "Semi Trucks: By the Numbers, HDS Truck Driving Institute, accessed November 1, 2025, https://hdstruckdrivinginstitute.com/blog/semi-trucks-numbers/.

4 "US ports by volume: How maritime cargo trends are stacking up," Supplychaindive, accessed November 1, 2025, https://www.supplychaindive.com/news/largest-us-ports-by-volume-month-coast-cargo-trends/693493/.

5 "Economics and Industry Data", American Trucking Association, accessed November 1, 2025, https://www.trucking.org/economics-and-industry-data.

6 "Long before Key Bridge collapse, Baltimore mariners warned of 'ship strikes'," *The Washington Post*, accessed November 1, 2025, https://www.washingtonpost.com/investigations/2024/05/23/key-bridge-warnings-ship-strikes/.

7 "What we know about the Baltimore bridge collapse," WEAA 88.9 FM, accessed November 1, 2025, https://www.weaa.org/local-news/2024-03-28/what-we-know-about-the-baltimore-bridge-collapse.

8 "Truck-to-truck worm could infect—and disrupt—entire US commercial fleet," *The Register*, accessed November 1, 2025, https://www.theregister.com/2024/03/22/boffins_tucktotruck_worm/.

9 The Colorado River serves as an agricultural water supply lifeline for numerous food-producing states, providing water to at least 40 million people in seven key states. It is estimated its continuing reduction in flow will be reduced an additional 20 percent in coming years. The Arizona Municipal Water Users Association calls the Colorado "the most endangered river in the United States." It is also the most important river for US agricultural production. "The Colorado River: An Overview of Its Present State and Challenges Ahead," Arizona Municipal Water Users Association, accessed November 1, 2025, https://www.amwua.org/blog/the-colorado-river-an-overview-of-its-present-state-and-challenges-ahead.

10 "USGS releases a comprehensive look at water resources in the United States," United States Geological Service, accessed November 1, 2025: "The assessment found that nearly 30 million people live in areas where available surface-water supplies are limited relative to water use, indicating a high level of water limitation." https://www.usgs.gov/news/national-news-release/usgs-releases-a-comprehensive-look-water-resources-united-states; "Water scarcity in agriculture: An overview of causes, impacts and approaches for reducing the risks,"PubMed Central, accessed November 1, 2025, https://pmc.ncbi.nlm.nih.gov/articles/PMC10392093/; "324 contaminants found in drinking water systems across US: Research," *The Hill*, accessed November 2, 2–25: "A survey of nearly 50,000 water networks nationwide revealed a staggering 324 different contaminants flowing out of American taps—with detectable levels of various pollutants showing up in nearly all water systems" https://thehill.com/policy/energy-environment/5164926-contaminants-american-tap-water-research/.

11 See, e.g., "The Ogallala Aquifer: When will the wells run dry? What then?," which estimates that the largest aquifer in North America could run dry in 25 years at current depletion rates. Myhighplains.com, accessed October 26, 2025, https://www.myhighplains.com/water-and-drought-on-the-high-plains/the-ogallala-aquifer-when-will-the-wells-run-dry-what-then/; "Ogallala Aquifer Could Dry Up in 20 Years—Yet It's Rarely Discussed," Climate Cosmos, accessed October 26, 2025, https://climatecosmos.com/climate-news/ogallala-aquifer-could-dry-up-in-20-years-yet-its-rarely-discussed/.

12 "Farmers are depleting the Ogallala Aquifer because the government pays them to do it," The Coversation, accessed November 2, 2025, https://theconversation.com/farmers-are-depleting-the-ogallala-aquifer-because-the-government-pays-them-to-do-it-145501.

13 For example, Joel Salatin and others report that in order to receive crop subsidies, cotton and other farmers in arid regions are required to continue watering dead crops following drought.

14 "Soil in Midwestern U.S. eroding 10 to 1,000 times faster than it forms," U.S. National Science Foundation, accessed November 2, 2025, https://www.nsf.gov/news/soil-midwestern-us-eroding-10-1000-times-faster-it#:~:text=In%20a%20discovery%20that%20has%20repercussions%20for%20everything,to%201%2C000%20times%20greater%20than%20pre-agricultural%20erosion%20rates.

15 "Midwestern US has lost 57. 6 trillion metric tons of soil due to agricultural practices," *Science Daily*, accessed November 3, 2025, https://www.sciencedaily.com/releases/2022/03/220316114958.htm.

16 "New Evidence Shows Fertile Soil Gone From Midwestern Farms," National Public Radio, accessed November 3, 2025, https://www.npr.org/2021/02/24/967376880/new-evidence-shows-fertile-soil-gone-from-midwestern-farms.

17 "Why is the San Joaquin Valley important?," Studycountry.com, accessed November 3, 2025, https://www.studycountry.com/wiki/why-is-the-san-joaquin-valley-important.

18 "SAN JOAQUIN VALLEY, CALIFORNIA Largest human alteration of the Earth's surface," USGS, accessed November 3, 2025, https://pubs.usgs.gov/circ/circ1182/pdf/06SanJoaquinValley.pdf.

19 "The deadly 1862 California flood that wiped out and reshaped the state," SFGate.com, accessed November 3, 2025, https://www.sfgate.com/weather/article/deadly-1862-flood-wiped-out-california-16761390.php.

20 "Will climate change cause a repeat of the Great Flood of 1862 in California?," AS.com, accessed November 3, 2025,https://en.as.com/latest_news/will-climate-change-cause-a-repeat-of-the-great-flood-of-1862-in-california-n/.

21 Arizona, which in 2018 was the nation's third largest producer of vegetables, boasts 26 million acres of land used for farms and ranches. In 1893, Arizona faced a devastating drought in which "The southern Arizona cattle population was decimated with up to 75% of all livestock dying. What was left was raced to market where prices plummeted." "Arizona Ranching in the Beginning . . ." Arizona Farm Bureau, accessed November 3, 2025, https://www.azfb.org/Article/Arizona-Ranching-In-the-Beginning.

22 "Drought and Agriculture," Food and Agriculture Organization of the United Nations, accessed November 3, 2025, https://www.fao.org/land-water/water/drought/droughtandag/en/.

23 "2023: A historic year of U.S. billion-dollar weather and climate disasters," climate.gov, accessed November 3, 2025, https://www.climate.gov/news-features/blogs/beyond-data/2023-historic-year-us-billion-dollar-weather-and-climate-disasters.

24 The US can surely increase domestic oil production, but even domestic supplies are not limitless. Treating limited natural resources as endless will simply kick these problems onto the backs of future generations (like the US debt and firehose of forever chemicals). Costs of fuel extraction will likely increase over time as easily accessible supplies are drawn down, regardless of whether the world has reached the "Peak Oil" production zenith. Over time, fossil fuel prices will steadily increase regardless of monetary inflation, but are vulnerable to sloppy monetary policy and overspending independently of supply threats.

25 This is offered as a theoretical, not necessarily a literal, forecast—much depends on improving agricultural efficiency and independence from energy price shocks preemptively.

26 "Russia: EMP Threat, The Russian Federation's Military Doctrine, Plans, and Capabilities for Electromagnetic Pulse (EMP) Attack," EMP Task Force on National and Homeland Security, accessed November 3, 2025, AD1124730.pdf (dtic.mil): "The United States and NATO allies regularly experience from Russia major cyber-attacks penetrating government agencies and critical infrastructures for electric power, telecommunications, transportation and other sectors vital to electronic civilization. These events practice a new way of warfare, including EMP attacks, that could blackout North America and NATO Europe, and win World War III at the speed of light. Any nuclear weapon detonated in outer space, 30 kilometers or higher, will generate a high-altitude electromagnetic pulse (HEMP) damaging all kinds of electronics, blacking-out electric grids and collapsing other life-sustaining critical infrastructures. . . . Russia probably remains the world's leader in Non-Nuclear EMP (NNEMP) weapons, also called Radio-Frequency Weapons (RFWs). Marriage of NNEMP to drones or cruise missiles, equipped with sensors to follow high-power electric lines and target control centers and transformers, introduces a major new threat to national power grids."

27 "The real-world impacts of cyberattacks," *Security Magazine*, accessed November 3, 2025, https://www.bing.com/search?q=The%20real-world%20impacts%20of%20cyberattacks%20Kimberly%20Johnson%2C&qs=n&form=QBRE&sp=-1&ghc=1&lq=0&pq=the%20real-world%20impacts%20of%20cyberattacks%20kimberly%20johnson%2C&sc=7-56&sk=&cvid=893E51FEAA6B470BB5398722767DF49A&ghsh=0&ghacc=0&ghpl=.

28 "Trends and disparities in concurrent tap water avoidance and household food insecurity among US children," *Nature Water*, accessed November 3, 2025, https://pmc.ncbi.nlm.nih.gov/articles/PMC12162046/.

29 "122 million more people pushed into hunger since 2019 due to multiple crises, reveals UN report," UNICEF, accessed November 3, 2025, https://www.unicef.org/press-releases/122-million-more-people-pushed-hunger-2019-due-multiple-crises-reveals-un-report.

30 "The hunger forecast: How a team of scientists studying drought helped build the world's leading famine prediction model," Science.org, accessed November 3, 2025, https://www.science.org/content/article/how-team-scientists-studying-drought-helped-build-world-s-leading-famine-prediction.

31 "US Population by Year," multpl.com, accessed November 3, 2025, https://www.multpl.com/united-states-population/table/by-year.

32 "USDA horse total, 1850–2012," Data padlock, accessed November 3, 2025, https://datapaddock.com/usda-horse-total-1850-2012/.

33 "2023 Economic Impact Study," American Horse Council, accessed November 3, 2025, https://horsecouncil.org/economic-impact-study/; "Business Briefs: Horse Industry Statistics Veterinarians Should Know," EquiManagement, accessed November 3, 2025, https://equimanagement.com/business-development/business-briefs/business-briefs-horse-industry-statistics-veterinarians-should-know/.

34 An estimated resident population of 341,701,720 as of November 1, 2025, census.gov, accessed November 3, 2025, https://www.census.gov/data/tables/time-series/demo/popest/2020s-national-total.html.

35 "A history of Vermont dairy," *Bennington Banner*, accessed November 3, 2025, https://www.benningtonbanner.com/opinion/columnists/a-history-of-vermont-dairy/article_ce657e9e-32c8-525c-8e48-4127a566a698.html.

36 "Vermont Dairy Data 2024 Production, Impacts, and Trends," Vermont Agency of Agriculture, Food, and Markets, accessed November 3, 2025, https://legislature.vermont.gov/Documents/2024/WorkGroups/House%20Agriculture/Topics%20in%20Agriculture/Dairy/W~Laura%20Ginsburg~Dairy%20Update%20Presentation~4-18-2024.pdf.

37 "What Experts Really Think About Diet Soda," *Time*, accessed November 3, 2025, https://time.com/6964018/diet-soda-health-effects/.

38 "Heavy metals in baby food? What parents should know and do," Harvard Health Publishing, accessed November 3, 2025, https://www.health.harvard.edu/blog/heavy-metals-in-baby-food-what-parents-should-know-and-do-2021030522088.; "Baby Foods Are Tainted with Dangerous Levels of Arsenic, Lead, Cadmium, and Mercury," Subcommittee on Economic and Consumer Policy Committee on Oversight and Reform U.S. House of Representatives, accessed November 3, 2025, https://oversightdemocrats.house.gov/sites/evo-subsites/democrats-oversight.house.gov/files/2021-02-04%20ECP%20Baby%20Food%20Staff%20Report.pdf.

39 *Recipe for a Livable Planet: Achieving Net Zero Emissions in the Agrifood System*, World Bank Group, 43, accessed November 3, 2025, https://openknowledge.worldbank.org/entities/publication/406c71a3-c13f-49cd-8f3f-a071715858fb.

Chapter 4

1 Ernest Hemingway, "Notes on the Next War: A Serious Topical Letter," *Esquire*, Sept. 1935."*The Hemingway Collection,*" 2014, 417.

2 Historian John Lukacs's presciently observed in 2002 that humanity now possesses an unprecedented capacity to destroy itself by toxification of the planet: "For the first time since Genesis (or: in the history of mankind) it has now become

not only imaginable but possible for human beings to destroy large portions (or, potentially, all) of humanity, and perhaps even most of life on this earth. This may happen by man-made explosions or by man-made posioning of the atmosphere by disastrous genetic manipulations: we (still fortunately) do not know." John Lukacs, *At the End of an Age* (Yale University Press, 2002), 192.

3 Grass-fed farmers will still face inflationary pressures, especially for winter hay stock-piling. This will vary to a great degree based on climate: Vermont farms must store about two hundred days of feed for winter: some farms in Florida pasture their livestock nearly year-round. All grass-fed livestock production will be more immune to input cost than for grain-fed animals: chickens and swine are highly dependent on grain crops.

4 Off-farm organic products such as lime, greensand, potash, rock phosphate, etc, will not be immune from inflation but may be reduced or eliminated in regenerative systems.

5 $1,572,000,000: "U.S. National Debt by Year," Investopedia, accessed November 5, 2025, https://www.investopedia.com/us-national-debt-by-year-7499291.

6 "When Does Federal Debt Reach Unsustainable Levels?," Penn Wharton Budget Model, accessed November 3, 2025, https://budgetmodel.wharton.upenn.edu/issues/2023/10/6/when-does-federal-debt-reach-unsustainable-levels.

7 Spending did drop as a percentage of GDP during Bill Clinton's presidency, but this was attributable to the explosive short-term wealth generated by the dot-com boom under his watch, not administration policymaking.

8 "National debt in the United States in relation to gross domestic product (GDP) from 2019 to 2022, with a forecast to 2029," Statista, accessed November 3, 2025, https://www.statista.com/statistics/269960/national-debt-in-the-us-in-relation-to-gross-domestic-product-gdp/#:~:text=The%20statistic%20shows%20the%20national%20debt%20of%20the,around%20120.03%20percent%20of%20the%20gross%20domestic%20product.

9 "'The Day the Dollar Died' is coming. What's the plan?," Committee for a Responsible Federal Budget, accessed November 3, 2025, https://www.crfb.org/blogs/mitch-daniels-day-dollar-died-coming-whats-plan.

10 This 120 percent number is cautiously conservative.

11 James Rickards, *Sold Out: How Broken Supply Chains, Surging Inflation, and Political Instability Will Sink the Global Economy* (Portfolio/Penguin, 2022), 194.

12 James Rickards, *Sold Out: How Broken Supply Chains, Surging Inflation, and Political Instability Will Sink the Global Economy* (Portfolio/Penguin, 2022), xix, 198.

13 James Rickards, *MoneyGPT: AI and the Threat to the Global Economy* (Portfolio/Penguin, 2024), 47–48.

14 "What is a BRICS currency and is the U.S. dollar in trouble?," Reuters, accessed November 3, 2025, https://www.reuters.com/markets/currencies/what-is-brics-currency-is-us-dollar-trouble-2024-12-17/.

15 "The BRICS Challenge and the US Response: A New Era of Gold," *The Jerusalem Post*, Accessed November 3, 2025, https://www.jpost.com/business-and-innovation/precious-metals/article-821429#:~:text=The%20BRICS%20challenge%20poses%20significant%20threats%20to%20the,nations%20to%20purchase%20gold%2C%20solidifying%20the%20BRICS%27%20leverage.

16 "What is Hyperinflation? Causes, Effects, Examples and How to Prepare," Investopedia, accessed November 3, 2025, https://www.investopedia.com/terms/h/hyperinflation.asp#:~:text=Hyperinflation%20is%20a%20scenario%20in%20which%20a%20country%27s,its%20financial%20obligations%20or%20produce%20goods%20and%20services

17 "Hyperinflation Throughout History: Examples and Impact," Investopedia, accessed November 3, 2025, https://www.investopedia.com/ask/answers/061515/what-are,-some-historic-examples-hyperinflation.asp.

18 Ibid.

19 "On the Measurement of Zimbabwe's Hyperinflation," *Cato Journal*, Vol. 29, No. 2 (Spring/Summer 2009), accessed November 3, 2025, cato123448v26n2_2up.q

20 "What caused hyperinflation in Venezuela: a rare blend of public ineptitude and private enterprise," *The Conversation*, accessed November 5, 2025, https://theconversation.com/what-caused-hyperinflation-in-venezuela-a-rare-blend-of-public-ineptitude-and-private-enterprise-102483.

21 "Venezuela inflation has cooled—but voters say they still can't make ends meet," Reuters, accessed November 5, 2025, https://www.reuters.com/world/americas/venezuela-inflation-has-cooled-voters-say-they-still-cant-make-ends-meet-2024-07-23/#:~:text=CARACAS,%20July%2023%20%28Reuters%29%20-%20The%20government%20of%20Venezuelan%20President.

22 "Modern monetary theory: the rise of economists who say huge government debt is not a problem," *The Conversation*, accessed November 5, 2025, https://theconversation.com/modern-monetary-theory-the-rise-of-economists-who-say-huge-government-debt-is-not-a-problem-141495#:~:text=This%20observation%20is%20the%20root%20of%20modern%20monetary%20theory%20%28MMT%29.

23 "Is modern monetary theory too good to be true?" The Brookings Institution, accessed November 5, 2025, https://www.brookings.edu/articles/is-modern-monetary-theory-too-good-to-be-true/.

24 "Why 43 million acres in US are owned by foreign nations," *Deseret News*, accessed November 5, 2025, https://www.ksl.com/article/51130319/why-43-million-acres-in-us-are-owned-by-foreign-nations--#:~:text=WASHINGTON%20%E2%80%94%20An%20Idaho%20congressman%20is%20asserting%20more%20than%2043.

25 John Maynard Keynes, *The Economic Consequences of the Peace*, Skyhorse Publishing, 2016, 121.

26 "Fiscal Cliff Debate Is About Size of Government, Not Taxing 'the Rich'," RealClearPolitics, accessed November 5, 2025, https://www.realclearpolitics.com/articles/2012/12/04/fiscal_cliff_notes_part_ii_116325.html.

27 Milton Friedman, *Money Mischief: Episodes in Monetary History* (Harcort Brace & Company, 1994), 49.

28 "What's Inflation?," accessed November 5, 2025, http://walterewilliams.com/what%27s-inflation/#:~:text=When%20there%E2%80%99s%20a%20general%20increase%20in%20prices,%20or%20alternatively,%20a.

29 "'The world's largest Ponzi scheme': Peter Schiff just blasted the US debt ceiling drama. Here are the 3 assets he trusts amid major market craziness," *Moneywise*, accessed November 5, 2025, https://finance.yahoo.com/news/world-largest-ponzi-scheme-peter-150000344.html?guccounter=1.

30 "U.S. Agricultural Trade at a Glance," US Department of Agriculture, Economic Research Service, accessed November 5, 2025, https://www.ers.usda.gov/topics/international-markets-us-trade/us-agricultural-trade/us-agricultural-trade-at-a-glance.

31 "U.S. Agricultural Trade at a Glance," US Department of Agriculture Economic Research Service, Figure 1 (U.S. exports of bulk and high-value commodities, 1994–2023) and 7 (U.S. imports of bulk and high-value commodities, 1994–2023), accessed November 5, 2025, https://www.ers.usda.gov/topics/international-markets-us-trade/us-agricultural-trade/us-agricultural-trade-at-a-glance.

Chapter 5

1 Quoted by Judith D. Schwartz, *Cows Save the Planet: And Other Improbable Ways of Restoring Soil to Heal the Earth* (Chelsea Green Publishing, 2013) 153.

2 "Ecological Impact of Lawns," NASA Earth Observatory, "[Researcher Cristina] Milesi says that a well-watered and fertilized lawn is a carbon sink [a place that absorbs more carbon than it releases]. If people recycle the grass clippings, leaving them to decompose on the lawn, the U.S. lawn area could store up to 16.7 teragrams of carbon each year. That's equivalent to about 37 billion pounds—the weight of about 147,000 blue whales. The fact that recycling the clippings on the lawn would be so productive is a little surprising, according to Milesi. . . . After all, decomposing grass is a source of carbon, with bacterial activity releasing carbon dioxide back into the atmosphere. The growth boost provided by the recycling of nitrogen from the decomposing grass clippings more than makes up for the carbon being released." accessed November 5, 2025, https://earthobservatory.nasa.gov/features/Lawn/lawn3.php. In language that recalls Judith Schwartz's remark that science as religion blocks critical thought, the NASA page regarding the ecological impacts of lawns claims "This page contains archived content and

is no longer being updated. At the time of publication, it represented the best available science."

3 "The beef industry is quick to point out that grain-fed (i.,e., corn-fed) beef produces *less* methane than grass-fed beef. Yes, less. Their reasoning goes like this: since they fatten the cows faster, CAFOs claim they produce less CO_2 and methane *per pound of beef produced.* However, this assertion disregards most of the greenhouse gases produced along the life cycle of CAFO meat production, from the fossil fuels to the fertilizer for the field corn, to the energy to transport that field corn to cows, to the pollution from manure lagoons." Josh Tickell, *Kiss the Ground: How the Food You Eat Can Reverse Climate Change, Heal Your Body & Ultimately Save the World* (Enliven Books, 2017), 197. The naturally grazed animals are also happier and healthier, and the products created for human consumption become more nutrient dense and healthy for humans as well. Gabe Brown explains: "From a livestock perspective, the goal of producing more and more pounds per animal led to raising animals in confinement. Dairy cows and beef cattle were taken off pasture, where they once benefited the ecosystem by grazing living plants, thus scycling [recycling?]more carbon. Instead, today they are raised in confined quarters. Their diets were changed by the all-knowing authorities from forages to high-starch grains, affecting the animals' health and longevity. . . . And the milk, cheeses, and other dairy products from this system are much less nutrient-dense, which is impacting human health as well." Gabe Brown, *Dirt to Soil: One Family's Journey into Regenerative Agriculture* (Chelsea Green Publishing, 2018), 177.

4 "There seems to be little correlation between methane levels and the number of ruminants. A joint report from the the UN's Food and Agriculture Organization (FAO) and International Atomic Energy Agency (IAEA) noted that since 1999 atmospheric methane concentrations have been stable while the population of ruminants worldwide grew at a rapid rate, raising the question of whether livestock play much of a role in the greenhouse gas situation." Judith D. Schwartz, *Cows Save the Planet: And Other Improbable Ways of Restoring Soil to Heal the Earth* (Chelsea Green Publishing, 2013), 27.

5 "Methane's role in climate change," Harvard John A. Paulson School of Engineering and Applied Sciences, accessed November 5, 2025, https://seas.harvard.edu/news/2023/02/methanes-role-climate-change; Over a 100-year span, methane is rated as 27–30 times more potent than carbon dioxide: "Understanding Global Warming Potentials," US Environmental Protection Agency, accessed November 5, 2025, https://www.epa.gov/ghgemissions/understanding-global-warming-potentials.

6 "Understanding Global Warming Potentials," US Environmental Protection Agency, accessed November 5, 2025, https://www.epa.gov/ghgemissions/understanding-global-warming-potentials.

7 "Livestock, Methane, and Climate Change: The Politics of Global Assessments," *Wiley Interdisciplinary Reviews*, accessed November 5, 2025, https://wires.onlinelibrary.wiley.com/doi/10.1002/wcc.790.

8 Ibid.

9 Ibid.

10 Scoones adds: "a number of well-known studies from the United Nations Food and Agriculture Organization have carried out such assessments, starting with the much-debated *Livestock's Long Shadow* (Steinfeld et al., 2006; see also Glatzle, 2014), and more recently the report, *Tackling Climate Change through Livestock* (Gerber et al., 2013). The latter came up with the now much-repeated "iconic fact" that 14.5% of total anthropogenic greenhouse emissions come from livestock." Ibid.

11 Ibid.

12 ". . . we're trying to World War II our way to better food. Nowhere is that more clear than with our use of copious amounts of synthetic nitrogen fertilizer. " Josh Tickell, *Kiss the Ground: How the Food You Eat Can Reverse Climate Change, Heal Your Body & Ultimately Save the World* (Enliven Books, 2017), 139, 141.

13 Josh Tickell, *Kiss the Ground: How the Food You Eat Can Reverse Climate Change, Heal Your Body & Ultimately Save the World* (Enliven Books, 2017), 140: "On a per-bushel basis our nutrient-use efficiency, especially nitrogen, has declined. So although we have increased the amount of crops we are producing per acre, it's actually taking more nitrogen on a per-bushel basis to produce a bushel of grain today than it took to produce a bushel of grain in 1960 . . ." Josh Tickell, *Kiss the Ground: How the Food You Eat Can Reverse Climate Change, Heal Your Body & Ultimately Save the World* (Enliven Books, 2017), 140, 141. See also, Gabe Brown, *Dirt to Soil: One Fanily's Journey into Regenerative Agriculture* (Chelsea Green Publishing, 2018), 175. "Breeders have been selecting for traits such as yield and not noticing that in the process other traits—such as the ability to form relationships with fungi—are lost."

14 "Manure that we currently treat as waste could, once again, meet as much as a third of global fertilizer needs. . . . Unlike many technologies to mitigate fossil fuel emissions, soil-building practices can be implemented immediately at low cost." David R. Montgomery, *Growing a Revolution: Bringing Our Soil Back to Life* (W. W. Norton & Company, 2017), 195, 228.

15 "Peter Sweden: UNREAL- Danish CARBON TAX on Cows," The Gateway Pundit, accessed November 5, 2025, https://www.thegatewaypundit.com/2024/10/peter-sweden-unreal-danish-carbon-tax-cows/.

16 Krasimir Bozhurin, "Fertilizer Trends & Market Insights for 2024 and Beyond," Vakichim, accessed November 5, 2025, https://growplant.org/blog/fertilizer-trends/.

17 "Fertilizer market review: What will 2024 bring?," AGProud, accessed November 5, 2025, https://www.agproud.com/articles/58574-fertilizer-market-review-what-will-2024-bring.

18 "Fertilizer Use and Price—Summary of Findings," USDA Economic Research Service, asscessed November 5, 2025, https://www.ers.usda.gov/data-products/fertilizer-use-and-price/summary-of-findings/.

19 Krasimir Bozhurin, "Fertilizer Trends & Market Insights for 2024 and Beyond," Vakichim, accessed November 5, 2025,https://growplant.org/blog/fertilizer-trends/.

20 ""Farm to Fork Initiative to Restrict European Union Agricultural Inputs May Increase Food Prices, Further Global Insecurity," USDA Economic Research Service, accessed November 5, 2025, https://www.ers.usda.gov/amber-waves/2021/march/farm-to-fork-initiative-to-restrict-european-union-agricultural-inputs-may-increase-food-prices-further-global-food-insecurity.

21 "Report: Fertilizer responsible for more than 20 percent of total agricultural emissions," *The Fern*, accessed November 5, 2025, https://thefern.org/ag_insider/report-fertilizer-responsible-for-more-than-20-percent-of-total-agricultural-emissions/#:~:text=The%20amount%20of%20synthetic%20nitrogen%20fertilizers%20used%20worldwide%20has%20grown.

22 "We can't live without industrially-produced fertilizer, a $212 billion industry, but it is responsible for 3% of greenhouse gas. More than one percent of the world's total energy production goes to produce nitrogen fertilizer. Developed countries contend with waterways polluted from leaching nitrogen, while adequate fertilizer is often inaccessible or too expensive for farmers in developing countries." "Synthetic fertilizer: Can't live with it, can't live without it," *Farm Progress*, accessed November 5, 2025, https://www.farmprogress.com/farm-operations/synthetic-fertilizer-can-t-live-with-it-can-t-live-without-it.

23 "Report: Fertilizer responsible for more than 20 percent of total agricultural emissions," *The Fern*, accessed November 5, 2025, https://thefern.org/ag_insider/report-fertilizer-responsible-for-more-than-20-percent-of-total-agricultural-emissions/#:~:text=The%20amount%20of%20synthetic%20nitrogen%20fertilizers%20used%20worldwide%20has%20grown ". . . researchers calculated emissions all along the production chain, from manufacturing to transport to application and even runoff of fertilizer into waterways. Taken together, these emissions amounted to the equivalent of 1,250 million tonnes of CO2 in 2018—more than a fifth of total estimated direct emissions from agriculture worldwide. In comparison, the commercial aviation industry—whose contributions to global warming are well recognized—emitted around 900 million tonnes of greenhouse gasses in 2018. . . . Fertilizers also are linked to a host of other environmental ills, including air and water pollution that occurs when the fertilizers aren't fully used by crops, dead zones and algal blooms in ocean and freshwater ecosystems, and depletion of the ozone layer."

24 "'I am not part of the problem': Bill Gates says his private jet and climate activism are compatible," Euronews, accessed November 5, 2025, https://www.euronews.com/green/2023/02/09/i-am-not-part-of-the-problem-bill-gates-says-his-private-jet-and-climate-activism-are-comp.

25 "Study shows EV owners have bigger carbon footprint than average because they are wealthier," Phys.org, accessed November 5, 2025, https://phys.org/news/2024-10-ev-owners-bigger-carbon-footprint.html#:~:text=The%20researchers%20found%20that%20people%20who%20purchase%20EVs%20tend%20to.

26 *The Great Plant-based Con: Why eating a plants-only diet won't improve your health or save the planet* (Piatkus, 2022), 301.

27 "These Ultra-Processed Plant-Based Foods Might Increase the Risk For Many Diseases," *Inverse*, accessed November 5, 2025, https://www.inverse.com/health/ultra-processed-plant-based-foods-unhealthy-study#:~:text=In%20fact,%20ultra-processed%20plant-sourced%20foods%20%28think:%20french%20fries%29%20can%20increase; "Study Says Processed Plant-Based Diets Can Hurt Heart Health," *Woman's World*, accessed November 6, 2025, https://www.womansworld.com/wellness/study-says-processed-plant-based-diets-can-hurt-heart-health#:~:text=Ultra-processed%20food%20has%20long%20been%20linked%20to%20potential%20negative%20heart.

28 "In 2021, the *New York Times* reported that serious questions about the environmental credentials of plant-based meat companies remained. 'One investor tracking firm gives Beyond Meat a zero when it comes to sustainability measures. Another rates it a "severe risk," the paper reported. The problem, say the critics interviewed, is that 'neither Beyond Meat, nor Impossible Foods discloses the total amount of the greenhouse gases emissions across all of its operations, supply chains or consumer waste.' . . ." Jayne Buxton, *The Great Plant-based Con: Why eating a plants-only diet won't improve your health or save the planet* (Piatkus, 2022), 293.

29 Judith D. Schwartz, *Cows Save the Planet: And Other Improbable Ways of Restoring Soil to Heal the Earth* (Chelsea Green Publishing, 2013), 145.

30 "Insiders Reveal Major Problems at Lab-Grown-Meat Startup Upside Foods," Wired, accessed November 6, 2025, https://www.wired.com/story/upside-foods-lab-grown-chicken/.

31 "Insect Farming: The Industry set to be Worth $8 Billion by 2030," *Hive Life*, accessed November 6, 2025, https://hivelife.com/insect-farming/.

32 "12 Signs That The Globalist Plan For Us To "Eat Ze Bugs" Has Already Become A Reality For Billions Of People," *The Most Important News*, accessed November 6, 2025, https://themostimportantnews.com/archives/12-facts-that-prove-that-people-all-over-the-globe-are-already-eating-the-bugs-on-a-regular-basis#:~:text=.

33 "A giant indoor farm in China is breeding 6 billion cockroaches a year. Here's why," *South China Morning Post*, accessed November 6, 2025, https://www.scmp.com/news/china/society/article/2142316/giant-indoor-farm-china-breeding-six-billion-cockroaches-year.

34 "The world's largest insect farm is being built in France," *Euronews*, accessed November 6, 2025, https://www.euronews.com/green/2020/10/26/the-world-s-largest-insect-farm-is-being-built-in-france.

35 "12 Signs That The Globalist Plan For Us To "Eat Ze Bugs" Has Already Become A Reality For Billions Of People," *The Most Important News*, accessed November 6, 2025, https://themostimportantnews.com/archives/12-facts-that-prove-that-people-all-over-the-globe-are-already-eating-the-bugs-on-a-regular-basis#:~:text=.

36 "CRISPR and Garlic could offer relief from climate-killing cow burps, farts," Interesting Engineering, accessed November 6, 2025, https://interestingengineering.com/innovation/crispr-garlic-solution-climate-killing-cow-farts.

37 "The amount of methane cattle generate has a lot to do with how livestock is managed. According to Anrea Malmberg, director of research at the Savory Institute, when cattle are in crowded feedlots, the manure is handled in liquid form, in lagoons or holding tanks—an ideal scenario for the production of methane. If, however, cattle graze on fields in lowered concentration, the manure becomes fertilizer. She adds: 'These are human decisions, not cows'.'" Judith D. Schwartz, *Cows Save the Planet: And Other Improbable Ways of Restoring Soil to Heal the Earth* (Chelsea Green Publishing, 2013), 27.

38 "Avoiding meat and dairy is 'single biggest way' to reduce your impact on Earth," *The Guardian*, accessed November 6, 2025, https://www.theguardian.com/environment/2018/may/31/avoiding-meat-and-dairy-is-single-biggest-way-to-reduce-your-impact-on-earth.

39 "Electric Vehicle Myths," US Environmental Protection Agency, accessed November 6, 2025, https://www.epa.gov/greenvehicles/electric-vehicle-myths#Myth2.

40 "The Environmental Impacts of Cobalt Mining in Congo, Earth.org, accessed November 6, 2025, https://earth.org/cobalt-mining-in-congo/.

41 "EV Juggernaut China Leads World in New Coal Power Plants," *Newsweek*, accessed November 6, 2025, https://www.newsweek.com/china-coal-power-plants-juggernaut-new-ev-1868930; "China builds more new coal plants than rest of the world," NPR, accessed November 6, 2025, https://www.npr.org/2023/03/02/1160441919/china-is-building-six-times-more-new-coal-plants-than-other-countries-report-fin.

42 "Tire Dust Makes Up the Majority of Ocean Microplastics: Study," The Drive, accessed November 6, 2025, https://www.thedrive.com/news/tire-dust-makes-up-the-majority-of-ocean-microplastics-study-finds.

43 "A dead battery dilemma," *Science*, accessed November 6, 2025, https://www.science.org/content/article/millions-electric-cars-are-coming-what-happens-all-dead-batteries.

Chapter 6

1 "On Farmers, Food, and France: An Interview with MEP Patricia Chagnon," *The European Conservative*, accessed November 6, 2025, https://europeanconservative.com/articles/interviews/this-globalist-right-and-this-ecological-extremist-left-have-found-a-common-enemy-european-agriculture-an-interview-with-rassemblement-national-mep-patricia-chagnon/.

2 Wendell Berry has cautioned of the folly of surrendering conservation to government authority: "If in order to protect our forest land we designate it a commons or commonwealth separate from private ownership, then who will care for it? The absentee timber companies who see no reason to care about local consequences? The same government agents and agencies who are failing at present to take good care of our public forests? Is it credible that people inadequately skilled and inadequately motivated to care well for the land can be made to care well for it by public insistence that they do so? The answer is obvious: you cannot get good care in the use of land by demanding it from public officials. . . . The idea that a displaced people might take appropriate care of places is merely absurd. . . . If we want the land to be cared for, then we must have people living on and from the land who are able and willing to care for it." Wendell Berry, *Private Property and the Common Wealth,* delivered as a speech at a conference on "The Forest Commons," March 31, 1995, Synergic Earth Network, accessed November 6, 2025, https://synearth.net/private-property-and-the-common-wealth/.

3 Judith Schwartz, *Cows Save the Planet* (Chelsea Green Publishing, 2013), 71.

4 "FACT SHEET: President Biden to Take Action to Uphold Commitment to Restore Balance on Public Lands and Waters, Invest in Clean Energy Future," US Department of the Interior, accessed November 6, 2025, https://www.doi.gov/pressreleases/fact-sheet-president-biden-take-action-uphold-commitment-restore-balance-public-lands#:~:text=The%20Executive%20Action%20will%20direct%20the%20Interior%20Department%20to%20outline.

5 "FACT SHEET: President Biden to Take Action to Uphold Commitment to Restore Balance on Public Lands and Waters, Invest in Clean Energy Future," US Department of the Interior, accessed November 6, 2025, https://www.doi.gov/pressreleases/fact-sheet-president-biden-take-action-uphold-commitment-restore-balance-public-lands#:~:text=The%20Executive%20Action%20will%20direct%20the%20Interior%20Department%20to%20outline.

6 "Post misrepresents John Kerry's speech at AIM for Climate Summit | Fact check," *USA Today*, accessed November 6, 2025, https://www.usatoday.com/story/news/factcheck/2023/06/06/john-kerry-proposed-farming-innovation-at-climate-summit-fact-check/70288331007/.

7 A similar question must be raised with regard to powerful international voices claiming a plant-based diet is the only way to feed the world and save the planet: "The head of the World Health Organization (WHO) has said a shift towards more plant-based diets is 'essential' for the health of people and planet. Dr. Tedros Adhanom Ghebreyesus . . . noted that food production is responsible for 'almost one third of the global burden of disease' and 30 percent of global greenhouse gas emissions. The majority of these emissions are from animal agriculture." "Transforming food systems is therefore essential, by shifting towards healthier, diversified, and more plant-based diets." ""World Health Organization Head Calls For Plant-Based Diet Shift," *Plant Based News*, accessed November 6, 2025, https://plantbasednews.org/news/environment

/world-health-organization-head-calls-for-plant-based-diet-shift/#:~:text=The%20head%20of%20the%20World%20Health%20Organization%20%28WHO%29%20has%20said.

8 The EU has sought to reduce pesticides, synthetic fertilizer and GMO crops as part of its Farm to Fork version of the US Green New Deal. There is no government push to reduce the nation's dependency on these inputs in domestic agriculture. In response to farmer revolts, the USDA, and globalist industrial interests, the EU has now paused its Farm to Fork policies. "The [EU] Commission is now hustling to authorize genetically modified crops on the European market, a measure that would have been impossible to pass just a few years ago. The tone has changed in Brussels." "Why Europe's 'Farm to Fork' policies collapsed," Competitive Enterprise Institute, accessed November 6, 2025, https://cei.org/blog/why-europes-farm-to-fork-policies-collapsed/; "From farm to flop? Political risks choke EU's green food plan," *Politico*, accessed November 6, 2025, https://www.politico.eu/article/blocked-and-delayed-political-risks-choke-eus-green-food-plan-farmers/.

9 "Operation Market Garden (1944): Summary, Date, & Significance, Britannica, accessed November 6, 2025, https://www.britannica.com/event/Operation-Market-Garden.

10 "Netherlands announces €25bn plan to radically reduce livestock numbers," *The Guardian*, accessed November 6, 2025, https://www.theguardian.com/environment/2021/dec/15/netherlands-announces-25bn-plan-to-radically-reduce-livestock-numbers.

11 Ibid. The article hinted at similar battles to come in other EU nations: "The Netherlands is not the only country in Europe facing a crisis over livestock emissions, with observers suggesting Denmark, Belgium and Germany may soon have to consider similar action. . . . The UK is reportedly on track to miss its own 2020 ammonia emissions reductions target by 20% and is likely to face legal challenges from environmental health campaigners."

12 "Memorial to victims of the Irish potato famine of the 1840s: Dublin, Ireland," wynninghistory.com, accessed November 6, 2025, https://wynninghistory.com/2025/01/09/dublin-memorial-famine/.

13 See Pat Coogan, *The Famine Plot: England's Role in Ireland's Greatest Tragedy* (Palgrave Macmillan, 2012).

14 "*Farms and farmland in the European Union—statistics,*" Eurostat Statistics Explained, accessed November 6, 2025, https://ec.europa.eu/eurostat/statistics-explained/index.php?title=Farms_and_farmland_in_the_European_Union_-_statistics#Farms_in_2020.

15 "What's happening with organic farming in Ireland?," *Irish Farmers Journal*, accessed November 6, 2025, https://www.farmersjournal.ie/life/features/whats-happening-with-organic-farming-in-ireland-676219#:~:text=Organic%20Farming%20Scheme%20to%20reopen%20in%20early%20February.%20Almost%203,000t.

16 "New rules for tagging calves—here's all you need to know," *Agriland*, accessed November 6, 2025, https://www.agriland.ie/farming-news/new-rules-for-tagging-calves-heres-all-you-need-to-know/.

17 Officially, the Irish government claimed "The animal identification systems are used to trace animal movements for cattle (formerly CMMS), pig, sheep and goats. The purpose of these systems is to reassure consumers that the food they eat can be traced back to its source." *"Animal Identification & Movement (AIM),"* Government of Ireland, accessed November 6, 2025, https://www.agriland.ie/farming-news/new-rules-for-tagging-calves-heres-all-you-need-to-know/.

18 "Benefits to using the AIM Bovine On Line System," www.agfood.ie, accessed November 6, 2025, https://assets.gov.ie/90387/10c4f866-17f7-4f1e-bd5b-546ffc78c58a.doc.

19 "Irish farmers pressured to cull up to 200,000 cows to meet climate goals," *Financial Times*, aaccessed November 6, 2025, https://www.ft.com/content/4028ae15-fea2-48fb-bcdb-228f61e1b098.

20 "Ireland Proposes Culling 200,000 Cows to Help Meet Climate Goals, Farmers Push Back," Dairy Herd Management, accessed November 6, 2025, https://www.dairyherd.com/news/business/ireland-proposes-culling-200000-cows-help-meet-climate-goals-farmers-push-back.

21 "R-CALF 2024: The Fight Against EID," *Tri-State Livestock News*, accessed November 6, 2025https://www.tsln.com/news/r-calf-2024-the-fight-against-eid/. (Congresswoman Hageman was criticizing the US EID service using Ireland as a warning example.)

22 "Ireland Isn't Culling Cows for Climate. But Maybe It Should Be?," *Bulletin of the Atomic Scientists*, accessed November 6, 2025, https://thebulletin.org/2023/10/ireland-isnt-culling-cows-for-climate-but-maybe-they-should-be/#:~:text=In%20the%20most%20recent%20MACC%20report,%20published%20in%202023%20by.

23 "French farmers up in arms over call to cut cow numbers for sake. of climate," Radio France Internationale, accessed November 6, 2025, https://www.rfi.fr/en/france/20230525-french-farmers-up-in-arms-over-call-to-cut-cow-numbers-for-sake-of-climate.

24 Ibid.

25 "Cutting cow numbers isn't the answer to curbing CO2 emissions, say French farmers," *Euronews*, accessed November 6, 2025, https://www.euronews.com/green/2023/05/25/cutting-cow-numbers-isnt-the-answer-to-curbing-co2-emissions-say-french-farmers.

26 "French farmers up in arms over call to cut cow numbers for sake of climate," Radio France Internationale, accessed November 6, 2025, https://www.rfi.fr/en/france/20230525-french-farmers-up-in-arms-over-call-to-cut-cow-numbers-for-sake-of-climate.

27 "How rioting farmers unraveled Europe's ambitious climate plan," *Vox*, accessed November 6, 2025, https://www.vox.com/future-perfect/24146466/europe-farmer-protests-eu-climate-environmental-policy-subsidies-livestock.

28 "Farms and farmland in the European Union—statistics, Eurostat Statistics Explained, accessed November 6, 2025, https://ec.europa.eu/eurostat/statistics-explained/index.php?title=Farms_and_farmland_in_the_European_Union_-_statistics#Farms_in_2020.

29 "On Farmers, Food, and France: An Interview with MEP Patricia Chagnon," *The European Conservative*, accessed November 6, 2025, https://europeanconservative.com/articles/interviews/this-globalist-right-and-this-ecological-extremist-left-have-found-a-common-enemy-european-agriculture-an-interview-with-rassemblement-national-mep-patricia-chagnon/#:~:text=So%20these%20ultra-liberal,%20globalist,%20capitalist,%20multinational%20companies%E2%80%94they%20want%20to%20be.

30 Email from Etienne Compagnon to John Klar, August 27, 2025.

31 A report by the Union of Concerned Scientists (UCS) concludes that Tyson Foods is responsible for dumping billions of gallons of contaminated water into American waterways. UCS does not propose to trust the company to clean up its own operations, instead advocating to regulate the entire industry: to expand EPA, USDA, and other federal oversight of the nation's 7,000 meat and poultry processors because of the alleged sins of Tyson, which operates 41 plants in the US. This echoes new EPA rules that expand its jurisdiction over nitrogen and phosphorous discharges by meat and poultry processors, despite the massive economic compliance costs this will place on small operators. The attack on Tyson Foods appears to be a Trojan Horse to advance sweeping government control of food and farming. The US federal assault on small farms looks more and more like the EU assault on farmers in many nations there. "Tyson Plans Release Pollutants in Local Waterways," Union of Concerned Scientists, accessed November 6, 2025, https://www.ucsusa.org/about/news/tyson-plans-release-pollutants-local-waterways.

32 "Texas farmers ask judge to block USDA from doling out disaster aid based on race or gender," *Just The News*, accessed November 6, 2025, https://justthenews.com/government/courts-law/montexas-farmers-ask-judge-block-usda-doling-out-disaster-aid-based-race-or.

33 Written Testimony from Renea Jones, Jones and Church Farms Inc. To the U.S. House of Representatives Financial Services Subcommittee on Oversight and Investigations, "Victims of Regulatory Overreach: How the SEC's Climate Disclosure Rule Will Harm Americans," accessed November 6, 2025, HHRG-118-BA09-Wstate-JonesR-20240318.pdf

34 "The EU's Landmark Climate Deal Is Being Stripped to the Bone," World Politics Review, accessed November 6, 2025, https://www.worldpoliticsreview.com/european-green-deal-climate/ : "EU Parliament approves weakened green rules for farmers," Reuters, accessed November 6, 2025, https://www.reuters.com/world

/europe/eu-parliament-approves-weakened-green-rules-farmers-2024-04-24/; "'With the smallest error, there are fines': EU farmers' frustration grows as paperwork piles up," *Euronews*, accessed November 6, 2025, https://www.euronews.com/green/2024/02/15/with-the-smallest-error-there-are-fines-eu-farmers-frustration-grows-as-paperwork-piles-up.

35 "Biden-Harris Administration Finalizes Rules to Strengthen Protection and Recovery of Threatened and Endangered Species and Their Habitats," U.S. Department of the Interior, accessed November 6, 2025, https://www.doi.gov/pressreleases/biden-harris-administration-finalizes-rules-strengthen-protection-and-recovery.

36 THE PEOPLE OF THE STATE OF NEW YORK v. JBS USA FOOD COMPANY and JBS USA FOOD COMPANY HOLDINGS, Complaint filed 2/28/24, accessed November 6, 2025, https://ag.ny.gov/sites/default/files/court-filings/jbs-complaint.pdf.

37 "Experts uncover 'game-changer' side effects of solar farms: 'The benefits are numerous'," The Cool Down, accessed November 6, 2025, https://www.thecooldown.com/green-tech/agrivoltaics-solar-farming-land-agriculture/.

38 Interview of Michael NicAoibh by John Klar, April 8, 2025.

39 "Indiana lost 350,000 acres of farmland in the last decade," Indiana Public Radio, accessed November 6, 2025, https://indianapublicradio.org/news/2024/07/indiana-lost-350000-acres-of-farmland-in-the-last-decade/.

40 "U.S. lost 142,000 farms according to ag census," *Farm Progress*, accessed November 6, 2025, https://www.farmprogress.com/farm-policy/u-s-lost-142-000-farms-according-to-ag-census.

41 "Down on the Farm: Why America's Food Producers Are Hurting," *Washington Examiner*, accessed November 6, 2025, https://www.washingtonexaminer.com/premium/3192197/america-food-producers-farms-hurting/.

42 "EU agriculture statistics: subsidies, jobs, production," European Parliament, accessed November 6, 2025, https://www.europarl.europa.eu/topics/en/article/20211118STO17609/eu-agriculture-statistics-subsidies-jobs-production-infographic; "The transition from small to large farms in developing economies: A welfare analysis," Knowledge for Policy, accessed November 6, 2025, https://knowledge4policy.ec.europa.eu/publication/transition-small-large-farms-developing-economies-welfare-analysis_en.

43 "Building bridges? EU, US collaboration on agriculture sounds alarm bells in Europe," Food Navigator Europe, accessed November 6, 2025, https://www.foodnavigator.com/Article/2021/11/05/Building-bridges-EU-US-collaboration-on-agriculture-sounds-alarm-bells-in-Europe#:~:text=The%20European%20Commission%20must%20%E2%80%98strongly%20resist%E2%80%99%20any%20attempt%20by%20the. Since then, the EU has been opening its markets to more GMOs: "The Commission is now hustling to authorize genetically modified crops on the European market, a measure that would have been impossible

to pass just a few years ago." "Why Europe's 'Farm to Fork' policies collapsed," Competitive Enterprise Institute, accessed November 6, 2025, https://cei.org/blog/why-europes-farm-to-fork-policies-collapsed/.

44 "EU-US Collaboration Platform on Agriculture," European Commission on Agriculture and Rural Development, accessed November 6, 2025, https://agriculture.ec.europa.eu/international/international-cooperation/eu-us-collaboration_en#:~:text=In%20November%202021,%20Commissioner%20for%20Agriculture%20Janusz%20Wojciechowski%20and%20United.

45 Ibid.

46 Ibid.

47 "U.S., EU Launch Collaboration Platform on Agriculture," USDA, accessed November 6, 2025, https://www.usda.gov/media/press-releases/2021/11/03/us-eu-launch-collaboration-platform-agriculture#:~:text=BRUSSELS,%20BELGIUM,%20Nov.%203,%202021%20%E2%80%93%20European%20Union%20Commissioner%20for.

48 "Who Is Tom Vilsack? Biden Reportedly Nominates 'Mr. Monsanto.' As Agriculture Secretary," Greenmatters, accessed November 6, 2025, https://www.greenmatters.com/p/tom-vilsack-monsanto.

49 Email from Chris Smaje to John Klar, October 16, 2024.

50 This has been exponentially compounded by 2024 proposals which would impose inheritance taxes on Irish farmowners, rekindling farmers' outrage there. See, e.g., Cormack McQuinn, *'Unfairness' and 'anomalies' in inheritance tax should be considered before budget, Taoiseach says, The Irish Times*, accessed November 6, 2025, https://www.irishtimes.com/politics/2024/07/16/unfairness-and-anomalies-in-inheritance-tax-should-be-considered-before-budget-taoiseach-says/.

51 Email from Chris Smaje to John Klar, October 16, 2024.

52 "How rioting farmers unraveled Europe's ambitious climate plan," *Vox*, accessed November 6, 2025, https://www.irishtimes.com/politics/2024/07/16/unfairness-and-anomalies-in-inheritance-tax-should-be-considered-before-budget-taoiseach-says/.

53 "Frustrated farmers are rebelling against EU rules. The far right is stoking the flames," Associated Press, accessed November 6, 2025, https://apnews.com/article/europe-democracy-farmers-protest-green-deal-elections-a0278919b2fe47c7476c0c56ccf4850b.

54 "Agricultural landscapes dominated the countryside in a few Member States; about 72 % of Ireland's land area was used as agricultural land and the share was also particularly high in Denmark (62.6 %). In Romania, Hungary, the Netherlands and Luxembourg, about one half of the total land area was used as agricultural land. This was in starkest contrast to Finland and Sweden where forests dominated the landscape. In these two Nordic Member States, agricultural

land use only represented the equivalent of 7.5 % and 7.4 % of their respective total land areas. Indeed, they were the only EU Member States where wooded areas belonging to agricultural holdings accounted for a higher share of the land area than that used for agricultural purposes." "Farms and farmland in the European Union—statistics," Statistics Explained, accessed November 6, 2025, https://ec.europa.eu/eurostat/statistics-explained/index.php?title=Farms_and_farmland_in_the_European_Union_-_statistics#Farms_in_2020.

55 "International Trade Association, Finland," *Finland Country Commercial Guide*, accessed November 6, 2025, https://www.trade.gov/country-commercial-guides/finland-agriculture; "*Market study: The Swedish market for processed food,*" Kommerskollegium National Board of Trade Sweden, accessed November 6, 2025, https://www.kommerskollegium.se/en/publications/market-studies/the-swedish-market-for-processed-food/.

56 "Countering Europe's Backlash to the Green Transition," Foreign Policy, accessed November 6, 2025, https://foreignpolicy.com/2024/07/15/europe-green-transition-backlash-climate-sustainability/.

57 Little discussed is that Canadian investors far outstrip China in US agricultural land holdings. *See* "Fact Check Team: How much US land and property is foreign-owned?," *The National News Desk*, accessed November 6, 2025, https://thenationaldesk.com/news/fact-check-team/how-much-us-land-and-property-is-foreign-owned-billionaires-timberland-farmland-agricultural-purchases-china-canada-netherlands-italy-united-kingdom-germany-senate-laws-realtor-residential-mexico-india-colombia-restrictions ("Canadian investors own the most land—31%—followed by the Netherlands, Italy, the United Kingdom and Germany."); *See also* "Foreign US Ag Land Ownership Grows," Progressive Farmer, accessed November 6, 2025, https://www.dtnpf.com/agriculture/web/ag/news/business-inputs/article/2025/01/14/afbf-foreign-ag-land-ownership-us-1. ("The expansion of renewable energy projects led to a growth in foreign ownership of agricultural land in the U.S. from 2022 to 2023. . . . Overall, the new analysis found a 1.58-million-acre increase in foreign-owned agriculture land in the U.S. from 2022 to 2023.)

58 The Saudi connection to Arizona includes a company named Fondomonte, which reputedly has been withdrawing unlimited amounts of water from lands it leases for merely $25 per acre: The value of the water extracted far exceeds the rent paid. Fondomonte is allegedly growing alfalfa year-round on its 3,500 Arizona acres to ship to other countries—like China. "Arizona to cancel leases allowing Saudi-owned farm access to state's groundwater," AP News, accessed November 7, 2025, https://apnews.com/article/saudi-arabia-drought-arizona-alfalfa-water-agriculture-0d13957edaf882690e15c0bd9ccfa59f.

59 "California drought: Why farmers are 'exporting water' to China," BBC, accessed November 7, 2025, https://www.bbc.com/news/magazine-26124989.

60 "RELEASE: Agricultural Census Shows Continued Shrinking of Ag of the Middle," National Sustainable Agriculture Coalition, accessed November 7, 2025,

https://sustainableagriculture.net/blog/2017-ag-census/#:~:text=A%20preliminary%20review%20by%20the%20National%20Sustainable%20Agriculture,agriculture%20was%20taking%20more%20medium-sized%20family%20farms%20out.

61 "Over 140,000 Farms Lost in 5 Years," American Farm Bureau Federation, accessed November 7, 2025, https://www.fb.org/market-intel/over-140-000-farms-lost-in-5-years.

62 "USDA: The United States lost 14,950 farms in 2024," On the Farm Radio, accessed November 7, 2025, https://www.onthefarmradio.com/single-post/usda-the-united-states-lost-14-950-farms-in-2024.

63 "Census22_HL_FarmEconomics_FINAL.pdf," USDA NASS, accessed November 7, 2025, https://www.nass.usda.gov/Publications/Highlights/2024/Census22_HL_FarmEconomics_FINAL.pdf: "The 105,384 farms in the top two categories (sales of $1 million or more) are fewer than 6% of U.S. farms; they sold more than three fourths of all agricultural products."

Chapter 7

1 "Not long after we met for the first time, [Medavoy] said to me, 'I can tell you how to run the world, you know. . . . You make up something complicated. Then you insert it into the bloodstream of the society, and you watch it bloom. You make it complex enough that it will take armies of people to sort it out and argue about it, and money.'" Jon Rappaport (interview with propaganda expert Ellis Medavoy), *Solari Report* 2023, no. 3.

2 "Dekulakisation as mass violence | Sciences Po Mass Violence and Resistance—Research Network," SciencesPo, accessed November 7, 2025, https://www.sciencespo.fr/mass-violence-war-massacre-resistance/en/document/dekulakisation-mass-violence.html.

3 "The term star chamber refers pejoratively to any secret or closed meeting held by a judicial or executive body, or to a court proceeding that seems grossly unfair or that is used to persecute an individual." "Star Chamber," The First Amendment Encyclopedia, accessed November 7, 2025, https://firstamendment.mtsu.edu/article/star-chamber/.

4 From Vietnam to Africa to Israel to Watergate, Kissinger established himself using his Cold War "cloak-and-dagger style" as extremely effective but notoriously dishonest, power-hungry, and self-serving. These hallmarks are woven through the shady cloth of his secret 1974 plan to persuade, cajole, bribe, manipulate and, if necessary, compel third-world countries to reduce their population numbers to "save the world" from overpopulation.

5 "National Security Study Memoranda 200," Nixon Library, accessed November 7, 2025, https://www.nixonlibrary.gov/sites/default/files/virtuallibrary/documents/nssm/nssm_200.pdf.

6 The Report states: "The real problems of mineral supplies lie, not in basic physical sufficiency, but in the politico-economic issues of access, terms for exploration and exploitation, and division of the benefits among producers, consumers, and host country governments. In the extreme cases where population pressures lead to endemic famine, food riot, and breakdown of social order, those conditions are scarcely conducive to systematic exploration for mineral deposits or the long-term investments required for their exploitation." Ibid.

7 Why is helping the poor people of the world avoid starvation a US "national security issue" requiring a massive top secret plan of implementation hidden from public view? Mr. Kissinger answered this question as a national security issue, requiring US domination in third-world nations so that its corporate interests would not be hampered from access to those nation's natural resources: "Countries suffering under such burdens will be more susceptible to radicalization. Their vulnerability also might invite foreign intervention by stronger nations bent on acquiring political and economic advantage. The tensions within the Have-not nations are likely to intensify, and the conflicts between them and the Haves may escalate. . . . The proposed strategy calls for a coordinated approach to respond to the important U.S. foreign policy interest in the influence of population growth on the world's political, economic and ecological systems." Ibid.

8 Ibid.

9 Ibid.

10 The Kissinger Report also advocated controlling American consumers' food choices: "There is an alternative view which holds that a growing number of experts believe that the population situation is already more serious and less amenable to solution through voluntary measures than is generally accepted. It holds that, to prevent even more widespread food shortage and other demographic catastrophes than are generally anticipated, even stronger measures are required and some fundamental, very difficult moral issues need to be addressed. These include, for example, our own consumption patterns, mandatory programs, tight control of our food resources. In view of the seriousness of these issues, explicit consideration of them should begin in the Executive Branch, the Congress and the U.N. soon."

11 *Solari Report* 2023, no. 3, 75, fn 210.

12 "National Security Study Memorandum NSSM 200, *Implications of Worldwide Population Growth For U.S. Security and Overseas Interests (THE KISSINGER REPORT),* accessed November 7, 2025, https://www.nssm200.com/wp-content/uploads/2015/09/NSSM-200.pdf.

13 "The World Population Plan of Action is not self-enforcing and will require vigorous efforts by interested countries, U.N. agencies and other international bodies to make it effective. U.S. leadership is essential. . . . The World Population Plan of Action and the resolutions adopted by consensus by 137 nations at the August 1974 U.N. World Population Conference, though not ideal, provide an excellent

framework for developing a worldwide system of population/family planning programs. We should use them to generate U.N. agency and national leadership for an all-out effort to lower growth rates. Constructive action by the U.S. will further our objectives." Ibid.

14 Ibid.

15 Kissinger's Report planted the propaganda metrics of the Cow Lie of the 21st Century: "Part of the rising per capita demand reflects improvement in diets of some of the peoples of the developing countries. In the less developed countries about 400 pounds of grain is available per person per year and is mostly eaten as cereal. The average North American, however, uses nearly a ton of grain a year, only 200 pounds directly and the rest in the form of meat, milk, and eggs for which several pounds of cereal are required to produce one pound of the animal product (e.g., five pounds of grain to produce one pound of beef)." This "analysis" ignored the fact that cows grow just fine without any grain at all—it is industrial agriculture that converted them to a grain diet. It also hints at the underlying discussion of targeting American meat diets back in 1974—allegedly, to save the world and the poor people.

16 "The Economic Bill of Rights," Ushistory.org, accessed November 7, 2025, https://www.ushistory.org/documents//economic_bill_of_rights.htm.

17 "12 Popular Foods That Are Vanishing From Store Shelves," Organically Human, accessed November 7, 2025, https://organicallyhuman.com/12-popular-foods-that-are-vanishing-from-store-shelves/#google_vignette.

18 "Week 63 Household Pulse Survey: October 18 – October 30, United States Census Bueau, accessed November 7, 2025, https://www.census.gov/data/tables/2023/demo/hhp/hhp63.html.

19 "A way out of Sri Lanka's food security crisis," *The Asian Review*, accessed November 7, 2025, https://asian-reviews.com/2024/02/25/a-way-out-of-sri-lankas-food-security-crisis/.

20 Buck v. Bell, 274 US 200 (1927), Justia U.S. Supreme Court Center, accessed November 7, 2025, https://supreme.justia.com/cases/federal/us/274/200/#opinions.

Chapter 8

1 "Impact of Business Cycles on US Suicide Rates, 1928–2007," PubMed Central, accessed November 7, 2025, https://pmc.ncbi.nlm.nih.gov/articles/PMC3093269/.

2 "Children and Adolescents, Impact of the Great Depression on," Encyclopedia.com, accessed November 7, 2025, https://www.encyclopedia.com/economics/encyclopedias-almanacs-transcripts-and-maps/children-and-adolescents-impact-great-depression.

3 "Bison/Buffalo: Bison Genocide," South Dakota State University, accessed November 7, 2025, https://libguides.sdstate.edu/c.php?g=1358402&p=10030696; "'Kill Every Buffalo You Can! Every Buffalo Dead Is an Indian Gone,'" *The Atlantic*, accessed November 7, 2025, https://www.theatlantic.com/national/archive/2016/05/the-buffalo-killers/482349/.

4 "The Dust Bowl," Library of Congress, accessed November 7, 2025, https://www.loc.gov/classroom-materials/united-states-history-primary-source-timeline/great-depression-and-world-war-ii-1929-1945/dust-bowl/.

5 Interview of Tink Camp at his home in Randolph, Vermont, on September 21, 2025.

6 Interview of Roland Greene, March 17, 2024.

7 "America's $28T Debt Explained in one Chart," Howmuch.net, accessed November 7, 2025, https://howmuch.net/articles/timeline-us-debt-history.

8 "U.S. National Debt Clock: Real Time," usdebtclock.org, accessed November 7, 2025, https://www.usdebtclock.org/.

9 "The U.S. national debt is rising by $1 trillion about every 100 days," CNBC, accessed November 7, 2025, https://www.cnbc.com/2024/03/01/the-us-national-debt-is-rising-by-1-trillion-about-every-100-days.html?msockid=064e1f6062fd68ca17a510db636f6974.

10 "Complete Measures of U.S. National Debt," Penn Wharton Budget Model, accessed November 7, 2025, https://budgetmodel.wharton.upenn.edu/issues/2025/1/27/complete-measures-of-us-national-debt.

11 "U.S. National Debt Clock: Real Time," usdebtclock.org, accessed November 7, 2025, https://www.usdebtclock.org/.

12 "Household Debt and Credit Report," Federal Reserve Bank of New York, accessed November 7, 2025, https://www.newyorkfed.org/microeconomics/hhdc.html.

13 "H. Rpt. 109-377: A Failure of Initiative: Final Report," govinfo.library, accessed November 7, 2025, https://govinfo.library.unt.edu/katrina/lawenforcement.pdf.

14 "Do Some People Really Think Chocolate Milk Comes from Brown Cows?," Live Science, accessed November 7, 2025, https://www.livescience.com/59666-do-people-believe-chocolate-milk-from-brown-cows.html.

15 "Turns out Americans really don't know how to cook anything but eggs," theladders.com, accessed November 7, 2025, https://www.theladders.com/career-advice/turns-out-americans-really-dont-know-how-to-cook-anything-but-eggs; "Majority Of Students Don't Know How To Boil An Egg, Half 'Not Confident' With Mashing Potatoes," *Huffington Post UK*, accessed November 7, 2025, https://www.huffingtonpost.co.uk/2013/09/17/students-dont-know-how-boil-egg-mash-potato_n_3940022.html.

16 "How many eggs are consumed each day in the US?," Answers.com, accessed November 7, 2025, https://www.answers.com/zoology/How_many_eggs_are_consumed_each_day_in_the_US.

17 "63+ Chicken Consumption Statistics," PreparedCooks.com, accessed November 7, 2025, https://preparedcooks.com/chicken-consumption-statistics/#:~:text=US%20consumption%20of%20%EE%80%80chicken%EE%80%81%20has%20reached%20an.

18 "Total number of hogs and pigs in the U.S. 2024," Statista, accessed November 7, 2025, https://www.statista.com/statistics/194365/total-number-of-hogs-and-pigs-in-the-us-since-2000/.

19 My Grammie Cesarine knew where the berries were and would often take us out berry picking like Roland Greene's grandmother. Grammie would bake dozens of pies and freeze them. She also knew where the dandelions and cowslips grew, and in her nineties foraged for butternuts—one of her favorites, and once again she knew where to hunt for them.

20 "FACT SHEET: President Biden to Take Action to Uphold Commitment to Restore Balance on Public Lands and Waters, Invest in Clean Energy Future," U.S. Department of the Interior, accessed November 7, 2025, https://www.doi.gov/pressreleases/fact-sheet-president-biden-take-action-uphold-commitment-restore-balance-public-lands.

21 "Vermont Enacts Community Resilience and Biodiversity Protection Bill (H.126)," Vermont Natural Resources Council, accessed November 7, 2025, https://vnrc.org/vermont-enacts-community-resilience-and-biodiversity-protection-bill-h-126/; "Draft Bill Template," Vermont Legislature, accessed November 7, 2025. https://legislature.vermont.gov/Documents/2024/Docs/ACTS/ACT059/ACT059%20As%20Enacted.pdf.

22 "'Kings Over the Necessaries of Life': Monopolization and the Elimination of Competition in America's Agriculture System," Farm Action, accessed November 7, 2025, https://farmaction.us/wp-content/uploads/2024/09/Kings-Over-the-Necessaries-of-Life-Monopolization-and-the-Elimination-of-Competition-in-Americas-Agriculture-System_Farm-Action.pdf.

23 "UN calls for urgent action to feed the world's growing population healthily, equitably and sustainably," United Nations Sustainable Development, accessed November 7, 2025, https://www.un.org/sustainabledevelopment/blog/2021/04/un-calls-for-urgent-action-to-feed-the-worlds-growing-population-healthily-equitably-and-sustainably/.

24 Ibid.

25 "EU Approves Insect-Infused Food: Mealworms in Bread and Pastries Now Permitted," RAIR Foundation USA, accessed November 7, 2025, https://rairfoundation.com/eu-approves-insect-infused-food-mealworms-bread-pastries/.

26 "A digital euro is coming. Here's what you need to know," World Economic Forum, accessed November 7, 2025, https://www.weforum.org/stories/2023/08/digital-euro-is-coming-privacy/.

27 "BASF Agricultural Solutions' blockchain platform enables tracing of sustainably produced FiberMax® cotton from seed to sew," BASF, accessed November 7, 2025, https://agriculture.basf.com/global/en/media/press-releases/2022/AP_221005.

28 "Agriculture in Iraq: Resources, Potentials, Constraints, and Research Needs and Priorities," ARS-USDA, accessed November 7, 2025, AgInIraq-092002A.PDF.

29 "Agriculture history: Achievements of Iraqs Civilizations," Iraqhistory.org accessed November 7, 2025, https://iraqhistory.org/en/agriculture/.

30 "Agriculture in Iraq: Resources, Potentials, Constraints, and Research Needs and Priorities," ARS-USDA, accessed November 7, 2025, AgInIraq-092002A.PDF.

31 Ibid.

32 "Biopiracy and GMOs: The Fate of Iraq's Agriculture," Global Research, accessed November 7, 2025, https://www.globalresearch.ca/biopiracy-and-gmos-the-fate-of-iraq-s-agriculture/1447#:~:text=Consistent%20with%20agricultural%20research,%20what%20Iraqi%20farmers%20need%20urgently%20is

33 "Iraq's Agricultural Industry Was Pillaged, Its Farmers Devastated, But It's Still Free Of GMO Seeds," *Mint Press News*, accessed November 7, 2025, https://www.mintpressnews.com/despite-decades-of-war-iraqs-agricultural-industry-remains-gmo-free/223169/.

34 "Biopiracy and GMOs: The Fate of Iraq's Agriculture," Global Research, accessed November 7, 2025, https://www.globalresearch.ca/biopiracy-and-gmos-the-fate-of-iraq-s-agriculture/1447#:~:text=Consistent%20with%20agricultural%20research,%20what%20Iraqi%20farmers%20need%20urgently%20is.

35 "Iraq's new patent law: a declaration of war against farmers," Grain.org, accessed November 7, 2025, https://grain.org/en/article/150-iraq-s-new-patent-law-a-declaration-of-war-against-farmers#:~:text=Eliminating%20competition%20from%20farmers%20is%20a%20prerequisite%20for%20these%20companies.

36 https://ejatlas.org/conflict/order-81s-effect-on-agriculture.

37 "The Monsanto Tribunal took place in 2016–2017 in The Hague. Five judges delivered a legal opinion and concluded that Monsanto's (now, Bayer) activities have a negative impact on basic human rights. Better regulations are needed to protect the victims of multinational corporations. International law should be improved for better protection of the environment and include the crime of ecocide." "International Monsanto Tribunal," monsanto-tribunal.org, accessed November 7, 2025, https://www.monsanto-tribunal.org/.

38 "Iraq's new patent law: a declaration of war against farmers," Grain.org, accessed November 7, 2025, https://grain.org/en/article/150-iraq-s-new-patent-law-a-declaration-of-war-against-farmers#:~:text=Eliminating%20competition%20from%20farmers%20is%20a%20prerequisite%20for%20these%20companies.

39 "Iraq Agriculture, Forestry, and Fishing," Britannica, accessed November 7, 2025, https://www.britannica.com/place/Iraq/Agriculture-forestry-and-fishing.

40 "Can Ukraine help green the EU's farming sector?," *The Parliament Magazine*, accessed November 7, 2025, https://www.theparliamentmagazine.eu/news/article/ukraine-agriculture-europe-accession-sustainability#:~:text=A%20moratorium%20on%20companies%20buying%20up%20agricultural%20land%20that%20expired.

41 "Ukraine War Exposes Folly of Anti-GMO Protectionism," American Council on Science and Health, accessed November 7, 2025, https://www.acsh.org/news/2022/03/22/ukraine-war-exposes-folly-anti-gmo-protectionism-16199#:~:text=Policymakers%20are%20working%20to%20relax%20import%20restrictions%20on%20transgenic%20(%E2%80%9CGMO%E2%80%9D).

42 "Ukraine Allows Farmland Sales For First Time Since Independence," Radio Free Europe Radio Liberty, accessed November 7, 2025, https://www.rferl.org/a/ukraine-agriculture-farmland-economy-/31336984.html.

43 The pattern of financial interests rescuing struggling nations from crisis is the hallmark of "soft colonialism" documented by John Perkins in *Confessions of an Economic Hit Man* (Plume, 2004).

44 "Corporations are expanding control over Ukraine's land with help from the IMF and the World Bank," Bretton Woods Project, accessed November 7, 2025, https://www.brettonwoodsproject.org/2023/04/oligarchs-and-corporations-are-expanding-control-over-ukraines-agricultural-land-with-help-from-the-imf-and-the-world-bank/#:~:text=New%20report%20from%20the%20Oakland%20Institute%20exposes%20the%20stealth%20take-over.

45 "Western corporations have already bought up half of Ukrainian agricultural land at a bargain price," *EurAsia Daily,* accessed November 7, 2025, https://eadaily.com/en/news/2024/07/14/western-corporations-have-already-bought-up-half-of-ukrainian-agricultural-land-at-a-bargain-price#:~:text=It%20is%20already%20known%20that%20three%20companies%20have%20purchased%2017.

46 "PolitiCheck: It is not true that GMO is legally grown in Ukraine or that the land is owned by American companies," Factcheck.bg, accessed November 7, 2025, PolitiCheck: It is not true that GMO is legally grown in Ukraine or that the land is owned by American companies - Factcheck.bg.

47 "Zelenskyy signs law legalizing production of GMO products in Ukraine," Interfax-Ukraine, accessed November 7, 2025, https://en.interfax.com.ua/news/economic/934644.html.

48 "Amidst Chaos of War, A New Report Exposes the Stealth Take-over of Ukrainian Agricultural Land," The Oakland Institute, accessed November 7, 2025, https://www.oaklandinstitute.org/new-report-take-over-ukrainian-agricultural-land#:~:text=One%20year%20into%20the%20war,%20a%20new%20report%20reveals%20how.

49 Ibid.

50 "Agro-Companies Buy Up 18 Percent of Ukraine's Legal Land Market," *Kyiv Post*, accessed November 7, 2025, https://www.kyivpost.com/post/37156#:~:text=Starting%20from%20Jan.%201,%202024,%20companies%20were%20legally%20free%20to.

51 "Western corporations have already bought up half of Ukrainian agricultural land at a bargain price," *EurAsia Daily*, accessed November 7, 2025, https://eadaily

.com/en/news/2024/07/14/western-corporations-have-already-bought-up-half-of-ukrainian-agricultural-land-at-a-bargain-price#:~:text=It%20is%20already%20known%20that%20three%20companies%20have%20purchased%2017.

52 "$100 million U.S. initiative boosts Ukrainian agriculture," U.S. Embassy in Georgia, accessed November 7, 2025, https://ge.usembassy.gov/100-million-u-s-initiative-boosts-ukrainian-agriculture/.

53 "US announces new partnerships to boost Ukraine's agricultural sector and grain production," CNN, accessed November 7, 2025, https://www.cnn.com/2023/03/02/politics/usaid-ukraine-grain-partnerships/index.html.

54 "USAID and Bayer expand partnership with additional $15.5 million from Bayer to support Ukrainian farmers," developmental aid, accessed November 7, 2025, https://www.developmentaid.org/news-stream/post/164922/usaid-support-ukrainian-farmers.

55 "USAID attracts nearly $1.75B to support Ukraine's agricultural sector," Ukrinform, accessed November 7, 2025, https://www.ukrinform.net/rubric-economy/3914934-usaid-attracts-nearly-175b-to-support-ukraines-agricultural-sector.html.

56 "45 years of AgriNews: 1970s boom turned into 1980s crisis," *Agrinews*, accessed November 7, 2025, https://www.agrinews-pubs.com/business/2022/03/21/45-years-of-agrinews-1970s-boom-turned-into-1980s-crisis/.

57 "'Kings Over the Necessaries of Life': Monopolization and the Elimination of Competition in America's Agriculture System," *Farm Action*, https://farmaction.us/wp-content/uploads/2024/09/Kings-Over-the-Necessaries-of-Life-Monopolization-and-the-Elimination-of-Competition-in-Americas-Agriculture-System_Farm-Action.pdf. .

58 "Agriculture Consolidation Data Hub," *Farm Action*, accessed November 7, 2025, *https://farmaction.us/agriculture-consolidation-data-hub/.*

59 "Under Siege: How the War on Farmers Threatens Western Values and Global Food Security," *The European Conservative*, accessed November 7, 2025, https://europeanconservative.com/articles/commentary/under-siege-how-the-war-on-farmers-threatens-western-values-and-global-food-security/.

60 "UN, World Economic Forum Behind Global 'War on Farmers': Experts," *The Epoch Times*, accessed November 7, https://www.theepochtimes.com/us/un-and-world-economic-forum-behind-global-war-on-farmers-experts-4622598.

Chapter 9

1 Wendell Berry, *Another Turn of the Crank* (Counterpoint, 1995). 60.

2 Sina McCullough, *Hands Off my Food!: How Government and Industry Have Corrupted Our Food and Easy Ways to Fight Back* (Watchdog Works, 2017), 112.

3 Seneff, Stephanie, *Toxic Legacy: How the Weedkiller Glyphosate is Destroying Our Health and the Environment* (Chelsea Green Publishing, 2021), 163.

4 Joel Salatin, *You Can Farm: The Entrepreneur's Guide to Start and Succeed in a Farming Enterprise* (Polyface, 1998), 34.

5 Mark Bittman, *Animal, Vegetable, Junk: A History of Food, from Sustainable to Suicidal* (Houghton Mifflin Harcourt, 2021), 299.

6 Ibid., 274.

7 Ibid., 267.

8 Wendell Berry, *Another Turn of the Crank* (Counterpoint, 2011), 72.

9 Partial credit for the policies proposed in *Small Farm Republic* must go to Wendell Berry, not only for his six decades of powerful writings, but because we sat at his dining room table where I solicited his counsel.

10 Many federal conservation programs do not currently permit livestock grazing on conserved farmlands—this is a tragedy that must be remedied by allowing farmers to return animals to the landscape using properly managed rotational grazing systems.

11 T. S. Eliot. *The Love Song of J. Alfred Prufrock,* 1915

12 Allan C. Carlson, "Distributism: A Short History," *Local Culture: A Journal of the Front Porch Republic*, 11–12.

13 E. F. Schumacher, *Small Is Beautiful:Economics as if People Mattered* (Harper Perennial, 2010), 167.

14 Allan C. Carson, "Distributism: A Short History," *Local Culture: A Journal of the Front Porch Republic*, 11.

15 Wendell Berry, *The Art of Loading Brush* (Counterpoint, 2017), 11.

16 Michael Moss, *Hooked: Food, Free Will, and How the Food Giants Exploit Our Addictions* (Random House, 2021),. 211.

17 Joel Salatin, *The Sheer Ecstasy of Being a Lunatic Farmer* (Polyface, 2010), 98.

18 Aldo Leopold, *The River of the Mother of God: and other Essays* (The University of Wisconsin Press, 1991) 298.

19 Wes Jackson, *Nature As Measure* (Counterpoint, 2011), 116,

20 "Why Antitrust Laws Matter More Than Ever in Agriculture and Food," *Food & Water Watch,* accessed November 8, 2025, https://www.foodandwaterwatch.org/wp-content/uploads/2023/05/Why-Antitrust-Laws-Matter-More-Than-Ever-in-Agriculture-and-Food.pdf.

21 "Antitrust enforcer Gail Slater on American innovation: 'We can win the AI race against the Chinese without becoming like China'," *New York Post,* accessed

November 8, 2025, https://nypost.com/2025/07/03/business/doj-antitrust-chief-is-betting-american-tech-will-beat-china/. .

22 Kirkpatrick Sale, *Dwellers in the Land: The Bioregional Vision* (The University of Georgis Press, 2000), 71.

23 Benjamin Lorr, *The Secret Life of Groceries: The Dark Miracle of the American Supermarket* (Avery, 2020). 268–269. Dr. Chris van Tulleken engages in a similar contemplation in *Ultra-Proceesed People: Why Do We All Eat Stuff That Isn't Food . . . and Why Can't We Stop?* (Penguin Books, UK, 2023), tracing the bizarre taxation of Pringles potato chips (crisps in the UK), of which only 40% of the content is actually potatoes (p. 250: "The true cost of Pringles").

24 "Lawn Surface Area in the United States," NASA Eartn Observatory, accessed November 7, 2025, https://earthobservatory.nasa.gov/images/6019/lawn-surface-area-in-the-united-states.

25 "Americans burn 800 million gallons of gas every year cutting their lawns—but there's a solution," Yahoo, accessed November 8, 2025, https://www.yahoo.com/lifestyle/americans-burn-800-million-gallons-220000120.html; "Grass Lawns are an Ecological Catastrophe—ONE Only Natural Energy," Only Natural Energy, accessed November 8, 2025, https://www.onlynaturalenergy.com/grass-lawns-are-an-ecological-catastrophe/.

26 "The Strange Psychology of the American Lawn," *Psychology Today*, accessed November 8, 2025, https://www.psychologytoday.com/us/blog/the-modern-brain/202002/the-strange-psychology-the-american-lawn.

27 Wes Jackson, *Nature As Measure* (Counterpoint, 2011), 116.

28 Smaje, Chris, *Finding Lights in a Dark Age* (Chelsea Green Publishing, 2025).

29 "Building an Agrarian Localist Present: A Review of *Finding Lights in a Dark Age*," *Front Porch Republic*, accessed November 8, 2025, https://www.frontporchrepublic.com/2025/11/building-an-agrarian-localist-present-a-review-of-finding-lights-in-a-dark-age/.

30 Greer, John Michael, *The Long Descent: A User's Guide to the End of the Industrial Age* (New Society Publishers, 2008), 168, 169. See also James Howard Kunstler, *Living in the Long Emergency: Global Crisis, the Failure of the Futurists, and the Early Adapters Who Are Showing Us the Way Forward* (BenBella Books, 2020).

Chapter 10

1 Wendell Berry, *Life is a Miracle: An Essay Against Modern Superstition* (Counterpoint, 2000), 55.

2 John Lukacs, *At the End of an Age* (Yale University Press, 2002), 42–43.

3 More than 30 percent of respondents in a 2018 poll believed the US would engage in a second Civil War within the next five years. "More than 30 per cent of Americans believe a second US civil war is imminent," *Daily Mail Online*,

accessed November 8, 2025, https://www.dailymail.co.uk/news/article-5894451/More-30-cent-Americans-believe-second-civil-war-imminent.html.

4 ". . . we do not look at the things which are seen, but at the things which are not seen. For the things which are seen are temporary, but the things which are not seen are eternal." 2 Corinthians 4:18, NKJV.

5 Wendell Berry, *Sex, Economy, Freedom & Community: Eight Essays* (Pantheon, 1993), xvii–xviii.

6 John Lukacs, *At the End of An Age* (Yale University Press, 2002), 37–38.

Resources

1 Joseph Mercola, "New Study Links Phthalates to Cardiovascular Disease," *The Epoch Times*, accessed November 9, 2025, https://www.theepochtimes.com/mkt_breakingnews/new-study-links-phthalates-to-cardiovascular-disease_4160936.html?utm_source=News&utm_medium=email&utm_campaign=breaking-2021-12-16-2&mktids=339f85ed4f93d036564993428f5fe355&est=tSesOd8br4ACUM1CIDpitQu11vT1XCdHjPoe1yPEj885PcLG9XbHscdurCAt1KPJ2gsaNA%3D%3D.

2 Shanna H. Swan & Stacey Colino, *Countdown: How Our Modern World Is Threatening Sperm Counts, Altering Male and Female Reproductive Development, and Imperiling the Future of the Human Race* (Scribner, 2021).

3 Ibid., 173 (Personal Pregnancy Protection Plan), 182 et seq.

Index

A

addiction, 13, 146
Agenda 2030, 130
Agricultural Improvement and Reform Act of 1996, 129
Agricultural Testament, An (Howard), 11–13
agroecology, 136
American Dream, 145
Amish, 139–140
ammonia, 17
Animal, Vegetable, Junk: A History of Food, from Sustainable to Suicidal (Bittman), 173
antitrust, 119–120, 128, 147–148
aquifers, 32–33

B

BASF, 122
batteries, 71–72. *See also* electric vehicles (EVs)
beef tallow, 68
Berry, Wendell, 5, 8, 12, 25, 29, 90, 134, 137, 155, 162–163, 165
Beyond Labels: A Doctor and a Farmer Conquer Food Confusion One Bite at a Time (McCullough and Salatin), 171
Biden, Joe, 51, 74, 118, 166
biodiversity, 3, 6, 28, 61, 64, 80, 83, 103, 118, 123
Bittman, Mark, 136, 173
Borlaug, Norman, 2
Bowman v. Monsanto, 20–21
BRICS nations, 50
Buck v. Bell, 107

C

CAFOs. *See* Concentrated Animal Feeding Operations (CAFOs)
Camp, Lawrence "Tink," 110–113
CAP. *See* Common Agricultural Policy (CAP)
carbon credits, 16, 33, 62, 67
carbon dioxide, 4, 14–16, 33, 60, 64, 71–72, 77, 93, 118, 121, 150, 166
carbon sequestration, 15–16, 87
Carson, Rachel, 163, 167
Carter, Jimmy, 120, 149
centralization, 3–4, 28, 165, 168
Chagnon, Patricia, 73, 81–82
Chávez, Hugo, 52
China, 6, 23, 31, 36–37, 41, 46, 50, 70–74, 93–94, 130
Clayton Act, 119
climate change, 14–17, 40–41, 59, 79–80, 97–98, 117–118, 152. *See also* carbon dioxide
Colino, Stacey, 173
Common Agricultural Policy (CAP), 87, 91–92
Concentrated Animal Feeding Operations (CAFOs), 29, 44–45, 60, 64, 66, 155
Cooperation Platform on Agriculture (CPA), 87
corn, 19, 23
cotton, 122
Countdown: How Our Modern World Is Threatening Sperm Counts, Altering Male and Female Reproductive Development, and Imperiling the Future of the Human Race (Swan and Colino), 173
COVID-19 pandemic, 4, 30, 41–42, 46, 53, 81, 161, 172–173
cows, 14, 33, 40–42, 59–60, 62–66, 69–71, 79, 81, 92, 102
CPA. *See* Cooperation Platform on Agriculture (CPA)
cross-pollination, 21, 23
currency, 7, 44, 46, 115–116. *See also* fiat currency
currency failure, 36
cyberattacks, 37–38

D

Daniels, Mitch, 48
debt, national, 45–50, 115–116
DEF. *See* diesel exhaust fluid (DEF)
deflation, 53
demographics, 89–95
de Waal, Alex, 102
diesel exhaust fluid (DEF), 6, 31–32
disaster relief, 83–84
Doors of Perception, The (Huxley), 163
drought, 34–35, 38
Dust Bowl, 110
Dwellers in the Land: The Bioregional Vision (Sale), 148

E

Eden, 4–5
ELDs. *See* electronic logging devices (ELDs)
electric vehicles (EVs), 15, 68, 71–72, 164
electromagnetic pulses (EMPs), 37–38
electronic logging devices (ELDs), 31–32
EMPs. *See* electromagnetic pulses (EMPs)
energy, fossil fuel, 3–4, 7, 29–30, 36–37, 60, 149, 151
energy crisis, 36–37
Engdahl, F. William, 123–124
environmentalism, 14–15. *See also* carbon dioxide; climate change
Equal Protection Clause, 84
EVs. *See* electric vehicles (EVs)

F

faith, in technology and science, 161–169
Fallon Morell, Sally, 171–172
famine, 27–42, 102, 153
Farm Aid, 128
Federal Deposit Insurance Corporation, 110
Federal Trade Commission (FTC), 148
fertilizer costs, 4, 30, 67
fertilizers, 3, 11–12, 18–21, 62, 65–68, 87–88, 100, 119–120, 127, 150, 157
Fesneau, Marc, 80
fiat currency, 2, 7, 36–37, 44–47, 56, 173
Finding Lights in a Dark Age (Smaje), 152
Finland, 93
Fitts, Catherine Austin, 173
flooding, 34
food addiction, 146
food liberty, 104–108
food security, 2–4, 13, 17, 19–20, 77–78, 85, 88–95, 106, 134–137, 145, 148, 153
Food Security Act, 128–129
food sovereignty, 109–131
forest regrowth, 15–16
fossil fuels, 3–4, 7, 29–30, 60, 149, 151
France, 80–83
Frank, Anne, 97
FTC. *See* Federal Trade Commission (FTC)

G

Galbraith, John Kenneth, 103
Gates, Bill, 67–68
GDP. *See* gross domestic product (GDP)
genetically modified organisms (GMOs), 3, 18–23, 60, 65, 70–71, 100–101, 107, 118, 125–126, 134–135, 138
Germany, 51
globalists, 40–41, 102, 104–105, 107
globalization, 8, 32
global warming. *See* climate change; greenhouse gases
glyphosate, 18–21, 29, 40, 61, 72, 105
GMOs. *See* genetically modified organisms (GMOs)
Gore, Al, 14, 166
Grapes of Wrath, The (Steinbeck), 110
Great Depression, 109–110, 119–120, 141, 156–157
Great Merger Movement, 119
Green Deal, 75, 92, 101
Greene, Roland, 113–117
greenhouse gases, 4, 14–16, 61–63, 79–80. *See also* carbon dioxide
Green New Deal, 24–25, 75, 87, 101
Green Revolution, 2–5, 11, 69, 74
Greer, John, 153
gross domestic product (GDP), 47
Gulf War, 123

H

Hageman, Harriet, 79
Hands Off My Food!: How Government and Industry Have Corrupted Our Food and Easy Ways to Fight Back (McCullough), 171
Hemingway, Ernest, 43
highway infrastructure, 31–32
Holmes, Oliver Wendell, 107

Homestead Act of 1862, 118–119
Howard, Albert, 11–13, 17
Huber, Don, 59
Hungary, 51
Huxley, Aldous, 163
hydrogenated oils, 68
hyperinflation, 36, 45–46, 50–57

I

I'll Take My Stand: The South and the Agrarian Tradition, 142
imports, 56–57, 67, 80, 115
inflation, 36, 43–45, 50–57, 152–153, 167
infrastructure, highway, 31–32
insects, as food, 70–72
International Treaty on Plant Genetic Resources for Food and Agriculture, 104
Iraq, 122–124
Iraq War, 123
Ireland, 78–80, 90–91

J

Jackson, Wes, 147, 151–153
James, Letitia, 84–85
JBS Foods, 84–85
Jones, Renea, 84

K

Kennedy, Robert F., 138, 166
Kerouac, Jack, 163
Kerry, John, 74
Keynes, John Maynard, 54–55
Kissinger Report, 99–105, 107, 130

L

Lange, Dorothea, 110
lawn mowing, 59, 150
Leopold, Aldo, 1, 24, 147
libertarianism, 146–147
López Obrador, Andrés Manuel, 19
Lott, Jeremy, 86
Lukacs, John, 160–161, 165, 167

M

MAHA, 138
McCarthy, Cormac, 27
McCullough, Sina, 171
meats, plant-based and synthetic, 15, 59, 69–70
Mercola, Joseph, 172
methane, 60, 62–64, 71
Mexico, 19, 23
microbes, 2–3, 17, 60
MMT. *See* modern monetary theory (MMT)
modern monetary theory (MMT), 53
MoneyGPT: AI and the Threat to the Global Economy (Rickards), 49
Monsanto, 20–21, 124
Mugabe, Robert, 51

N

national debt, 45–50, 115–116
Netherlands, 76–78
NicAoibh, Michael, 85, 90–91
nitrogen, phosphorus, and potassium (NPK), 12, 16
nitrous oxide, 4
NPK. *See* nitrogen, phosphorus, and potassium (NPK)

O

O'Hara, Edwin, 144
oil, 29–30, 36–37, 158
On the Road (Kerouac), 163
Order 81, 124
organic, 137
overpopulation, 99–101

P

pesticides, 3–4, 21–23, 35, 61, 70, 87–89, 111, 127
PFAS. *See* polyfluoroalkyl substances (PFAS)
plant-based meats, 15, 59, 69–70
plastic, 151
pollinators, 35–36
polyfluoroalkyl substances (PFAS), 6, 162
population, 99–101
prepping, 140–141
psychological health, 144–153

R

Reagan, Ronald, 55, 120, 128, 158
refrigeration, 7
rewilding, 15–16, 54, 73–74, 115, 138, 146
Rickards, James, 48–49, 53
Roosevelt, Franklin D., 104, 120, 138
Roundup, 18, 20

S

Salatin, Joel, 138, 146–147, 171

Sale, Kirkpatrick, 148
Saudi Arabia, 94
Schiff, Peter, 55
Schumacher, E. F., 142
Scoones, Ian, 63–65
seeds, 6–8, 20–23
Seneff, Stephanie, 173
Sherman Act of 1890, 119
Silent Spring (Carson), 163
Slater, Gail, 147–148
Smaje, Chris, 90–91, 152
soil, 1–9, 12–13, 17
soil erosion, 2, 12, 33–34
Sold Out: How Broken Supply Chains, Surging Inflation, and Political Instability Will Sink the Global Economy (Rickards), 48–49
Sowell, Thomas, 55
spiritual health, 144–153
Sprengel-Liebig Law of the Minimum, 12
Steinbeck, John, 110
supply chains, 49–50
Sustainable Development Goals (SDGs), 130–131
Svalbard Global Seed Vault, 104
Swan, Shanna h., 173
Sweden, 93
synthetic meat, 15, 59, 69–70

T

TCI. *See* Transportation Climate Initiative (TCI)
Terminator technology, 22
Toxic Legacy: How the Weedkiller Glyphosate is Destroying Our Health and the Environment (Seneff), 173
toxification, 14, 72, 147, 165
transportation, 6–7, 30–32
Transportation Climate Initiative (TCI), 149–150
Trump, Donald, 54, 74, 118
Truth About COVID-19, The: Exposing the Great Reset, Lockdowns, Vaccine Passports, and the New Normal (Mercola), 172

U

Ukraine, 37–38, 54, 73–75, 78, 93, 124–127
ultra-processed foods, 68–69, 89, 102, 116, 134, 173
Ultra-Processed People: Why Do We All Eat Stuff That Isn't Food . . . and Why Can't We Stop? (van Tulleken), 173
United Nations, 5, 33, 75, 130
United States Agency for International Development (USAID), 127
Unsettling of America, The (Berry), 29
urea, 4

V

van Tulleken, Chris, 173
Venezuela, 43–44, 52–54, 56–57
Vilsack, Tom, 74, 88–89
Volcker, Paul, 51
von Liebig, Justus, 12

W

war, 36–37
water aquifers, 32–33
WEF. *See* World Economic Forum (WEF)
WHO. *See* World Health Organization (WHO)
Wojciechowski, Janusz, 87–88
World Bank, 41–42, 97, 103, 126
World Economic Forum (WEF), 5, 33, 40, 75, 97, 103, 120–121, 130
World Health Organization (WHO), 5, 33, 97, 103, 130

Y

You Can Farm: The Entrepreneur's Guide to Start and Succeed in a Farming Enterprise (Salatin), 138

Z

Zelenskyy, Volodymyr, 126
Zimbabwe, 51–52
zoning laws, 106